The Stages of A-Khrid Meditation

Dzogchen Practice of the Bon Tradition

by

Bru-sgom rGyal-ba g.yung-drung

(1242 -- 90)

Translated by

Per Kvaerne and Thupten K. Rikey

LIBRARY OF TIBETAN WORKS & ARCHIVES

First published in 1996

ISBN: 81-86470-03-4

Published by the Library of Tibetan Works and Archives, Dharamsala, H. P. (India) and printed at Indraprastha Press (CBT), 4 Bahadurshah Zafar Marg, New Delhi 110002.

To

the Venerable Abbot Lungtog Tenpe Nyima Rinpoche, the present *sMan ri khri 'dzin*, whose affectionate guidance has always been a source of inspiration.

CONTENTS

PREFACE

The main part of the present work appeared in the journal *Kailash*, published in Kathmandu, in 1973.[1] Some of the basic ideas of the Bonpo tradition of the Great Perfection had been presented to Western readers in 1967 by Professor David L. Snellgrove in his translation of excerpts from the *gZi brjid*.[2] However, the text of which I published and translated roughly one third in *Kailash* is older than the *gZi brjid*, which is assigned to the 14th century. It also has the advantage of being a systematic, practical manual written for the benefit of teachers who have set themselves the task of guiding others in achieving enlightenment through the practice of the Great Perfection.

The Great Perfection (*rdzogs pa chen po*) is a tradition of spiritual training and philosophical insight which is found in the Nyingmapa school of Buddhism as well as in the Bon religion. Probably there is a certain amount of common ground, historically as well as philosophically, between Bon and Nyingmapa Buddhism as far as the Great Perfection is concerned, but the nature and extent of this relationship still awaits study.[3]

The Great Perfection of Bon is found in three distinct traditions, each with its own texts and spiritual lineage. This was pointed out for the first time in Western literature by Samten G. Karmay in his short but useful work, "A General Introduction to the History and Doctrines of Bon", published in 1975.[4] The three traditions, sometimes known as *a rdzogs snyan gsum*, are the *A khrid*, 'the Teachings regarding the Ultimate Origin (A)', the *Zhang zhung snyan rgyud*, 'the Aural Transmission of Zhang zhung', and a tradition which, though quite separate and distinct, is simply known as *rDzogs chen*, 'the Great Perfection'. While the latter two have been transmitted through lineages of masters reaching, so the Bonpos claim, back to supra-human spheres, the *A-khrid* is held to have an historical origin which can be precisely defined, being initiated by the lama known as rMe'u dGongs-mdzod, 'the Great Hermit' of the rMe'u clan, who lived from 1038 to 1096. The following passage from the above-mentioned work by Samten G. Karmay can serve to introduce the present translation:

"*A-Khrid* was promulgated by the great hermit, dGongs-mdzod (1038-1096). His system is divided into 80 periods called *A-khrid thun-mtshams brgyad-cu-pa*, each period lasting one or two weeks. After completing this course the adept is qualified and given the title *rTogs-ldan*. However, the system of 80 periods was reduced to 30 by 'A-zha Blo-gros rgyal-mtshan (1198-1263) and a little later this was further reduced to 15 by Bru rGyal-ba g.yung-drung (1242-1290). Since then the system has been known as *Bru'i a-khrid thun-mtshams bco-lnga-pa*—the fifteen period A-khrid of Bru" (p.215).

Publications (other than texts in Tibetan) relevant to the Great Perfection of Bon have not been numerous. Brief excerpts from texts belonging to the *Zhang zhung snyan rgyud* and the *bsGrags pa skor gsum* traditions were translated by Giacomella Orofino in 1985: *Insignamenti tibetani su morte e liberazione. Testi inediti dalle piú antiche tradizioni del Tibet*, Roma (Edizioni Mediterranee); English revised edition 1990.[5] A short but important contribution was Chap. VIII, "rDzogs chen in the Bonpo Tradition", in Samten G. Karmay, *The Great Perfection. A Philosophical and Meditative Teaching of Tibetan Buddhism*, Leiden (E.J. Brill), 1988, pp. 201-205.

In 1993 two books on this topic appeared. Tenzin Wangyal, a Geshe from the Bonpo Monastery at Ochghat, Himachal Pradesh, presented the Great Perfection according to his own training and experience in *Wonders of the Natural Mind. The Essence of Dzogchen in the Native Bon Tradition of Tibet*, Barrytown, N.Y (Station Hill Press). The other book, entitled *Heart Drops of Dharmakaya. Dzogchen Practice of the Bön Tradition*, Ithaca, N.Y. (Snow Lion Publications), is a composite volume. The main part of the book is a somewhat free English rendering of a work by the famous Bonpo lama Shar-rdza bKra-shis rgyal-mtshan (1859-1934), with the comments (based on tape-recordings) of *slob dpon* bsTan-'dzin rnam-dag, probably the greatest Bonpo scholar alive today and a master of the Great Perfection. In addition, it contains short biographies of Shar-rdza bKra-shis rgyal-mtshan and of bsTan-'dzin rnam-dag, an essay on the phenomenon of the 'rainbow body' (*'ja' lus*), a short history of Bon, illustrations, Tibetan text, a preface by the editor of the volume, Richard Dixey, and a short Introduction and a Bibliographic Essay by myself. An article on the A-khrid which I published in 1983 is reprinted as the Introduction to the present volume.

Per Kvaerne

INTRODUCTION[1]

One of the most fascinating—and least known—aspects of Tibetan religion is the system of meditation known as 'The Great Perfection', *rdzogs pa chen po,* or *rdzogs chen* for short.[2]

rDzogs-chen is of considerable interest for the study of Buddhist meditation, as well as for the study of mysticism in general, being a system of spiritual training and realization which is practised to this day by Tibetan adepts. However, it is also interesting from a historical point of view. It is generally recognized that for the study of the complex question of the formation of Tibetan Buddhism, a better understanding of this meditational tradition is of crucial importance. Giuseppe Tucci puts it in the following way (Tucci 1970 p.19):

> The development of Tibetan Buddhism in its initial phases is by no means as uncomplicated as the orthodox tradition would have us believe. Only systematic research in the history and beginning of the rdsogs c'en may permit one to judge the extent to which the tradition must be revised as regards these events.

Accordingly there should be no lack of incentive to study this tradition.

The study of rDzogs-chen raises a number of questions which have far-reaching consequences for the history of Tibetan religion. The first question, which is perhaps of the greatest immediate interest in the context of the present volume, is the relationship between rDzogs-chen and the Chinese meditational school known as Ch'an. It is a well-known fact, of course, that Chinese monks belonging to Ch'an were extremely active in Tibet in the eighth century, and that they came into conflict with representatives of Indian Buddhism. This conflict, which had not only religious, but also political implications, culminated in the famous debate in which exponents of the Chinese instant path' were pitted against the Indian 'gradualists' who advocated the more orthodox view of a step-by-step approach to Enlightenment.[3] Whatever the actual outcome of this debate (the Chinese party claimed that they were the victors), or whether an actual debate ever took place or not,[4] the later Tibetan tradition as recorded, for instance, by Bu-ston, adopted the view that the Chinese were soundly defeated, and any doctrine advocating an 'instant path' of 'no effort'—or which could be construed as advocating such a path—ran the risk of being branded as 'Chinese' and hence unorthodox. This fact is significant for the study of rDzogs-chen, for many of its Tibetan critics accused it of being precisely such a 'Chinese' doctrine, an innovation not sanctioned by the orthodox Indian Buddhist texts.[5] The Ch'an element in rDzogs-chen has also been stressed by Tucci,[6] and we shall return to this question at the end of the Introduction.

The second question of general significance for the study of the history of Tibetan religion concerns the relationship between the varieties of rDzogs-chen found in the Nyingmapa and the Bonpo traditions respectively. As pointed out by David L. Snellgrove (Snellgrove 1967 p.15), a comparative study of their literature would be extremely important for elucidating the whole question of the relationship between the two schools in general, and hence for coming to grips with the problem of how a religion, in many respects convergent with Buddhism but styling itself Bonpo, arose after the collapse of the national dynasty in the ninth century; but before a comparison of this kind can be carried out, we have to know what to compare. Accordingly, I propose to present a small contribution to our knowledge of rDzogs-chen by focusing on one particular tradition. Only when this kind of basic work has been undertaken on a much larger scale, will it be possible to compare Nyingmapa and Bonpo doctrines, and to approach the question of possible connections between Ch'an and rDzogs-chen with greater confidence.

The Bonpos recognize not only one, but three different traditions of rDzogs-chen, which are considered to be quite distinct, at least as far as their respective lineages are concerned. In the characteristic Tibetan shorthand fashion, these three traditions are known as *a rdzogs snyan gsum* (Karmay 1975a p. 215):

1. A-khrid, "The System Leading to the Ultimate (=A)"
2. rDzogs-chen, "The Great Perfection"
3. Zhang-zhung snyan-rgyud, "The Oral Tradition of Zhang-zhung".

I shall deal briefly with the second and the third of these, before going into detail concerning the first.

The second, which is explicitly styled rDzogs-chen, has been less explored than the other two. Its basic text, *rDzogs chen yang rtse'i klong chen*, was discovered by the *gter ston* ('Treasure-Discoverer') gZhod-ston dNgos-grub grags-pa in 1088 as part of the gter-ma ('Treasure') known as Lho-brag-ma i.e. the 'Treasure' discovered at the temple of Khom(s)-mthing in Lho-brag (Karmay 1972 pp.154-56). It is apparently very closely connected with the rDzogs-chen of the Nyingmapas, gZhod-ston being an important gter-ston in the Nyingmapa tradition also, under the name of Grub-thob dNgos-grub (ibid. p.154 n.1). Perhaps it is significant (although this is mere conjecture) that this particular 'Treasure' is said to have been found "behind the statue of Vairocana at Khom-mthing" (Kvaerne 1971 p. 230), in view of the important role which the eighth century Tibetan Buddhist monk Vairocana is supposed to have played in the introduction of rDzogs-chen into Tibet, at least according to the later tradition.[7] The *rDzogs chen yang rtse'i klong chen* is supposed to have been composed by sNya-chen Li-shu stag-rings, one of the siddhas who according to later Bonpo tradition were active in Tibet during the religious struggles of the eighth century. It is included in the Tenjur of the Bonpos (T 225).[8] sNya-chen also hid the text in the temple of Khom-mthing, and gZhod-ston is regarded as his emanation (Karmay 1972 p. 154 n.1.)

The basic text of the third tradition enjoys the status of *bka' ma* ('Belonging to the Word'), i.e. of uninterrupted transmission without having been hidden as a 'Treasure'. This term further implies that it was originally proclaimed by sTon-pa gShen-rab himself, and it is thus included in the Bonpo Kanjur (K 108). The *Zhang zhung snyan rgyud* is supposed to have been brought from Zhang-zhung and introduced into Tibet by the Zhang-zhung siddha Gyer-spungs sNang-bzher lod-po in the eighth century.[9] In recent years it has been published twice, together with a biography of the lamas of the lineage written by Spa bsTan-rgyal bzang-po (fifteenth cent.).[10]

It is worth noting that the Bonpos have, without hesitation, included rDzogs-chen texts not only in their Tenjur, but also in their Kanjur; in both collections, such texts constitute separate sections, and are regarded as expressing the supreme doctrines (Kvaerne 1974, passim). While certain rDzogs-chen texts are included in the Buddhist Tenjur (Tucci 1958 p. 122 et seq.), and a single rDzogs-chen tantra is to be found in the Kanjur (Karmay 1975b), the rDzogs-chen literature of the Nyingmapas is on the whole to be found outside these collections, above all in the great collections of Nyingmapa texts like the *Vairo rgyud 'bum*, the *rNying ma'i rgyud 'bum*, and the *Rin chen gter mdzod*.[11]

Turning, finally, to the first tradition, the A-khrid, we shall study it in greater detail. There are two reasons for focusing on this tradition. The first is practical: a certain amount of groundwork has already been done and the results published (Kvaerne 1973a), while the second reason is one of method: the basic texts of the A-khrid are neither *bka' ma* nor *gter ma*, but have been written by certain lamas whose biographies are available, so that the tradition can be traced back to a historically identifiable source. Once again we are led back to the eleventh century, i.e. a crucial period in the formation of Tibetan Buddhism, a period when the various schools and centres of religious life arose which gradually developed into the so-called 'sects', as well as into the Bon religion in its present form.

The founder of A-khrid is rMe'u dgongs-mdzod ri-khrod chen-po, 'The Meditation-Treasury, the Great Hermit, of (the family of) rMe'u', who lived 1038-1096. He is regarded as a person of exceptional sanctity, and he is therefore often referred to simply as *dam pa*, 'The Saint'. As I have translated a version of his biography elsewhere, I shall only mention a few points of his life-story here.[12]

Having in his youth left his family in order to devote himself to the religious life, he stayed with various lamas and was finally ordained as a monk at the age of twenty-four. Thereafter he lived as a hermit in various places in his native province of gTsang, attracting to himself many disciples, teaching and ordaining. Although he composed several works dealing with the practice of meditation (for example a *sgom rim*, Kvaerne 1973 p. 33), his energies were on the whole directed towards the practice of meditation, rather than literary activities, and he was, at least as a young man, emphatic in rejecting scholastic studies. Thus his biography relates that having studied for some time with two lamas,

> Reflecting carefully, he thought: "As for those two, they will exercise the abbatial function, so the teaching of the Word is firmly established. However, in this there is no profit for me; I require the spiritual realization (*dge sbyor*)[13] resulting from the full comprehension of the (esoteric) Sense of the Word" (Kvaerne 1973 p. 31).

His continuous practice of meditation is especially stressed, but so are the supernatural powers which ensued:

> Having instantaneously traversed all the stages (*sa thams cad dus gcig la non nas*), he strode forth in the sky, went through mountains without being impeded, and, firm stone becoming like mud, the master left clear imprints of his hands and feet at Brag-spyang thag-mo (ibid. p. 32).

His disciple sGom-chen 'bar-ba is perhaps the most colorful and unconventional personality of the A-khrid lamas.[14] His impetuous (or is it ironic?) rejection of worldly life, following impulsively upon his meeting his future guru, is characteristic:

> Upon arriving at the bank of the river Nyang-chu, violent disgust with samsāra was born, and he threw his trousers and carrying-frame into the water and said: "Go down from here! I will go upwards—our period of companionship has been (too) long" (ibid. p. 37).

After he had become the disciple of dGongs-mdzod, there followed a period of three years in which he unsuccessfully strove for spiritual realization (*dge sbyor*), his mounting frustration being increased by his guru's reluctance to impart spiritual counsel. His realization was reached in a remarkable way, through sudden, violent physical movement:

> Thereafter, having one day said: "Come up from here!" and having brought him to a grassy bog, he (i.e. dGongs-mdzod) said: "'Bar-ba! As you are said to have been very strong when young, make a leap here!" 'Bar-ba, acting accordingly, slipped and fell, and his body tumbled down very violently. Spiritual realization arising at that very instant, he cried and laughed without stopping (ibid. p. 39).

The rest of his career was apparently of a rather conventional kind, consisting of teaching, distributing alms, and exhibiting various miraculous powers. It is perhaps noteworthy that he did not receive ordination, but remained a layman and "showed great respect to the monks"; he died at the age of seventy-six (ibid. p. 40).

A third lama in the A-khrid lineage must be mentioned—Bru-chen rGyal-ba g.yung-drung (1242-90).[15] He is a typical monk-scholar—learned in a wide range of disciplines, active as a teacher and writer, but at the same time proficient in the art of meditation. From his biography we shall note two points: first, that he also figures in the spiritual lineage of the Oral Transmission of Zhang-zhung (ibid. p.21); second, that he is the author of the basic, authoritative text of the A-khrid tradition, the *Man ngag khrid kyi rim pa lag len thun mtshams dang bcas pa*, usually known as the *A khrid thun mtshams bco lnga*, "The Fifteen Periods of A-khrid". Our investigation of the A-khrid system will be based on this text, which, together with various ancillary texts and an auto-commentary, is considered to be sufficiently authoritative to be included in the Bonpo Tenjur (T 284).[16] This text is a typical work of systematization and codification, and it is stated in the colophon (p. 115 l.6) to have been written "in accordance with the practice of dGongs-mdzod". It was, however, certainly not without predecessors; thus we know that a text styled *gYas ru'i a khrid chen mo* was composed by 'Gro-mgon gYor-po me-dpal (1134-68) (Kvaerne 1973 p. 24). It has also continued to retain the attention of Bonpo lamas up to our own times, as the commentaries written by Shar-rdza bKra-shis rgyal-mtshan (1859-1935) testify.[17] We shall now study the actual system of meditation as outlined in the *A khrid thun mtshams bco lnga*, restricting ourselves, however, to a general survey of this text and reserving the detailed discussion of its terminology for later and more comprehensive treatment.

The text is divided into three main parts. The first part, which covers the first four 'periods' (1)-(4), deals with the 'preliminary procedures' (*sngon 'gro*). It is sufficient to mention these briefly, the important thing being to note that although they are preliminary, they are also indispensable, as they serve "to ripen the unripe consciousness (*rgyud*)". The preliminaries, then, are as follows:

(1) Meditation on transitoriness to counteract desire.
(2) Resolution to gain Enlightenment, the taking of the Refuges, the confession of sins.
(3) Accumulation of merit.
(4) Offering of prayers and request for benediction.

There exists a commentary to this section written by Shar-rdza bKra-shis rgyal-mtshan.[18]

The second part contains the 'basic subject-matter' (*dngos gzhi*), showing how the "ripened consciousness is set free". It is perhaps the most interesting part, in which the characteristic traits of the actual meditational procedure are clearly set forth. It consists of six 'periods',[19] divided into three major steps: "grasping mentally that which has attributes" (5); "equipoising (the mind) on that which is without attributes" (6)-(7); "confronting (the mind) with the meaning of Ultimate Nature (*gnas lugs*)" (8)-(10).

(5) Meditation, then, initially focuses on a concrete, visible object, for example the outline of the Tibetan letter A,[20] "written on a piece of indigo paper" (p. 79), and fastened on a stick in front of the disciples who are seated in rows in a quiet and secluded spot. The cross-legged posture of meditation is described in detail, and it is said that "by virtue of this control of the body, the humors are balanced, the consciousness assumes its natural state;... psychic veins, wind and seed are brought under one's control—such is its virtue" (p. 79).

Thereafter the way in which the eyes should be controlled is described:

> One should staringly, unblinkingly, without looking up or down or to the right or to the left, directly in front regard the A without opening fully nor closing the eyes, without being distracted by thoughts of the past or imaginings regarding the future, by sudden reflections or thoughts or recollections of good or evil... staring down uninterruptedly as if boring a hole, being straight like the shaft of a spear, being tense like the string of a bow, being insensate like a corpse: without wavering, without recollection, without forgetfulness, without mental vacancy, without thinking of anything in particular, without being tired even for a moment (p. 80).

The length of each session is indicated as being initially equal to the time required to recite the mantra *a oṃ hūṃ a a kar sale 'od a yang oṃ 'du* two hundred times. After two or three days of assiduous practice, certain signs (*rtags*) of spiritual progress will manifest themselves. These are the 'signs' (*nimitta*) which in Theravāda Buddhism are said to ensue from the practice of 'mindfulness' (*sati*), and which appear before entering into the first stage of trance (*jhāna*).[21] Our text differentiates, in what appears to be a very empirical manner, between 'internal signs' and 'external signs'. The internal signs are, among others:

> Like a tortoise placed in a basin, one is unable to move; like the wind hitting a small bird, shuddering slightly and feeling cold, one's mind becomes (as it were) numb; like water drawn from an iron pipe, the mind, subtle and even, continuously gushing forth, remains one-pointed...(p. 81).

External signs are, in the best disciples, "absence of bodily movement or unsteadiness. In the others, a strong desire to weep, laugh, dance and run will occur; turning the face away, not shutting the mouth or eyes, feeling a pricking sensation, sweating, shuddering, and falling to the ground" (p. 82).

These symptoms are of course well known from other sources in connection with the initial stages of meditation, particularly as a result of exercises regulating the breath, and it is interesting to note that although nothing is said about regulating the breath, the explanation offered in our text is that the 'mild wind' has entered the *avadhūti* (the central psychic channel).

(6) The next stage is continued meditation, but now without any fixed or defined object. Bodily posture and gaze are as before: "without forcing it, without relaxing it, (the body) is simply equipoised entirely in its own natural disposition ... abandoned, stupefied, and relaxed like a corpse" (p. 84). Likewise the gaze is as before, but no longer focused on an object: "One should look straight ahead, emptily, unblinkingly, staringly, without looking up or down or near or far" (p. 85). Thus the consciousness (*shes pa*) comes to rest "and samādhi void of discursiveness is produced spontaneously" (p. 84).

Accordingly the attention now shifts from the body and the gaze to the mind itself, which is viewed in its natural state of an 'eternal now':

> Without effacing former traces, without interest in the future, one equipoises one's present mind (*da ltar gyi rig pa*) ever fresh, shining and even ... The mind having no support, grasping is loosened by itself, mental restlessness disappears by itself; one equipoises (the mind) in its spontaneous self-nature (*ma bcos rang lugs*). [So]

the mind is equipoised intently without support, without depending on anything at all; without being covered by the notion of object and subject, it is equipoised unveiled and naked; isolated without being corrupted by discursive thought, it is equipoised brightly; not bound by the ego, it is equipoised unhurriedly according to its own disposition; without discursiveness through mental activity, it is equipoised relaxedly and clearly; without being obscured by darkness, it is equipoised shiningly in luminosity (p. 86).

Or again:

Shining, discerning, and firm; deep, luminous and bright; shining, without root; stunned in its own luminosity; naked, without discursiveness; unblinking, without grasping; spontaneously balanced; freely sparkling in its own arising—let it always remain in that condition (p. 89).

Our text, which is a manual for giving instruction in meditation, written, in other words, for the guru rather than for the disciple, is careful to give precise indications: "If the sessions of meditation are long, he will become languid and indifferent; if they are short, there being no stability (*gnas cha*), he will not grasp his innate nature (*rang so*)" (p. 87). He gradually extends the sessions of meditation, from the time it takes to recite one hundred to the time it takes to recite three or four hundred times the mantra *a oṃ hūṃ a a kar* etc., and he reduces the interval between the sessions, being careful to avoid sinful, violent, or exhausting actions, abstaining from speech, his mind being "like a corpse", keeping away excessive heat and cold, "beer and pungent herbs"; nor should he feel joy at improvement or dismay at diminishment of success in meditation. Constant diligence in meditation is all-important, for thereby—thus concludes the sixth 'period'—ensues the threefold 'tranquility' (*zhi gnas*): first the 'mind-created tranquility' is born, then the 'tranquility of one's innate nature' arises, and finally 'the firmness of ultimate tranquility' is obtained (p. 88).

(7) There follows the description of a procedure whereby the mind, thus equipoised in meditation, is identified with the universal void. This process has three elements or phases—'Example' (*dpe*), 'Meaning' (*don*), and 'Sign' (*rtags*):

> When the bright sky is without cloud or wind, let him assume the gaze and the bodily posture set forth above. Fixing the mind on empty space, the sky and the mind become indistinguishably intermixed, gradually harmonious with one another, undivided without separation... At that time, externally the sky does not consist of any substance, form, color, dimension, direction or characteristics at all that can be discerned, it is perfectly stainless, freely sparkling in the Void—this is the Example.
>
> Internally, this constantly discerning, lustrous one called 'the mind of the self' regards blankly and discerns clearly outwards and inwards without distinction—that is the Sign.
>
> The identity of those two... this state of non-dual Great Equality... is the Meaning (p. 90).

(8) The eighth 'period' introduces the third stage, the 'confrontation with the Meaning of Ultimate Nature'. This consists—somewhat surprisingly in view of the preceding emphasis on 'blankness' etc.—of a particular yogic procedure involving the visualization of three psychic channels connected with the imagery of masculine/feminine polarity, and the performance of certain breathing exercises. It is not necessary to go into this in detail; we may, however, note that the procedure is stated to "separate the pure and impure aspects of the consciousness" (p. 93) whereby "Spontaneous Wisdom" (*rang 'byung ye shes*) arises. This Wisdom is nothing but the mind itself, in its essential purity and luminosity:

> without recollection of former propensity to passion, without anticipation of what is to come; unmoved by mental flash-backs; not overpowered by drowsiness; without making the mind itself an object; without the six 'perceptive groups' following the five senses; without attachment to the taste of samādhi; the present consciousness being bright in its own luminosity, without grasping, with joy it shines steadily (p. 93).

We note that the disciple is now admonished not to be attached to the 'taste of samādhi', which is, obviously, nothing but a particularly subtle form of desire and attachment, and hence is known as 'the internal Māra' (p. 96). Any conscious effort to meditate is a hindrance; indeed, what is felt to be a painful absence of meditation is—provided the mental anguish becomes sufficiently acute and all-embracing—nothing but Spontaneous Wisdom itself:

> Accordingly, the constant hoping for the arising (of realization) through one's own practice of and meditation on that which one's guru has taught and instructed, the great and vociferous insistence on the need of it (i.e of realization) when it does not arise—that is precisely That; it is not elsewhere. Impress this on your mind; strive spiritually; make a firm resolution! (p. 94).

The text adduces several quotations in this connection which merit being reproduced in full:

Thus also the *Lung drug* says: "It is That; feel it and look at it. Looking, there is nothing to be seen. By means of That, That itself is seen." Li-shu has said: "As it is nothing but precisely This itself, why do you say 'I do not know it'?" The *'Bum* says: "The Wisdom of Self-Knowledge does not arise from without, nor does it arise from within; it arises by itself in itself" (p. 94).

Before proceeding, it is worth noting that the visualizations referred to above involving psychic channels etc., far from being a superfluous interpolation, seem to play a crucial role in turning 'tranquility'—which might otherwise become mere stupor (*ldengs po*)—into a dynamic process of spiritual liberation; for "one session of visualization of psychic channels and wind is swifter and more beneficial than innumerable precious and profound methods" (p. 95).

(9) The mind has thus returned to a state of being which is perfectly quiescent, natural, luminous and equipoised, and the text now returns to the theme of doing away with the very consciousness of being in a state of meditation, for "by seeking it is lost, by regarding it is obscured, by meditation it is corrupted" (p. 96), and "by contemplation on the thought 'I meditate', the bodhi-mind is obscured" (ibid.). In other words, the time has come to dissolve, once and for all, the false dichotomy between 'I' and 'it', between subject and object. So, "dissolving it relaxedly, all that which was meditated upon is dissolved so that it becomes non-meditated upon" (p. 96). This mental state is neither the stupor to which meditation might lead, nor the equally 'profane' state of

mental dispersion, for one should "exert oneself spiritually without letting the thoughts wander" (p. 95). Yet this exertion is really a non-exertion, for it simply consists in the effort to "relax it (i.e. the consciousness) unconcernedly, dissolve it unhurriedly, loosen it completely, like one who having, carried on his back a heavy load of wood, is able to put it down at last" (p. 96).

The consciousness having been 'relaxed', "After dissolving, one should without purposely meditating, spontaneously extend the string-of-recollection ('stream-of-consciousness') and retain it without either meditating or letting the thoughts wander" (p. 97). "After relaxing, loosening, and dissolving, rest in your consciousness without meditating or letting your mind wander, without thinking discursively or grasping" (ibid.).

Neither meditating nor inattentive, one should simply rest uninterruptedly in the spontaneous flow of one's consciousness; thus all mind-produced defilements are destroyed and the first stage of the spiritual quest, the practice of 'periodical meditation' (*thun sgom*), is brought to its conclusion.

(10) The adept now enters the second stage, that of 'permanent meditation' (*ngang sgom*) in which Wisdom free from defilements is realized. Permanent meditation, which is not an 'ordinary' (*tha mal*) state, being neither meditation nor inattentiveness, involves, in a certain sense, the return to the 'ordinary', everyday life. For whereas the adept, while training himself in the basic skill of equipoising, was enjoined to avoid violent or exhausting movements, passions, even speech itself, he may now indulge in any activity at all, provided his 'permanent meditation' is not interrupted.

In other words, the basis for what follows is a dialectical movement from dispersion (lack of balance) to equipoise, i.e. samādhi, which, unless meditation on psychic channels etc. is resorted to, may become prolonged indefinitely in the form of 'stupor'. Both dispersion and equipoise are, however, in different ways, 'ordinary' conditions; their synthesis, so to speak, is a state of 'neither meditation nor non-meditation', and involving a return to the world of human activity.

The text deals with this 'synthetic stage' under the conventional headings of 'body', 'speech', and 'mind', which are now, no matter how they are engaged, regarded as "the body of a god", "the sound of sacred recitation", and as "wisdom" itself. Thus all actions, words and thoughts whether pure or not, are "raised to the path" (*lam-du slong-ba*), i.e. transmuted into Means towards Enlightenment, provided one remains in a state of continuous spiritual realization (*dge sbyor gyi ngang du*) (p. 98). The text is so explicit at this point as to merit being quoted at length:

> Firstly, on the basis of the above 'knowledge of retaining', he will accompany it with looking upwards and downwards, moving hither and thither, being twisted, unsteady, and careless. If this does no harm, he rises gently and accompanies it with salutations and circumambulations, which are pure. Thereafter he will accompany it with rendering them (i.e. these 'pure' actions) energetic. Thereafter he accompanies it with various actions like leaping, running, etc., which are neutral. Thereafter he accompanies it with actions like beating, furious anger, etc., which are impure. Engaging even in all these actions, all pure and impure physical acts and behavior are raised to the Path while in a condition of spiritual realization.
>
> Secondly, again while in a state of spiritual realization, he should recite the formulas, the Refuge, the bodhisattva's vow, prayers and sūtras, which are pure. He accompanies (realization) with speech and chant of every sort, benign and fierce. If this does no harm, he accompanies it with the speaking of nonsense, loose talk, jokes, questions, and abuse etc. of every sort, which are neutral. Thereafter he purposely utters shouts, harsh words, lies etc., which are impure. If one raises all this to the Path, there is accompaniment of speech (by spiritual realization).
>
> Thirdly, while in a state of spiritual realization, he accompanies it with the turning of his own body into that of a tutelary deity... He accompanies realization with various thoughts and reflections, which are neutral. Thereafter he accompanies it with all the impurities like the Three Poisons, the Five Poisons, etc. If all these are intermixed, mind and spiritual realization are likewise intermixed (pp. 98-99).

We have come a long way from the bodhisattva's vow and the simple taking of the Refuge referred to at the outset. The adept plunges right back into the whirl of life, not only in external mode of life, but in his very thought and feeling.

> He indulges in feelings of fear and terror, fright and anguish, disgust and aversion, disease and pain, anger and fury, worry and shame, desire and passion, misery and suffering, joy and happiness, etc. Discursiveness, doubt, hope and fear, suffering—unsuitable and disagreeable unfavorable circumstances; from eating and chewing, walking and sitting, all actions and behavior at the present moment right up to, finally, death—with regard to these the mind's essence does not escape (*rig pa'i gnad ma shor*); one is not separated from the potential friends, viz. recollection and grasping, and they are carried to the path in a condition of spiritual realization; they are cut off just as they are; they are accepted unquestioningly; defeat and victory are intermixed (p. 95).

In short:

> When in the condition of the Great Vehicle, the Foundation, one can carry everything to the Path, acts of body or speech, behavior pure or impure, virtuous or non-virtuous, good, bad, or neutral—whatever one has done goes towards spiritual realization (p. 100).

Thus is completed the 'confrontation with Ultimate Reality'.

The third section of the text is styled 'the consummation' (*mthar phyin pa*): it is the "instruction in bringing the liberated consciousness to its final end" (p. 100). A summary of the salient features of this process must suffice.

(11) The eleventh 'period' has the heading "suppressing the psychic-impressions (*bag chags*) in the evening"; in other words, the psychic forces which until now have operated independently of spiritual realization are now also brought under control. So, lying down at night in the sleeping posture of the Buddha, full of compassion and faith in one's guru and tutelary deity, one visualizes one's mind (*rig pa*) in the form of an A from which rays of light shoot forth and are reabsorbed; thereby the entire body is felt to be suffused by light. Concentrating on the A and suppressing the shooting-forth and the reabsorption of light, one lies down (as it

were) in the Void, having no particular sensation. The best disciple, mixing sleep and contemplation (*bsam gtan*), goes straight off to sleep; he is not separated from spiritual realization for a single moment, and while in sleep he experiences nothing but pure luminosity, i.e. mind itself in its absolute mode of being. Disciples of medium capability recognize their dreams as such, so their dreams and wishful imaginings are 'raised to the Path' and their spiritual realization increases even more at night than it did during the day. Even the least skilled disciples will gradually learn to recognize their dreams as such (p. 101). Likewise all sensations are to be regarded as dreams, and all dreams as sensations, so that everything appears as dream or illusion (p. 103). Whatever mental form the psychic-impressions create, to whatever place the mind wanders, whatever sensations may arise—all is to be regarded as the illusory appearances of dreams and hence 'raised to the Path' (p. 140).

(12) The heading of the following 'period' is "training the reflective-power (*rtsal*) on the sensations during the day". The 'reflective-power' is "the consciousness consisting of thoughts and recollections" (p. 95); and while previously, for the purpose of attaining samādhi or 'equipoise', this 'reflective-power' was to be rendered unmoving (pp. 95-96), it is now to be 'exercised' or 'purified' by being allowed to play freely on all the objects of sensation, without discriminative thought, without acceptance or rejection (for thereby it would slip back into an 'ordinary' condition).

> In the best disciples, who are in a state of continuously seeing (the truth), the 'reflective-power' will arise in itself and dissolve in itself, like snow and rain falling on a lake; in those of medium skill, who are in a state of meditation, it will be seen in its nakedness and dissolve in its nakedness, like a long-sought-for person whom one finally meets; while in the least skilled ones the 'reflective-power' will be exercised, the string-of-recollection, one's constant companion, being like water gushing forth from an iron pipe (p. 105).

It is possible to remain unruffled by all appearances,

> For appearances (*snang ba*) are mind (*sems*), and mind appearance: hence appearances and mind are not-two;

> in appearance itself is Emptiness, and in Emptiness itself is appearance: hence appearance and Emptiness are not-two—they arise luminously without being hindered, they dissolve sparklingly having no own-nature, and their arising and dissolving are simultaneous. So in the best disciples they arise in themselves and are dissolved in themselves; in the medium ones they are seen in their nakedness and are dissolved in their nakedness; in the least skilled ones the grasping recollection is (as it were) a friend whose form is seen (as) Emptiness, whose voice resounds (as) Emptiness, whose smell is smelt as Emptiness, whose taste is enjoyed as Emptiness, whose touch is put on as Emptiness, whose Doctrine is recollected as Emptiness, etc.—one strives spiritually, leaving everything just as it is (p. 106).

Summing up this 'period', the text states:

> One exercises the 'reflective-power' with regard to the appearances (caused by) the six sense-fields, but that is not enough: no harm must result. Harm not resulting is not enough: they (i.e. the appearances) must arise as friends. Arising as friends is not enough: one must enjoy their flavor as not-two (with regard to Emptiness) (p. 106).

(13) The adept is now approaching the final goal, and must train himself to "raise, at morning and at night, his discursive-thoughts to the Path". So whatever illusions or discursive-thoughts trouble his consciousness (*rgyud*), he lets them arise and dissolve without any feeling of there being anything to suppress or any intellect to suppress it (p. 107), for just as waves do not ruffle the essential tranquility of the ocean nor a rainbow that of the sky, thus that which arises as the mind (*sems*) is essentially at rest in the mind-itself (*sems nyid*)—"everything is 'great tranquility', everything is 'great spontaneity' " (ibid.).

(14) Finally one lives in a state of "perpetual confrontation" (*rgyun du rang ngo sprad pa*) which reaches its consummation in a final dialectical movement: all appearances are 'confronted' as mind (*sems*); the mind is 'confronted' as limitlessness; limitlessness is 'confronted' as the 'three bodies' (p. 109).

As for the first phase, there is nothing except mind; everything is the magic-appearance (*cho 'phrul*) of the mind, yet apart from appearances there is no mind. According to the psychic-impressions of their mind, beings experience hell, the state of the tormented ghosts, etc.; likewise in this life, humans experience illusory sensations due to sleep, the intermediate state, possession by spirits, medicine, or food; and by illusion of the senses one may see two moons, take a rope to be a snake, etc. All these appearances are nothing but mind (pp. 109-10). In fact, whatever appearances arise in a being who has been corrupted by the sleep of ignorance are false, like a dream or an illusion. So all appearances should be seen simply as mind, and left as such, mind and appearance having one single flavor (p. 111).

But the mind, thus recognized, has neither beginning nor end; sparkling, brilliant, naked, pliant, it is the producer of Buddha and of beings, pure and impure, inner and outer; although various things arise, it remains unborn in its own-nature; its play arises unhindered, its essence is non-dual, being limitless it has no characteristic, it surpasses all speech, all thought (p. 111).

Thirdly, this limitless mind which permeates everything, itself being neither great nor small, many nor few, good nor bad, coarse nor subtle, exists internally in the 'heart' (*tsi ta*) as the 'three bodies': the Mother, the 'universal foundation', the Void, is the 'absolute body' (*bon sku*); the mind, self-luminous, non-grasping, shining and unmoving, is the 'perfect body' (*rdzogs sku*); the 'reflective-power', self-arising, self-dissolving, is the 'illusory-body' (*sprul sku*) (p.112). Or again: the absolutely pure Wisdom of one's own-mind (*rang rig*) is the 'absolute enjoyment-body', and all actions are the 'illusory body'. Thus externally the essential emptiness of all the sense-fields like form etc. are the 'absolute body', the luminosity of their unhindered shining is the 'perfect body', the instability of their `magic-appearance' is the 'illusory body'—these three bodies, gathered into a single essence, exist inseparably. Internally, whatever instability there is due to sudden thoughts or recollections, their emptiness is the 'absolute body', their appearance is the 'perfect body', their luminosity is the 'illusory body'—whoever knows this is the Lord of the 'three bodies' (p. 113).

This instruction—thus we may terminate our résumé—one first learns and understands, thereafter impresses on one's mind, and finally experiences for oneself (p. 114).

Having reviewed the fifteen 'periods' of the A-khrid system of the 'Great Perfection', there remains only to make a few concluding observations.

Firstly, it is quite clear that the term rDzogs-chen is an ambiguous one, covering a variety of doctrines and meditational procedures. Our text, for instance, makes no mention of the emanation of phenomenal existence in the form of five rays of light of different colors from the original, universal luminosity, a feature of Nyingmapa rDzogs-chen texts to which Tucci has drawn attention (Tucci 1958 p. 106 n. 1; 1970 p. 102).[22] After all, this diversity is not so surprising, for both of the traditions in which rDzogs-chen is to be found are characterized by the absence of an institutionalized *magisterium* and by the predominance of an open, individualistic spirit, more ready to assimilate than to reject. As far as rDzogs-chen is concerned, it is simply too early to generalize; we can only, as in the present case, say that such and such a doctrine is to be found in a given text. Perhaps if research could be undertaken on a wider scale, a more comprehensive and coherent picture—both in the historical and the systematic sense—might gradually emerge.

Secondly, we are obviously very far from being in a position to solve all questions concerning the historical origins of rDzogs-chen. However, certain preliminary conclusions may nevertheless be ventured. Thus it seems that the main features of rDzogs-chen—certainly this would seem to be true of the text we have studied here—may be explained in terms of Indian Buddhism. In particular, the doctrines of the Buddhist siddhas, as expressed in the *Dohākoṣas* of Saraha, Kāṇhapa and Tillopa, with their background in the main philosophical systems of Mahāyana Buddhism, would seem to provide sufficient material out of which rDzogs-chen could be developed. I say 'developed', for there can hardly be any doubt that a specific rDzogs-chen system is a Tibetan creation (indeed, this point is made by its Tibetan critics), and in the case of the present text at least, one has the feeling that its author has been animated by a desire to be as comprehensive and inclusive as possible, welding together elements from a number of different sources. This conclusion is, I believe, all the more sound as Tucci, in spite of his repeated assertions (Tucci 1958 pp. 21, 45, 60) that Ch'an elements are to be found in rDzogs-chen, nowhere demonstrated that these elements must necessarily, or even preferably, be interpreted as emanating from Ch'an. Nevertheless, when dealing with the question, subsequent writers speak of Ch'an elements in rDzogs-chen as if this were an established fact, and refer to Tucci 1958 (Neumaier 1970 p. 136; Stein 1972 p. 22). The possibility of specifically Ch'an elements having contributed to the development of the 'Great Perfection' cannot, of course, be ruled out *a priori*, and Stein 1971 pp. 23-28 and 1972 p. 23 n. 3 has pointed out some striking parallels in the field of vocabulary and concepts; however, it is extremely difficult to positively identify such traits on internal, textual criteria, as Ch'an has to a large extent the same Indian sources as those which, through the siddhas, may be taken to have influenced rDzogs-chen.[23] The question of the continued presence of Ch'an in Tibet after the eighth to ninth centuries, would therefore seem to be more appropriately dealt with independently of rDzogs-chen. Discussing this question, S.G. Karmay concludes (Karmay 1975a p. 215) that "even though in rDzogs-chen there may be parallel ideas and practices to those of Chan, rDzogs-chen must be considered as of Indo-Tibetan origin whilst the tradition of Chan in Tibet may be studied as an independent movement."

Thirdly, limiting myself to the present text (although it clearly holds true for rDzogs-chen as a whole), I would point out that it is of considerable general interest for students of mysticism, being a manual intended for those engaged in guiding others on the Path, and disclosing a coherent, dynamic, and profound method of spiritual development and liberation. One may note that while this system does involve, at a certain stage, a quietistic mode of life, it nevertheless leads finally to a life of mental and physical activity where even the emotions are 'raised to the Path', and where the paraphernalia of tantric ritualism plays no necessary part.

More specifically, the present text indicates a particular kind of spiritual development which may be taken to be closely related to that motivating the highly unconventional behavior of the Tibetan *smyon pa* (madmen), the 'holy fools' who have been, down through the centuries, a typical—and highly cherished—part of the religious scene in Tibet.[24] Some of these engaged (usually with impunity!) in the kind of 'violent' or 'impure' behavior mentioned in our text—"leaping, running, beating, anger, nonsense, loose talk, jokes, abuse, shouts, lies" (p. 98). Even a mind apparently clouded over by all kinds of passions, doubts, and delusions, by "anger and fury, worry and shame, desire and passion, joy and happiness" (p. 99), may become the vehicle of profound spiritual realization, or so our text maintains.

The Stages of A-Khrid Meditation

Dzogchen Practice of the Bon Tradition

Homage to the gracious lama!

Passed down to the lamas, siddhas and yogis through the lineages of mind and miracle transmission, this guide to the individually transmitted instructions constitutes the highest level of [the Enlightened One's] view and intention. Described in prose, it shows the meaning at one's fingertips; it employs skilful means to illustrate the instructions; it strikes [the disciples] in such a way that their practices become spontaneous; it brings one to the state from which wisdom is encountered in its pure state; it introduces the mind face to face; it holds the meaning from its root; it grasps the words, deriving their main points; and it pursues the primordial state of mind nakedly. This guide to the jewel-like individually transmitted instructions to accomplish the state of enlightenment by forceful methods has practices in three stages:

I. The Preliminary Practice: bringing the unripened mind to the ripened state.

II. The Actual Body of Practice: setting free the ripened consciousness.

III. The Final Stage of Practice: bringing the freed mind to the accomplished state.

Part One

The Preliminary Practice:

Bringing the Unripened Mind to the Ripened State

I. PRELIMINARY PRACTICES

The Preliminary Practices are in four parts:

1. Meditation on Impermanence: a means to turn away from attachment.
2. Taking Refuge after Having Cultivated Bodhicitta: a means to open the door to the right path.
3. Maṇdala Offering: a means to complete the accumulation of merit.
4. Entreaty: a means to receive full blessings.

1. Meditation on Impermanence

(Session One)

First one assumes the fivefold sitting posture or sits with one's body straight. All of a sudden one says *Phat!* as mentioned in the *Lung* and does an intense contemplation on 'self-eradication of attachment'. This is done to such an extent that a shudder of fear runs through the skin. After having abided in this meditation for a long period, one thinks in the following manner:

This imputed "I" constitutes a wandering consciousness from the intermediate state forced inside an uncut whole body of flesh, blood and bones and covered by a thin skin. It is certainly a house of pain and impurities. In its nature, it is a corpse, a skeleton scarecrow, a net of nerves, and, in its appearance, a cemetery. When thought of, it is frightening. When examined, it arouses a shudder of fear. *A-tsa-ma!* Look at it! One has devoted oneself to nursing this "I" nicely, fondling it, and providing ornaments and clothing in the hope it would be something immortal. Now it is the source of sicknesses and an ocean of pain. Eventually, it will end up leaving behind either a handful of burnt bones, or a piece of rotten carcass, or a ditch full of insects, or something to be destroyed by birds and animals. Time rolls on, months absorbed in the sky and days in the earth. One might not be ready, but the time [of death] will come. In such circumstances, the time of death is not predetermined, nor is the place and cause. Yet, death is definite. None will accompany one then. *Ang!* One does not know when one will die. At the time of death, the wealth one has accumulated, the friends one is acquainted with, the kith and kin one is related to, the castle one has built, the food one has relished, the clothes one has put on, and all other things in this illusory world are not going to accompany or help. *Ang!* Instead of being helpful, they could cause desire, pain and deception. Alone and naked, one will wander in unknown lands. Deprived of one's physical body, one will be like an orphan. Driven by bloodthirsty and murderous ghosts, one will suffer. When the results of one's own bad karma have befallen one, only the lama and the tutelary deity can give one hope, for whatever they do, they do it with a kind heart.

Furthermore, in the course of many lives down to the present, one has been born so many times, but has one achieved any result? One thinks about it. One has wandered in so many places, but has one found any place of safety etc.? One thinks about it. One has done so many deeds, but has there been any essential meaning one is now seeing? One thinks about it. One has suffered a lot in those past lives, but do those sufferings have any effect on this present life? One thinks about it.

Also, one thinks: it is evident that in the days to come, no one escapes the fact that birth eventually invites death. It is known that anything that is accumulated eventually runs out and that the food and other properties [one has accumulated] are illusory. One eventually gets separated from anything with which one has come into contact and [the very concept of] enemy or relative is deception. Apparently, life cannot be made short or prolonged. One has mistaken the goal in those good months and years in the past, which is now clear. Should one knowingly deceive oneself in the future?

Also, one thinks about the changing nature of appearances, their formation, continuity, dissolution and extinction; [the changing nature of time, such as] year, month, number of days, moments and the shortest fraction of a moment; the changing condition [in the lives] of other living beings, such as being happy, unhappy, rich, poor, of high position, low position, death, birth, good and bad. Turning to oneself, one thinks about the changes taking place in the surrounding objects, such as the place one is living in, friends one is keeping in touch with, deeds one is doing, food one is relishing, clothes one is putting on, paths one is walking on and so forth.

In this way, if [this meditation on] impermanence becomes

fully integrated into one's mind-stream, then the sensation of fear, skin-startling shudders, hyperventilation or a feeling of disgust at oneself will occur. Also, for every sort [of people engaged in this practice], since they have understood the manner in which things become manifest and the nature of karma, it is impossible that a positive change will not occur in their mind.

If this is seen to happen, then the meditation on impermanence is accomplished. For that person all appearances are illusory, clinging to inherent existence is cut off, saṃsāra is seen as disgusting, worldly deeds are seen as lacking essence, the devilish concept of friend and foe is eradicated and knots of attachment and desire are undone. The real purpose comes spontaneously in one's mind. One will regard nothing except the lama as the source of advice, Eternal Bon as the object to rely upon single-pointedly, the practice of the Great Vehicle as the mind and body training, and caves and secluded sites as the places to live in. In this way, one becomes a person integrated into the practice. Gyer-mi says:

For one who has taken birth it is impossible not to die.
For one who is dead it is impossible not to be reborn.
Being born it is impossible not to wander in saṃsāra.
Isn't it clear that returning to saṃsāra is of no joy?

Also, Bla-chen says:

O my follower *gshen pos!*
If you have realized impermanence
And have remembered death,
You have done the right thing.

2. *Taking Refuge after Having Cultivated Bodhicitta*

(Session Two)

Homage to holy lamas!

This session has three parts:

(a) Bodhicitta Cultivation
(b) Taking Refuge
(c) Confession of Sins

(a) Bodhicitta Cultivation

As for the first, generally taking refuge and Bodhicitta cultivation come in the beginning of all paths. Here also, in order to follow this special instruction, one cultivates Bodhicitta in the first place. The manner in which it is done is as follows:

The fact that all these living beings in the six realms, whose population is as vast and great in number as space itself, have all been one's father, mother and relatives can be understood if one examines closely the fact that one has taken many different lives and has travelled in every high and low realm. Thus, the kindness that they have extended cannot be repaid through any means except by cultivating Bodhicitta. Thinking thus, one concentrates on the benefits of Bodhicitta cultivation. One assumes the fivefold sitting posture or the posture of sitting straight or any other sitting posture that is proper. Holding one's eyes in between the eye-brows (*smin mtshams*), one thinks thus: all these living beings of the three realms who indeed are my parents and to whom I owe my gratitude are born again in this ocean of saṃsāra and remain wandering there. They undergo different karma and pain. They are deprived of chances to be free and happy even for a short moment. Since their situation is gruesome, it is I who should have no choice but to work for their well-being. However, my attitude at this stage is like that of a person who is equally being carried away in the water current; my mind is spiritually unripened and lacks power and capability. Therefore, aiming at their welfare, I should enter the door of this practice of individually transmitted instructions, the most special of all the methods to accomplish the Enlightened state, and should make myself attain Enlightenment in this lifetime in this illusory body itself. Furthermore, I should, by the power of my compassion, deliver living beings [from saṃsāra] to such an extent that this world is emptied. As far as [working for] the purpose of living beings is concerned, the time sequence of doing so is flexible. Therefore, I must persevere to attain Enlightenment at this very moment, so that my body, speech and mind become a means for the well-being of all. May all these be fulfilled! In this way, one prays not simply from the mouth in unclear words or superficially, but from the depth of one's heart, well-disciplined and single-pointedly; while reciting the verse, "*Phyogs bcu ...*" and so forth. The *Sems lung* says:

One without Bodhicitta cultivated in the first place
Is like a farmer who has forgotten his cause.
A *gShen rab* who has Bodhicitta in deed,
Is like rain from the sky—an asset to the ocean.

(b) Taking Refuge

Secondly, as for the refuge-taking, one assumes the sitting posture as before, with the hands folded. Then, one visualizes in the space in front a seat of lion, elephant, horse, dragon and garuda uplifted from the corners by strong elephants with a gleaming sun and moon disc located above. One's root guru sitting on the seat is transformed into light and appears in the form of Kun-bzang gShen-lha 'od-dkar, white in color, with one face and two arms; marked with the thirteen characteristics of peace and nine of purity; glowing in the illuminating lights; setting free living beings by the power of his immeasurable compassion; and overpowering other appearances by his glorious rays. It is said, "all those who have been one's lama, even those who taught the alphabet *Ka, Kha* and so forth, should be thought of as having emanated from him." Immeasurable light shines forth from his body, speech and mind. As a result, hosts of inner and outer divine beings, Buddhas in the ten directions, hosts of Bodhisattvas, *rgod lcam ḍākinīs* and the lineage-holder lamas are invited from beyond visible space. Their bodies radiant like rainbows, they sit on the lotus seats located in the space in front of the central figure. The holy objects representing Buddha's body, speech and mind and located behind the central figure are also radiant, illuminating and standing as steadily as mountains and rocks.

Then one imagines that one has manifested oneself into many hundreds, each one leading an immeasurable number of living beings from the three realms. All, in deep faith, devotion and respect, make circumambulations and prostrations and go for refuge:

> From this point until the time we attain the heart of Enlightenment, we take refuge in you, O holy and compassionate ones! May the inner and outer undesirable causes and obstacles be pacified! May this life, the life in the intermediate state and the next be protected from fears! We are without guidance, please be our

holy protectors and escorts! Look upon us always with
your compassionate minds!

In this way, one cultivates a strong will-power and recites the verse, *"bDag dang..."* and so forth.

Finally, one imagines that lights shine forth from the heart region of hosts of deities and eradicate undesirable causes and obstacles; one is taken under their protection and guarded by their compassion. The *Sems lung* says:

Those gone for refuge in the Four Swastikas
Are the ones best protected.

(c) Confession of Sins

As for purification, one neither conceals nor keeps secret but feels guilt and regret in front of the holy ones and offers to purify the hosts of negative karma committed by oneself and others in the course of many past lives down to the present, either by direct means, by encouraging others or by condoning the negative karma done by others, whether it be very subtle or gross, done with or without awareness and so forth—in short, the hosts of negative deeds of different types that have been carried out due to ignorance, lack of understanding and deception. In this way, one should cultivate a will-power which is unfabricated, so real that it can make the flesh and bones shudder.

By virtue of this, showers of light shine forth from the heart region of hosts of deities and absorb into one's own body and that of all living beings through the crown of the head. As a result, all kinds of impressions [stored in the mind] and the factors that obscure wisdom are ejected as blackness from the bottom base orifices and from under the toenails, as well as in the form of vapors, red-blue in color, from the sense doors and the pores in the crown of the head. In this way, one imagines that all negativities and the factors that obscure wisdom are purified. It is said:

If regretted deeply afterwards,
Then karma and the factors that obscure wisdom will
certainly be purified.

Now, from this time to the time I attain the state of Enlightenment, I will strictly avoid negative deeds, be wary of them and train myself indiscriminately in the line of virtuous deeds. Also, I will encourage others to follow this line. Those who follow and practise virtuous deeds are extremely wonderful and admirable.

In this way, one should think deeply and recite the verse, *"bDag dang 'gro ba..."* and so forth. It is said, "Rejoicing [in others' good deeds] is an inconceivable root of virtues."

Lastly, reciting the verse, *"dGe ba de dag..."* and so forth, one should dedicate for the attainment of Enlightenment the root virtues accumulated by oneself as well as all living beings in the past, present and future.

From the series of individually transmitted instructions, this ends the parts dealing with refuge-taking, Bodhicitta cultivation, and confession of sins written according to the teachings of 'Dulba Rinpoche. This ends the second session, the duration of which is either nine or seven days.

3. Maṇḍala Offering

(Session Three)

Homage to the holy lamas!

The maṇḍala offering, which is meant for accumulating merit, is the practice that brings forth greater merit than any other general composite root virtue. This is said in the *Klu-'bum* as well as by the great lamas of the *Secret Cycle* and other past masters.

As for this, an object of concentration [i.e the maṇḍala baseplate] is used. The best types are made from gold or silver and the middle type from brass or bronze. As a last choice, one should at least make one for offering from wood or clay, and its surface should be smooth. It should be free from any inauspicious signs. If it lacks lustre, undesirable visions cannot be suppressed; if its face is uneven, the merits accumulated will be unsteady; if it has creases or cracks, there will be obstacles to one's life-span; if it lacks the required length, one can't achieve the essential goal; and if its width is not up to standard, one will be reborn in the impure realms. Hence, one should be aware of its faults and virtues. Both the practitioner and his sponsor should cultivate Bodhicitta mentally as well as practically and create the mandala base-plate in such a way that its material, shape and size are just right. Such a mandala base-plate is similar to a skull marked with special characteristics. If kept, it will fulfil one's wishes and accomplish special as well as common spiritual power.

As for its decoration, the best ones use jewels, and the middle ones use sea-shell clusters. As a last choice one should, at least, use grains or medicinal herbs to make seventeen beautiful clusters. It is said:

> If the maṇdala is made from jewels, its diameter can be that of four fingers measure or more. If it is made from wood or clay, it should not be less than a cubit or a span measure in diameter, lest it resemble the one used by heretics.

Hence, one should be aware of what is to be avoided and what is not.

While one is offering the maṇdala, first of all one should cultivate Bodhicitta, go for refuge and do the confession of sins and so forth. Then, one should wipe clean the maṇdala base-plate thinking that, by virtue of this, all sins and obscurations are eradicated, and one should recite the verse, "*Bon nyid...*" and so forth. It is said:

> By virtue of wiping it clean, one becomes in [one's next life] a handsome, sharp-minded and intelligent person who eventually will eradicate all negative karma and obstacles.

From this point on, the maṇdala base-plate is not to be separated from one's hands [till a cycle of the maṇdala offering is completed]. If it is, one will be reborn among the nihilists. Therefore, the maṇdala offering is to be performed in one activity as follows:

Recite the text, "*Bhrum ri ti gar ma la ho,*" and add a cluster in the centre. Then recite, "*A yam ram mam kham brum shak sa le sang nge ye swa' ha',*" and add clusters in the four cardinal directions and the eight corners, starting from its eastern face, which is the face towards you, and moving to the right. As the recitation continues "*Phyod-phur sa-le ha-lo seng,*" add four more clusters in the centre. These clusters should be neither too close to each other nor too far apart; neither should they touch each other nor should there be any one missing. Fully aware of these faults and virtues, one should add them beautifully in the right manner. It is said thus:

> If they are too close to the centre, the sense organs will not be complete [in one's next life]. If they are too close

to the edge, one will be reborn in the land of barbarians. If the spaces in between them are not equal, one will come across disciples of good and evil manners.

After the maṇḍala is arranged, it is offered as follows:

Firstly, one visualizes clearly in the space in front one's root lama in the form of a tutelary deity sitting on a seat of lion, elephant, horse and garuda with cushions of sun and moon disk and the lotus; the lineage-holder lamas sitting one above the other in the space above, resembling a staircase; the holy objects representing the body, speech and mind of Buddhas displayed in the background; and the Buddhas from the ten directions, the host of meditational deities, *rgod lcam dākinīs* and the oath-bound protector deities assembled in the front in inconceivable numbers filling the whole earth and space, just like the sky thickly covered with clouds or stars.

As for the mentally created madala, one visualizes the earth with its entire range as a vast spread of precious golden sands; the great mountain of Sumeru located in the centre and surrounded by the seven mountains of gold and the seven lakes of gentle waves; the four great continents located in the four cardinal directions and the eight subcontinents in the eight corners; and the whole complex surrounded by a single giant iron fence. Inside this pure realm, one visualizes a great many offerings resembling hosts of assembled clouds, such as the eight types of auspicious objects, seven types of jewels, precious flowers of gold, flowers of turquoise, nine types of beautiful objects, nine types of desirable sounds, nine types of aromas, nine types of sweet tastes, nine types of soft touches, nine types of desirable Bon, the heavenly garments, divine horse and elephants, the city of Indra, a hundred thousand varieties of lotus, and as many offerings of gods and men as could fill this whole realm.

Having done so, one visualizes oneself transformed into innumerable beautiful youths from heaven adorned with beautiful ornaments of many varieties. Spread far and wide in this big realm, each in his respective region encourages and guides an inconceivable number of living beings, who also are adorned with ornaments of many varieties in similar manner. Positioned in a dancing gesture, thrilled by the power of joy and faith, and holding offerings of many varieties in their hands, they sing in chorus clearly modulated songs and make offerings.

In this way, without any negative inclination and attachment, the realm and the hosts of offerings one has thus visualized are offered to the assembly of holy ones visualized in the space in front thus:

> O compassionate ones! Please accept them and bless us. May the special realization of the practice of the Great Vehicle be born in us right now. May the undesirable interferences from within and without be pacified and the karma and obstacles be purified.

Having done so with deep concern, one recites, *"Zhing khams..."* and so forth. It is said, "The mentally created maṇḍala and assembly of holy ones are to be visualized millions at a time," but this should be done according to one's capacity to visualize.

After having done so, one should recite, *"Mya ngan mi 'da'..."* and so forth, and should do the prayer of entreaty. Finally, reciting, *"bDag gi lus sku..."* and so forth, one should dedicate the merits.

If one intends to dissolve the maṇḍala, one should do so anticlockwise from the edge following the correct order and reciting the verse, *"Bon nyid sems nyid..."* and so forth. One should visualize the assembly of holy ones [in the space in front] absorbing into the central figure, which transforms into light and absorbs into oneself and others. The realm and the offerings [that one has visualized] merge into the nature of space and become invisible.

Before the cluster in the centre is dissolved, one should do the refuge taking, Bodhicitta cultivation and purification. Soon after the central cluster is dissolved, the maṇḍala base should be wiped clean.

This maṇḍala offering as explained above should be repeated one hundred times during the day and one hundred in the night or in whatever manner time permits. When one is undergoing the course of post-preliminary practices, it is done ten to fifteen times or more. In case maṇḍala offerings are to be made without a baseplate in the early morning or in the late evening, they should be done with the mentally created maṇḍala.

This ends the third session, which deals with the instructions on maṇḍala offering for merit accumulation, explained and taught according to the teachings of the past masters.

4. Entreaty

(Session Four)

Homage to the holy lamas!

The fourth session, entreaty and receiving blessings, the past masters considered as a part of the maṇdala offering and never a separate session. However, 'Gro-mgon says:

> Milk is the source of butter
> But if not churned,
> Butter won't be there.
> Flint-stones are the source of metals
> But if not heated so as to melt and be refined,
> Metals won't be there.
> Faith and aspiration are the sources of blessings
> But if not entreated for,
> The blessings won't nourish your mind-stream, will they?

Also, 'Dul-ba Rinpoche says:

> For most beginners, spiritual progress happens because of their faith and aspiration. For them, to entreat [for blessings] is important.

As for its practice, on the crown of the head of one's ordinary physical body, one visualizes one's root lama in the form of Sambhogakāya Buddha gShen-lha 'od-dkar with an appearance of the tutelary deity, sitting on a seat of lion, elephant, horse, dragon, and garuda with cushions of sun and moon disk and lotus; in him merge all who have been one's lamas. Thus Tshe-dbang says:

> His body is gShen-rab, speech Bon and his mind the Buddha mind. In him are the four holy objects.

In the space above him, one visualizes the lineage holders sitting one above the other resembling a staircase, which includes the eight lamas of the mind transmission lineage of siddhas, holders of the entrusted teachings of the Bru and Zhu lineage, the treasure rediscoverers of the gShen, Gyer, rMa and dByil clans, Eight gShen known as Learned Translator, Four Learned Ones, Thirteen Lineage-Holders, Six Great Masters, and the holders of the Tathagata mind transmission lineage. As a matter of fact, one visualizes all the lineage holders from Kun-tu bzang-po in the 'Og-min paradise down to one's root lama all glowing with light; sending forth illuminating rays in the ten directions and guiding living beings by the power of their immeasurable compassion; self-illuminating like rainbows but free from an inherent self. In the outer circle of space, one visualizes the assembly of meditation deities; Buddhas of the ten directions; and hosts of siddhas, Bodhisattvas and the lamas in whom one has faith. Next to them, in the outer circle of space one visualizes the protector deities sitting in such a manner that they are driving away undesirable circumstances.

To them, one does prostration with immense devotion and respect and imagines that one is leading as many living beings from the three realms as could fill the whole earth, while praying as follows:

> May undesirable circumstances that have befallen unfortunate living beings like me and others be pacified. May the negativities and obscurations caused by bad karma be purified. O compassionate ones! There is no one except you in whom we could place our hope and upon whom we could rely. Protect us, O compassionate ones! Eradicate the undesirable circumstances, show the right path, and bless us fully!

In this way, deeply concentrated, fully resolved and absolutely surrendered, one prays from the depth of one's heart.

Seeing them as they are, the holy ones send forth inconceivable lights of different colors from their heart region. The lights transform into streams of water and purify the negative impressions and obscurations in oneself and others, as quickly as frost melts in the sunshine. Also, streams of water from the heart region of Kun-bzang descend gradually through the lineage holders and absorb into one's body from the heart region of one's root lama. The water spreads on all living beings, purifying all their karma and obscurations; the impurities inside [the body] are dissolved; the forms of material aggregates outside are destroyed; and the complete transformation of [the material body into] a body of rainbow takes place. Abiding in this state, one deeply cultivates faith and devotion and prays:

> O holy ones! Please bless me instantly with all the good qualities that your body, speech and mind have attained, the views and realization that are within you, the manner in which you work for living beings, your skilful method, your compassion, your knowledge, your love and so forth. May my mind-stream be ripened, liberated and awakened.

One maintains such a state of concentration as deeply and focused as to produce a feeling of one's hair standing on end or tears rolling down. By virtue of this, streams of water of blessing descend as before and gradually absorb into one's body from the heart region of one's root lama. The water spreads on all [living beings], and purifies them as clean as glass jars filled with water or white balloons with butter.

Abiding in a natural state of mind, one develops deep faith and devotion. "Just like me, all living beings are also reciting the prayers in chorus in clearly modulated tones." Thinking thus, one recites the prayer of the lineage holders.

In the end, one visualizes as follows: all [one has visualized] turns into light and absorbs into the lineage holders. They too turn into light and gradually absorb into the root lama who, together with his cushions and seat, transforms into light and absorbs into oneself and other living beings, as they receive the power of direct accomplishments from the body, speech and mind of the holy ones. Lastly, one does the dedication for the attainment of Enlightenment.

As for this practice, one should devote mornings and evenings to the prayers of entreaty and the afternoons to maṇḍala offerings. Also, one should devote to other practices as much time as possible.

If carried out in this manner, the best ones will see by the power of blessings a spontaneous progress in their practices. The ones in whom so much [progress] is not seen will at least see in themselves a feeling of disgust towards saṃsāra, a willingness to attain liberation and a power to see all appearances as nothing but illusions.

This practice to cultivate indissoluble bonds of faith and devotion and to entreat steadfastly for blessings is my instruction called *White Panacea*. If it is true or not will come to light when one puts it into practice. Do not be suspicious! Don't hesitate! Spiritual progress will appear in the course of time.

Generally, one has to be linked with this practice until one attains the result. However, during the course of post-preliminary practices, it can be done either monthly or on certain days of every month, such as the tenth, fifteenth and so forth.

This ends the session on entreaty: a means to receive full blessings, written according to the teachings of past masters.

PART TWO

The Actual Body of Practice

Setting free the ripened consciousness

II. THE ACTUAL BODY OF PRACTICE

Homage to the holy lamas!

The Actual Body of Practice has three parts:

1. The mental grasping of that which has attributes.[25]
2. The equipoising[26] on that which is without attributes.
3. The confrontation with the Substance of Ultimate Nature.

1. *Mental Grasping*

(Session Five)

At the first streak of dawn, at the very moment when the sky becomes bright, sprinkle water on the disciples. Seating them on comfortable seats, let them engender joy and reverence and recite prayers.

Fastening the letter "A" written on a piece of indigo paper to a stick the height of which is just right, one places it on top of a sacrificial cake in front of the disciples.

One makes the surroundings (*tho skor*)[27] free from the clamor of men and dogs, very solitary and secluded; (such a place having been found,) that which is to be the object of guidance has three subdivisions:

(a) control of the body;
(b) the 'gaze';[28]
(c) the 'vow'.[29]

(a) CONTROL OF THE BODY

One assumes the fivefold posture:

i. as for the legs, pressing the left on the right, one assumes a cross-legged posture;
ii. as for the hands, pressing the thumb on the third finger, one places them so that they are equipoised;
iii. as for the spine, without twisting it or leaning against anything, not letting it become crooked or letting it lean for-

wards,[30] but holding it perfectly straight, one should hold the shoulders high;

iv. as for the neck, bending it a little, one holds the throat straight;

v. as for the eyes, looking neither up nor down, one regards unblinkingly the letter "A" directly in front.

Controlling at this time the body by means of the rules mentioned above and subduing it by means of discipline, one must concentrate intently:[31] the body must not lean backwards or forwards, be twisted or unsteady; the eyes must neither wink nor be fully opened or closed; one allows saliva, mucus and tears to flow unrestrained.

By virtue of this control of the body, the humors are balanced; the consciousness assumes its natural state; bones and joints are joined together;[32] psychic veins, wind, and semen are brought under one's control—such is its virtue.

(b) The Gaze

The mind conforms to the eye, as the great dGongs-mdzad[33] says: "If the eyes are fully open, one will grasp external objects; if they are shut, one sinks into drowsiness." Therefore one should staringly, unblinkingly, without looking up or down or to the right or to the left, directly in front regard the "A" without opening fully nor closing the eyes; without being distracted by thoughts of the past or imaginings regarding the future, by sudden reflections or thoughts and recollections of good and evil—as if one were rolling one's spear on one's shield;[34] or as if one were shooting an arrow at a target; controlling one's mind so that it becomes one-pointed, subduing it by means of discipline—staring down uninterruptedly as if boring a hole, being straight like the shaft of a spear, being tense like the string of a bow, being insensate like a corpse; without wavering, without recollection, without forgetfulness, without mental vacancy,[35] without thinking of anything in particular, without being tired even for a moment.

(c) The Vow

At this time, the eyes do not waver, the eyebrows do not move, the body does not shake, saliva is not swallowed, one does not cough, saliva etc. is allowed to flow without being restrained.

As for the length of the meditation session, each at first lasts for as long as it takes to recite the formula called "*Sale 'od*"[36] about two hundred times; thereafter, starting with subsequent sessions, the length becoming for example three hundred, it is gradually extended, and until a sign (of spiritual progress) is produced, let the disciple subdue himself and meditate.

As for the visualization-support of the uninterrupted meditation:[37] let him use a dot, an image, the letter "A", a swastika or whatever is agreeable.

Thus, while all the signs of spiritual progress will appear in the best disciples as soon as such an object of meditation is given to them, the remaining will for the most part show such signs within two or three days. This is the purport of the *Gab pa* when it says: "Control of[38] one's thoughts is obtained in three and a half days."

Guiding and watching the disciples again and again at all sessions of meditation, both initial and subsequent, it is very important to note where they are in need of improvement.

If, having done this, spiritual progress is still difficult to acquire, one should make a semi-circular row of disciples on a piece of high ground. If they are numerous, let them form several rows, one behind the other. The rules concerning bodily posture being as before, their eyes should stare into empty space.

Let them without wavering concentrate their minds on a (suitable) sound. By letting them recite neutral sounds like *HUM HRI* or *HU HUM* or *HI HING* from one hundred to one thousand times as required, it is impossible that signs of spiritual progress should not be produced; further, this guidance by means of sound is praised in certain texts as the best for people who are lazy,[39] for the blind, for old people, and for those of mild disposition.

Although there are many signs of spiritual progress, they may, if they are summed up, be grouped into internal and external signs. Internally, there are eight signs that the mind has been brought under control:

i. like a tortoise placed in a basin, one is unable to move;
ii. like the wind hitting a small bird, shuddering slightly and feeling cold, one's mind becomes tense;
iii. like grapes spread out (?), one dwells in a sensation of bodily and mental plenitude and overflowing;
iv. like a tinderbox which is struck, sometimes giving fire and sometimes not, at some sessions the success is only partial (?);[40]

v. like water drawn from an iron pipe, the mind, subtle and even, continuously gushing forth, remains one-pointed;
vi. like a bee desirous of nectar, being unable to separate oneself from material objects and quite unable to abandon them, one remains attached to them as if fixed by nails;
vii. like a fish swimming about in the ocean, one does not abandon one-pointedness, being like one roaming freely wherever one wishes without impediment;
viii. like the wind blowing through a fruit tree, the mind, subtle and even, becomes free from passion directed towards visible objects.

Thus, in some these signs will all appear; in others, not more than one or two will appear.

At that time, as external signs, absence of bodily movement or unsteadiness will occur in the best disciples. In the other disciples, a strong desire to weep, laugh, dance, and run will occur; turning the face away, not shutting the mouth or eyes, feeling a pricking sensation, sweating, shuddering, and falling to the ground will occur; this is said to be a sign that the 'mild wind' has entered the central psychic channel as the mind has been grasped.

Further, if the humours corresponding to the elements earth and water predominate, signs of spiritual progress will appear late, but subsequently they will turn into constant companions. If fire and wind predominate, signs of spiritual progress will appear early, but subsequently they will turn into hindrances.

Thus, if at the time of sitting down for meditation the beginning of the session is successful but the termination unsuccessful, let the disciple exert himself on that which has attributes; for as this is a sign of regeneration, the seed of meditation having been sown in previous lives, it will now be difficult to sow that seed once more.

Or if, the beginning being unsuccessful but the termination successful, all that which comes later becomes progressively better than that which preceded; let him subdue himself by some effective means and meditate without ill-will, for as he has a fresh mind it will be easy to sow the seed of meditation.

If, although unsuccessful at the time of guidance with regard to that which has attributes, he is nevertheless successful with regard to that which is without attributes, he has no need of that which has attributes as his faculties are excellent.

If he is successful at all times, this is a sign that his consciousness has (a high degree of realization?).

Early in the morning when no trace on the ground can be seen due to darkness he becomes drowsy;[41] later, the performer of everything, the root of evil, the basis of strife, the aggregate of good and evil being that itself (i.e. the mind), let him look inwards at its (i.e. the mind's) own nature. Letting him observe its origination, its going, and its staying, and (letting him) carefully trace its own form and figure, and inquiring of him again and again, examine his faults and virtues.

As soon as the practitioner gets an insight and roughly understands this, he should be guided as follows: upon the basis of the simile of Prince Tong-thun, he should be introduced to his mind by seeing that although the prince wandered for kalpas, [the royal blood in him] was neither lost nor separated [from him]. Similarly, the self is constant except that its experience of pain and pleasure is very different. Upon the basis of the simile of the human face, he should be introduced to his mind [which like the face] is not hidden anywhere but yet is never seen; it is within oneself in its natural state. Upon the basis of the simile of the man called 'Od-mdzes, he should be introduced [to his mind], which has the same identity but is seen differently, although it is not more than one. Upon the basis of the simile of the mustard seed and the oil, he should be introduced [to his mind] which is present within oneself as it is one's cherished property. Upon the basis of the simile of the lamp-pot and the flame, he should be introduced to the fact that mind and body are interdependent and the essence of the mind shines in the eyes. Upon the basis of the simile of the imprisoned king, he should be introduced to the fact that to follow virtue and avoid fault and to hold the mind as it is are of great importance. These six, if comprehended and employed during this course of training, will bring success, according to my experience. If after giving guidance as it should be given, through guidance with attributes, guidance with recitation, search of mind and so forth, one fails to hold the mind as it is with vitality, then instruction has not been effective. In such a case, let the disciple do the accumulation of merit, purification and so forth, receive initiation from a renowned lama, and begin again, following the instructions suggested by all the past lamas. Or let him cultivate faith and devotion in prayers of entreaty from time to time.

The change of meditative objects, wind control and the yantrayoga practices should be done with perseverance according to the *Geg sel*. Done in this manner, it is impossible not to be successful. It is said by the past great siddhas:

> Whether or not the lama's blessing is powerful, the instruction is profound, the method of teaching is effective, the intellectual capacity [of the disciples] is sharp, the causes and conditions are powerful, the four elements [concerned] are intact, and whether or not the faith and devotion [one has] are powerful, might make a difference in terms of how fast one achieves it, but it is impossible that one will never be successful.

Thus, it is at this stage that many attain insight. Due to the fact that the intellectual capacity differs from person to person, some attain insight from meditation without attributes, while others do so from the practice of channel and wind, or from the introduction. Also, it appeared to me that many attain insight simply from certain irrelevant good or bad causes. Thus, this instruction is such that it tames the untamed ones. As it is said in the *Lung*, it should be practised three times during the night or until signs of spiritual progress have appeared.

This ends the part dealing with the session of meditation with attributes, written according to the teachings of past masters. (For Similes, see Appendix 1.)

2. *The Equipoising*

(Session Six)

Homage to the holy lamas!

The equipoising on that which is without attributes has two parts, namely the two stages of equipoising:

(a) Spiritual exertion for the obtaining of stability.
(b) Spiritual exertion for the procuring of benefit from stability.

(a) Spiritual Exertion for the Obtaining of Stability

Part (a) has four subdivisions:

i. assuming a bodily posture—control of the body;
ii. the gaze—control of the senses;

iii. equipoising—control of the mind;
vi. guarding spiritual realization—control of the 'vow'.

i. Assuming a Bodily Posture

One places the body on a comfortable seat according to its nature in the fivefold posture taught above; without purposely disciplining the body, without forcing it, without relaxing it, it is simply equipoised entirely in its own natural position. In short, without being seized by any consideration, thought, hope, or fear[42] concerning the body even for a moment, one equipoises it, abandoned, stupefied, and relaxed like a corpse.

By equipoising the body thus, the humours are balanced; psychic channels, wind, and semen attain their natural state; the consciousness comes to rest and samādhi void of discursiveness is produced spontaneously. In short, as one's physical acts, one's conduct, one's going, sitting, all pure and impure deeds—during all lives down to the present—have only turned to suffering accompanied by exertion, the psychic channels have been twisted, the winds agitated, the humours unsettled, and the mind disturbed; subsequently hindrances in the producing of samādhi without discursiveness have been created; now, therefore, one must feel weariness and disgust, one must feel fright, one must feel terror.

ii. The Gaze

The fierce wrathful deities look upwards; the tranquil bodhi-minded deities look downwards; looking to the right is Method, to the left Wisdom—although many ways of keeping the eyes are described, as the manner now in question is that of the Buddhas and Mahāsattvas when they are immersed in profound samādhi, the mind conforms to the eye in empty space directly in front (of the eyes); without moving the eyeballs or the eyebrows, without opening or closing (the eyes), one looks emptily straight ahead.

'Od zer dpag med has said: "In particular, if you know the precepts concerning the gaze, you will perceive the Pure Reality;[43] one is elevated above the state of saṃsāra. Therefore, it is called 'The gaze of the saints'.

As it is thus said, one should look straight ahead, emptily, unblinkingly, staringly, without looking up or down or near or far.

iii. Equipoising

As for one's thoughts, considerations, whatever one has had of good or evil recollections—during all lives down to the present—as they have all only become the cause of suffering accompanied by painful exertion, one must now feel weariness and disgust; without effacing former traces, without interest in the future, one equipoises one's present mind ever fresh, shining and even.

In fact, one equipoises the mind unaffectedly in the unmoving expanse of the 'basis'; without even a single recollection of repeated wishes, hopes, wants, yearnings and thoughts, one transforms the host of wrathful (passions?) into the Unborn;[44] one equipoises (the mind) spontaneously in the state of equality. The five senses of themselves become vacant; the mind has no support; grasping is loosened by itself; mental restlessness disappears by itself; one equipoises (the mind) in its spontaneous self-nature.

The great dGongs-mdzad has said: "One equipoises (the mind) on that which is without attributes; one equipoises it gently, unhurriedly, relaxedly."

And the *'Bum* says: "One should equipoise (the mind) in the one ever-fresh bindu. And having equipoised it, one possesses the 'seals' of the basic precepts—what a wonder!"

The *rTsa rgyud* says: "Without perceiving the Expanse itself through meditation, equipoise (the mind) in a state which is luminous and without visualization."

The *Kun bzang zhal gdams* says: "Equipoise the mind ever anew. Do away with hope and fear. Loosen all effort. Be one-pointed. Envelop (the mind) in the Expanse. Equipoise it in the Essence."

The *Zhal chems* says: "Thus, as for the luminous contemplation, equipoise (the mind) without the consciousness then grasping it."[45]

The *mDo* says: "If, without unsteadiness, one does not think discursively of Reality, that is the very foundation of meditation.

"If, without discursive thoughts, (the mind) is all-pervading and luminous, that is the very substance of meditation.

"If, without desire, one possesses 'the Castle of Diligence', that is the very fruit of having meditated."

Further, although one may adduce and explain teachings of every sort that may cause disgust with saṃsāra to arise, in reality the mind is equipoised intently without support, without depending on anything at all; without being covered by the notion of object and subject, it is equipoised unveiled and naked; isolated without being corrupted by discursive thought, it is equipoised brightly; not bound by the ego, it is equipoised unhurriedly according to its own disposition; without discursiveness through mental activity, it is equipoised relaxedly and clearly; without being obscured by darkness, it is equipoised shiningly in luminosity.

Deciding the number and length of the meditational sessions, let the disciple meditate.

iv. Guarding Spiritual Realization

If the sessions of meditation are long, he will become languid and indifferent; if they are short, there being no stability, he will not grasp his innate nature; accordingly, he first makes the meditational sessions about as long as a hundred (repetitions of the formula called) *"Sale 'od"*; as for subsequent sessions, they are gradually extended every day. It is said that after a short while the sessions of meditation will be observed for as long as three or four (hundred repetitions of *"Sale 'od"*). It is very important to meditate on the Essence naturally.

Ne-gu has said: "Do not effect a harmful release (of your thoughts), effect a beneficial release!" Therefore, one should stop while its (i.e. the meditation's) continuation is good and take a rest. At first make the intervals between the sessions somewhat long. Thereafter, extending the sessions, gradually shorten the intervals. Further, in the intervals between the sessions of meditation, concentrate on joyful reverence, compassion, and the contemplation of impermanence.

As contemplation is like nursing a baby, avoid mental obscuration, sin, immorality and so on.

As right conduct is like a patient with a broken head, do not perform violent actions involving leaping, running, carrying loads, walking, becoming exhausted, and so on.

As one's speech should be like one who is dumb, without clamor, idle talk, muttering, conversation, or uttering even a single word, abstain from speech.

As one's thoughts and recollections should be like a corpse, be without recollections, thoughts, discursiveness and examinings.

Avoiding impediments, rely on favorable circumstances: one should not stay near the fire or in the sun, nor expose oneself to wind and chilly breezes; one should avoid food like beer and pungent herbs that upset the humours and cause drowsiness.

Relax and rest a little at midday and midnight when insight grows dim; be moderate as to diet and clothes; secure the retreat firmly, do not feel joy at improvement, do not feel dismay at diminishment (of success).

In reality, as diligence above all is important when, being utterly immersed (in meditation), one first meditates, it is important that one does not permit oneself to be idle even for a moment. If one lets oneself (be idle), blaming oneself one reproaches oneself so that the hair on one's body rises and one's skin creeps and flesh shudders.[46]

"One should not meditate at midday or midnight, the times of drowsiness. One should perform one's spiritual exercises at night, at day-break, in the morning and in the evening. Relax the senses in a moist place". Thus Bla-chen has said.

"As for the spiritual exercises of one who meditates for the first time, a hundred occasions for joy[47] and a hundred occasions for weeping arise." Thus the Hermit has said.

By meditating thus, first the mind-created tranquility is born; intermediately the tranquility of one's innate nature appears; finally the obtaining of the firmness of ultimate tranquility arises. Therefore one will obtain firmness as this instruction is the foundation of spiritual realization.

In particular, when imparting instruction concerning spiritual realization, let him (i.e. the disciple) exert himself for fifteen days, twenty days, or a month.

The chapter dealing with the equipoising on that which is without attributes, obtained from gracious gurus and explained in detail, is the sixth.

(b) The Spiritual Exertion for the Procuring of Benefit

(Session Seven)

Homage to the holy lamas!

The spiritual exertion for the procuring of benefit has three parts:

i. the gaze—the essence of visualization.
ii. the mode of arising (of mental sensations while meditating)—the essence of spiritual realization.
iii. the confrontation[48]—the essence of the means, i.e. the path.[49]

i. The Gaze

The *'Bum* says: "Having entered into the samādhi of 'The Lofty Banner of Victory', you will obtain the Great Liberation."

Bla-chen has said: "If the bird has no feathers, it lacks the means of flying. Exercise the 'reflective power'; heighten vigour,[50] be alert; regard the brightness (of your mind)!"

And the Hermit has said: "Relax unconcernedly, equipoise (the mind) without restraint! The one important point of spiritual realization consists therein."

Accordingly, one assumes the bodily posture as (explained) above: thereafter, in accordance with what *'Od zer dpag med* has said—"The yogin who has not closed his eyes is particularly exalted above all yogins; practise the so-called 'Lion's Gaze'!"—the mind accordingly conforms to the eye; therefore one directs the gaze staringly into empty space; as for the senses, let their outflow be without interruption (?); as for the mind, one produces vigor; as for the illusory body, one causes brightness to shine forth."[51]

The consciousness becomes luminous and unblinking; discursiveness vanishes blankly,[52] feeling is dispersed (?)[53]—one does not desire external objects, one does not scrutinize the internal mind. The luminous mind being firm and stable, shining from within and bright; shining, without root; stunned in its own luminosity; naked, without discursiveness; unblinking, without grasping; spontaneously balanced; freely sparkling in its own arising—let it always remain in that condition.

Gradually extending the sessions of meditation, one meditates as set forth above. Avoiding impediments in connection with food, behavior, and conduct of body, speech and mind, relying on favorable circumstances, one should do everything as set forth above and continually exert oneself spiritually without becoming tired.

ii. The Mode of Arising

Through the observing of these precepts, in a short while all external and internal modes of arising (of mental sensations) are by themselves entirely and utterly cut off, and whatever one has done, the mind without exerting itself does not abandon relaxed outflow.

One exerts oneself to obtain the following advantages: in the consciousness, courage like that of an eagle flying across the sky arises; 'hardness' (*'thas pa*),[54] instability (or 'stupor'),[55] drowsiness, sluggishness, and all the other faults vanish by themselves for him who seeks spiritual realization; benefit is obtained at the very same instant; the net of the mind being without directions (i.e. limits), it is torn apart;[56] Wisdom of Insight flames by itself; one cannot be moved by recollections arisen suddenly (*tol skyes pa'i dran pa*);[57] external and internal hindrances disappear by themselves.

As luminosity arises, one should firmly spread the foundation of the tranquilities mentioned above. As it establishes the basis of spiritual realization, this instruction is very precious for the procuring of benefit.

iii. The Confrontation

When the bright sky is without cloud or wind, let him assume the gaze and the bodily posture set forth above. Fixing the mind on empty space, the sky and the mind become indistinguishably intermixed, gradually harmonious with one another, undivided without separation. At that time he is confronted (with the true import of his psychic experiences) by means of Example, Meaning,[58] and Sign.

The *Gab pa* says: "As for this equality of Example, Meaning and Sign—in the mind of the fortunate it is meditated upon as being of one inseparable Reality."

Accordingly, at that time, externally the sky does not consist of any substance, form, color, dimension, direction or characteristics at all that can be discerned, it is perfectly stainless, freely sparkling in the Void—this is the Example.

Internally, this constantly discerning, lustrous one called 'the mind of the self' regards blankly and discerns clearly outwards and inwards without distinction—that is the Sign.

The equality of those two (Example and Sign) is established (?): the mind is just like the sky; the sky is just like the mind—indistinguishably intermixed, undivided without separation. Always remaining blankly insensate (?) (*kad de*) in this state of non-dual Great Equality, the Absolute called the *bon sku* is the Meaning.

Giving examples by means thereof (i.e. by means of Example, Meaning and Sign), one may employ (the dichotomy of) object and consciousness with regard to everything.

The *Lung drug* says: "As for all these various appearances, they are Kun-tu bzang-mo; all actions, being Means, are her male counterpart. And the state of not being moved from there is gShen-lha ('od-dkar)." These quotations must be understood to be of the same purport.

The *'Grel ba* says: "Although one makes the division into Example, Meaning and Sign, that is only in order to guide the living beings of saṃsāra."

Thereafter, at the time of imparting instruction in spiritual realization, let him follow these precepts also for nine, eleven, or fifteen (days) etc., and produce inseparably united the tranquilities and supreme insight.

The section dealing with the procuring of benefit, written down in accordance with the words of the Guru, the protector of living beings, is the seventh.

3. *The Confrontation with the Substance of Ultimate Nature*

(Session Eight)

Homage to the holy lamas!

The confrontation with the Substance of Ultimate Nature has three parts:

(a) The discerning of spontaneous wisdom.
(b) The casting off of defilements produced by the intellect.
(c) The gaining of control over stainless wisdom.

(a) The Discerning of Spontaneous Wisdom

This part has two subdivisions:

i. the instruction as to the manner in which one should meditate—the subject-matter;
ii. the confrontation therewith.

i. The Instruction as to the Manner in Which One Should Meditate

The *lDe mig* says: "Abiding and bliss are grasped in the central indigo-colored psychic channel".[59]

The *Drang don* says: "The secret (refuge) being the psychic channel, wind and bindu, the highest refuge is to meditate on the going out and the coming back of the mind."

The Great Guru says: "In the crystal cavity of one's own body, there are three psychic channels having cakras with roots and petals wide open. In the house of light, the internal wind is shot out like an arrow; the external wind is drawn back like a bow-string; the central wind is churned in that very place like milk. Thereby the three powers of meditation are perfected."

As it is thus said, as far as the essential points concerning the bodily posture are concerned, one accordingly assumes the five-fold posture as set forth above and controls (one's body) by means of the rules and concentrates intently.

It is also said that one may observe the seven essential points concerning 'fire' (?).[60]

As for the manner of visualization when meditating: as for the three psychic channels (that rise) to the top of the head like cut reed-hollows from the interior of the trunk of the body upwards, at the organs of generation the right and left (channels) like the loops of the letter *CHA* thrust upwards into the central channel.[61] As for their dimensions, the left and the right are like a medium arrow-shaft, while the central channel should be visualized as slightly thicker. As for their colors, the right is white, the left red, and the central channel is indigo.

In the space directly to the right and to the left of the top of the head, conceive the letter *A* and *MA* (respectively). The letters having dissolved into light, visualize the male deity mKha'-la Rig-pa'i rgyal-po[62] and the female deity sKos-kyi nyi-ma like rain-bows.

Conceive that those two, having dissolved and turned into a white and a red bindu like two boiled peas, congeal on the opening of the right and the left channel (respectively), and conceive that by letting the wind fly out three times, it departs together with evil propensities and defilements.

Thereupon, drawing (the wind) in just as it may come, draw up the lower wind; press down the upper wind; the bindus of the right and the left psychic channels enter; cause them to enter the central channel. Being situated one on top of the other, or else mixed together, they (i.e. the bindus) arrive at the top of the head; imagine that they (once more) congeal on the opening of the right and left channel. If you cannot subdue the wind, expel it completely. Thereafter again drawing in the wind, perform the exercise as before.

One should thus perform the complete circuit three times, or five, or seven; or, intermediately, nine, eleven, or fifteen; or, finally, seventeen, nineteen, or twenty-one times etc. As for the 'wind',[63] it is said to be important to exercise it in the lunar fashion;[64] as for the sessions of meditation (?).[65] Accordingly, perform (a suitable number of) circuits so that the intervals (between the sessions of meditation) should not be empty.

After about ten, fifteen, or twenty wind-exercises, conceive that it (i.e. the bindu) comes straight to the heart at the time when it is drawn upwards, and disappears without a trace. Firmly uttering (?) a suitable syllable like *HA* or *PHAṬ*, just relax effortlessly while in the natural state, holding the eyes in the correct way; in a state of realization equipoise (the mind) just as it remains. Meditate in a state of spiritual realization for about five or ten sessions. Again concentrating as before on the visualization of the psychic channels and the wind, it is important to be diligent at night, at dawn, in the morning and in the evening.

Further, having practised the 'gentle wind' at the first sessions, when one acquires a little training, chiefly perform the 'violent wind' as its benefit is greater. As for the wind, quickly seize it before 'the horse escapes'.[66] Breathing thus continuously, the practitioner envelops himself in a neutral wind; he must understand the essence of 'letting fly', 'entering', 'pressing down', and 'sending forth'.

Teaching this little by little, it is important that it does not become a hindrance. If it nevertheless becomes a hindrance, it is very important to know how to set things right. In short, one must understand that both the benefits and the dangers of these precepts are great.

ii. The Confrontation

After having made the disciple meditate for one session on the visualization in accordance with the method set forth above, one imparts instruction while he is in the natural state. As a result, having at that time by means of that profound method separated the pure and the impure aspects of the consciousness, at that time for a little while....[67]

The *sNyan rgyud* says: "Impurity having been dissolved in the Void, purity shines in luminosity. The garment of intellect having been taken off, the mind shines forth nakedly. The clouds of discursiveness having disappeared, wisdom shines without the covering of obscuration. Thus in the consciousness of one and all is the mind which exists according to its own self. Spontaneous wisdom is like the sun shining forth from between the clouds. It arises free from obscuration in stainless luminosity.

"As for its (i.e. wisdom's) manner of being: without recollection of former propensity to passion; without anticipation of what is to come; unmoved by mental flashbacks; not overpowered by drowsiness; without making an object of the mind; without the six 'perceptive groups' following the five senses; without attachment to the taste of samādhi; the present consciousness being bright in its own luminosity, without grasping, with joy it shines steadily.

"The arising of a sensation like that of a dumbly stupid person eating molasses, or of a young girl experiencing delight[68] (for the first time), is also called Innate Wisdom, the Nature of the Sense of Mahāyana, the Insight of the Buddhas of the Three periods, or the Spontaneous gShen-lha dkar-po of the mind.

"Accordingly, the constant hoping for the arising (of realization) through one's own practice of and meditation on that which one's guru has taught and instructed, the great and vociferous insistence on the need of it (i.e. realization) when it does not arise—that is precisely That; it is not elsewhere. Impress this on your mind; strive spiritually; make a firm resolution!"

Thus also the *Lung drug* says: "It is That; feel it and look at it. Looking, there is nothing to be seen. By means of That, That itself is seen."

Li-shu has said: "As it is nothing but precisely This itself, why do you say 'I do not know it'?"

The *'Bum* says: "The wisdom of self-knowledge does not arise from without, nor does it arise from within; it arises by itself in itself." As for these quotations, the disciple is confronted in detail (with them so that he realizes that) "It is thus!"

Thereafter, as for the procuring of benefit through means, i.e. the Path: the pure and impure aspects of the consciousness are separated; spontaneous wisdom shows itself clearly; mind and Void—mother and son—are brought into harmony; the benefit of insight is born at that instant. Accordingly, it is very important.

When Sad-ne-ga'u,[69] tranquility having arisen as he was able to remain in vacant meditation for years and months, addressed the Ācārya Ne-gu, (the latter) said: "That (achievement) of yours, tranquility, is mere stupor. Not taking that as the highest, meditate on my instruction concerning the nourishing of the central psychic channel. Subsequently spiritual realization will come." Having meditated in accordance with (Ne-gu's) words, he abandoned his former spiritual attitude like a snake its skin, and a wholesome insight arose; this story is told.

Again, experiencing for themselves that one session of visualization of psychic channels and wind is swifter and more beneficial than innumerable precious and profound methods, it is important that all the disciples constantly devote themselves to this.

At the time of observing this (instruction concerning meditation) in particular, let the disciple meditate for ten or fifteen days, etc.

The section dealing with the discerning of spontaneous wisdom, a systematization of the practice of the eminent gurus, is the eighth.

(b) The Casting Off of Defilements Produced by the Intellect

(Session Nine)

Homage to the holy lamas!

The teaching of the method of intermediately casting off the defilements produced by the intellect has three parts:

i. Equipoising.
ii. Dissolving.
iii. Retaining—concentration on these three is of great importance.[70]

i. Equipoising

The method of equipoising, the *gShen rab 'da' dga' chi drod* says: "Thus, as for the luminous contemplation, one equipoises (the mind) without the consciousness then grasping it. One equipoises the five senses so that they become self-vacant; one equipoises the mind so that it becomes all-absorbing: one equipoises body and mind naturally..."

The *Gab pa* says: "As for the way of mind, being natural, it is bliss."

The Great Guru has said: "Whatever you perceive, meeting with the self-arisen sphere of external objects, one equipoises it (i.e. the consciousness) naturally, one equipoises, purposelessly (?*rgya yan*) and uninterruptedly, the consciousness which is without grasping, passion or desire; one equipoises, without meditating or letting the thoughts wander, the consciousness which does not distinguish between object and subject."

The Hermit Father and his spiritual Son[71] have said: "While in the natural state equipoise (the mind) luminously according to its own nature, equipoise it gently, unhurriedly, relaxedly."

In reality, on the basis of the Mother, the nature of the 'basis' in the Son, the natural unruffled mind, render unmoving the 'reflective-power', namely the consciousness which consists of thoughts and recollections; the mind is thereupon equipoised blankly in its own place.

The Great Guru has said: "By seeking it is lost, by regarding it is obscured; by meditation it is corrupted. If actions are many, you run the risk of wandering about in saṃsāra."

These quotations being of one purport, they should be borne in mind; 'knowledge of equipoising' is very important.

ii. Dissolving

The method of dissolving intermediately, not entering a state of stupor after equipoising, one must firmly do away with the immediately preceding (?) state of consciousness. Dissolving it relaxedly, all that which was meditated upon is dissolved so that it becomes non-meditated upon. The string of recollection of him who meditates is completely severed, and he exerts himself spiritually without letting his thoughts wander.

The *rGyud* says: "By meditating, Buddhahood is not found—let spontaneous wisdom arise. By the arising (of spontaneous wisdom), the Void is not discerned—equipoise it (i.e. spontaneous wisdom) according to its own nature, luminous and without contemplation."

Ne-rgyung has said: "By meditating, (the mind) is not composed—equipoise it naturally on the foundation of Buddhahood. By equipoising it, one errs into a profane condition—let the wisdom of luminous recollection arise. By arising, the Void is not grasped—without letting the thoughts wander, rely on non-meditation. Relax, loosen, or dissolve—whichever you prefer—the present tirelessly busy consciousness."

The Great Guru has said: "Like one bearing a load of wood, relax it (i.e. the consciousness) unconcernedly, dissolve it unhurriedly, loosen it gently."

Accordingly, intermediately 'knowledge of dissolving' is very important.

Certain gurus have said: "As for stupor after the tranquility of meditation, it is like falling asleep while on one's way to see to a matter." Further: "As for the desire to taste samādhi, it is the internal Māra."

And the *Gab pa* says: "By the contemplation of the thought "I meditate", the 'basis', the bodhi-mind, is obscured."

Do not all these quotations have that purport?

iii. Retaining—Concentration

Further, as for the retaining finally, one should, without again meditating, spontaneously extend the 'string of recollection' and retain (realization) without either meditating or letting the thoughts wander.

The *Cog bzhag* says: "He shows that the flow of the mind is luminous by the instruction stating that there is nothing at all on which to meditate and nothing with regard to which to be inattentive."

dPon-gsas Tha-mi thad-ge has said: "Although you scatter the pebbles of calculation this way and that, make sure that you are not separated from the great depth of the luminous substance."

The Great Guru has said: "After relaxing, loosening, and dissolving, rest in your consciousness without meditating or letting your mind wander, without thinking discursively or grasping."

Accordingly, the string of recollection is extended spontaneously; one retains (realization) at all times and in all ways.

Thus, when one who has begun meditating performs the full succession (of equipoising, dissolving, and retaining) he (first) assumes the bodily posture and gaze as when in samādhi; he equipoises the mind naturally in its own nature.

Intermediately he dissolves (the consciousness); improvement is seen immediately in him who meditates (?);[72] that on which one meditates is dissolved unhurriedly so that it becomes non-meditated upon.

Finally he retains (realization); he does not again meditate. By means of the string of recollection one does not let the mind escape to its ordinary state. Without being separated from either absence of meditation or absence of inattentiveness, one rests in one's consciousness and retains (realization).

Thus, first make the dissolving shorter, the period of equipoising and retaining about equal; thereafter gradually extending the duration of the 'knowledge of retaining', when finally there is nothing except 'knowledge of retaining', equipoising and dissolving are not necessary. At that time periodical meditation is brought to its completion.[73]

Therefore, as this is precisely the actual content of that which is without attributes and the very essence of spiritual exertion of the present time of meditation, one should know that this instruction in spiritual-exertion-at-all-times is effective generally (?). In particular, when imparting (this instruction), one should let one's disciple meditate for ten or fifteen days, etc.

The section dealing with the method of casting off defilements, set down in accord with the words of the Precious Saint, is the ninth.

(c) GAINING OF CONTROL OVER STAINLESS WISDOM

(*Session Ten*)

Homage to the holy lamas!

The production of Stainless Wisdom while yet on the Path has four parts:

i. Body—the body of a god.
ii. Speech—recitation.
iii. Mind—wisdom.
iv. Yogic devices[74] connected with various means.

i. Body

On the basis of the above 'knowledge of retaining', the disciple will accompany (retaining of realization) with looking upwards and downwards, moving hither and thither, being twisted, unsteady, and careless. If this does no harm he arises gently and accompanies (realization) with salutations and circumambulations, which are pure. Thereafter he will accompany (realization) with rendering them energetic. Thereafter he accompanies (realization) with various actions like leaping, running etc., which are neutral. Thereafter he accompanies (realization) with actions like beating, furious anger etc., which are impure.

Having engaged even in all these actions (while retaining realization), all pure and impure physical acts and behavior are indulged in on the Path (i.e. they are converted into means when one is) in a condition of spiritual realization.

ii. Speech

Secondly, again while in a state of spiritual realization, he should recite the formulas, the Refuge, the bodhisattva's vow, prayers and sūtras, which are pure. He accompanies (realization) with the recital of sounds and chants, benign and fierce, of every sort. If this does no harm, he accompanies (realization) with the speaking of nonsense, loose talk, jokes, questions, and abuse etc. of every sort, which are neutral. Thereafter, he purposely utters shouts, harsh words, lies etc., which are impure.

If one indulges in all these (actions) on the Path, there is accompaniment of speech (by spiritual realization).[75]

iii. Mind

Thirdly, while in a state of spiritual realization, he accompanies (realization) with the turning of his own body into that of a tutelary deity. Further, he accompanies (realization) with the entering into the samādhi of *Bya cha dge spyod*[76] and the performing of the utpattikrama of outer and inner mantras.[77]

Engaged therein, he accompanies realization with various thoughts and reflections, which are neutral. Thereafter he accompanies realization with all the impurities like the Three Poisons, the Five Poisons, etc.

If all these are intermixed, mind and spiritual realization are likewise intermixed.

iv. Yogic Devices Connected with Various Means

He indulges in feelings of fear and terror, fright and anguish, disgust and aversion, disease and pain, anger and fury, worry and shame, desire and passion, misery and suffering, joy and happiness, etc. Discursiveness, doubt, hope and fear, suffering— unsuitable and disagreeable unfavorable circumstances; all eating, walking, sitting, (in short) actions, behavior, from the present ones right up to death finally—with regard to these (feelings, actions etc.) the mind's essence does not escape; one is not separated from the (potential) friends, viz. recollection and grasping, and they are carried along on the Path (i.e. changed into means) in a condition of spiritual realization; they are cut off just as they are; they are accepted unquestioningly; defeat and victory are intermixed.

The *Lung drug* says: "He who—if he makes the mighty effort—acts without consideration for good or evil, he is praised as the vessel of the Great Perfection." Further: "Not being hindered (by considerations of good and evil), that is the correct conduct."

Accordingly, understanding (these precepts) and, as for the manner of gaining control over these (feelings etc.), being skilled in gentle means, having gently prolonged the state (of spiritual realization), intermixed (this condition and the feelings etc.), and separated (the mind's essence from these feelings), he should exert himself with regard to that which is without attributes.

He who is a beginner intermixes body, speech, and mind one by one (with realization); after some time, he intermixes the three simultaneously; when he is fully confident he intermixes so that they are utterly cut off (?).

Thus, at first not separating, one can only intermix; intermediately, having intermixed, this is merely not harmful; finally, there is a sensation of (the feelings etc.) appearing as friends (of realization).

The *Drang don* says: "When the feelings are harmful, one relies on a beneficial friend." Further: "When the feelings are beneficial, everything appears as friends."[78]

When in the condition of the Great Vehicle, the 'basis', one can gain control over everything, the actions of body and speech, behavior pure and impure, virtuous and non-virtuous, good, bad or neutral—whatever one has done goes towards spiritual realization.

The *gSal byed* says: "When one understands the one reality of the foundation, although he has acted sinfully for many aeons, he who is without virtue is (nevertheless) separated from sin." Further: "If you are not united with the substance of the Great Vehicle, although you perform many pure austerities of body, speech, and mind, you do not obtain the result; if you do not understand the one reality of the 'basis', although you have acted virtuously for many aeons, you are bound by the sin of thinking discursively on virtue."

The *Lung drug* says: "That is not in the wishing for physical suffering[79] to become the cause of Enlightenment. How can you get butter from water? Virtue and sin are identical; sin itself is Enlightenment." Further: "This is not in another—he is an empty sack; there is nothing else in this one—he is a golden vessel."[80]

As for these quotations, perceiving their meaning to be thus, until he has spread the foundation of spiritual realization the beginner accordingly, with much wavering and unsteadiness, is similar to one who, his feet not steady on the ground, performs dance movements with his arms. Accordingly, for him it is very important to be disciplined. If he does not know how to spread the Foundation and gain control (over all feelings etc.), he is like a rivulet run dry due to drought; as he cannot overcome accidents and circumstances, this instruction is the most important.

Accordingly, in short, as for his constant spiritual exertion, at the time of guidance concerning the foundation, one imparts instruction privately for ten or fifteen days.

The section dealing with the production of stainless wisdom (while yet) on the Path, set forth in accordance with the words of the Holy Guru, is the tenth.

SUMMARY

1. One assumes correct bodily posture which causes physical and mental relaxation and equilibrium, and correct gaze which causes a condition of blankness of the mind (*rig pa*) corresponding to and dependent on the blankness of the gaze.

This forms the basis of meditation (*bsgom*) which is performed during sessions (*thun skor*), the number and length of which are gradually increased. The nature and method of this meditation is not detailed, but a visible 'support' (*dmigs rten*) is employed. The meditation should result in the mind being 'brought under one's control', which is manifested by certain 'signs of spiritual progress' (*zin rtags*), the ultimate being that of the mind becoming "subtle and even, free from passion directed towards visible objects".

2. Thereafter follows meditation without visible 'support' i.e. 'equipoising' (*mnyam bzhag*) which ultimately leads to the identification of the psyche (*sems*) with the Unconditioned.

First one obtains 'stability' (*gnas cha*). Bodily posture and gaze are as before, but without conscious effort; thereby 'samādhi void of discursiveness' (*rnam par mi rtog pa'i ting 'dzin*) is produced spontaneously. The mind is then equipoised in perfect vacancy and tranquility on the Unconditioned, whereby the senses cease to register external stimuli and the mind becomes without support (*brten med*) and appears in its spontaneous self-nature.

The length of each session of this effortless meditation is gradually extended and the intervals between the sessions reduced. Through this meditation, the three 'tranquilities' (*zhi gnas*) are obtained, of which the final is connected with 'firmness' (*brtan pa*) i.e. 'stability'.

This condition of 'stability' having been acquired, the mind is caused to remain in the condition of spontaneous luminosity described above. All 'modes of arising (of mental sensations)' (*'char tshul*) are 'cut off', i.e. one makes them cease to appear. This is followed by the 'confrontation' (*ngo sprod pa*) by means of which the identification of the psyche (*sems*) with the Unconditioned (the Void) becomes possible; the 'confrontation' is effected by means of Example (*dpe*), Sign (*rtags*), and Meaning (*don*):

Example—the clear and infinite sky is identified with the Void.

Sign—the psyche is blank and luminous as described above with reference to the mind.

Meaning—the sky (the Void) and the psyche become indistinguishably intermixed.

3. The final stage is now possible: the confrontation with the 'substance of ultimate nature'. i.e. the Void.

First, one acquires spontaneous wisdom (*rang 'byung gi ye shes*). Through psycho-physical mastery of the mind (in its aspect of 'psychic fluid'), the pure and impure aspects (*dangs snyigs*) of the consciousness (*shes pa*) are separated, and spontaneous wisdom shines forth of its own accord.

Thereafter, one does away with the defilements produced by the intellect (*blo*), in which process there are three stages:

(a) On the basis of the 'basis' (the Void), in the mind the 'reflective power' (*rtsal*), i.e. the consciousness, is brought to rest, equipoised (*'jogs*).

(b) The mind being thus equipoised, the stream-of-consciousness (*dran thag*) is utterly cut off, 'dissolved' (*bshigs*)

(c) A new stream-of-consciousness which seems to be of a transcendent nature ("neither meditation nor non-meditation") arises, and this stream-of-consciousness is 'retained' uninterruptedly thereafter (*skyong*).

Until this stage, meditation has been characterized as *thun sgom* 'periodic meditation', i.e. meditation performed during definite sessions separated by periods of non-meditation. At this third stage, however, meditation becomes permanent and spontaneous (*ngang sgom*), although outwardly the adept may lead an active, perhaps even worldly life.

The arising of stainless wisdom (*dri ma med pa'i ye shes*) now becomes possible: in this state all actions of body, speech, or mind are permissible as they merely serve as means on the Path (*lam du khyer, lam du slang*) towards the final merging with the Void.

The third section of our text (*mthar pyin pa*, "The Final Release"), which has not been translated (for a summary, see the Introduction), deals with the ultimate meditation, *klong sgom*, in which meditation becomes one with the Void.

APPENDIX I

The Similes

Prince Tong-thun

Once upon a time there was a king who had two sons. The elder son, who was successor to the throne, died. The younger son went out one day to play when he was very young and didn't return. When the king died, there was none to succeed him. Then, a minister suggested that the lost son might still be found because he had the marks of sun and moon on the right and left shoulder and marks of dice on his thighs.

Thus the attendants were sent to search, and they found one with such marks. The foundling was consecrated, given new clothes and was crowned. By virtue of this, the land prospered. Such is the example.

The meaning that this example conveys is:

Just as a prince remains a prince always, even though he changes his lifestyle, likewise the origin of living beings, i.e. Buddha-nature, remains the same. Not seeing one's own true nature, living beings wander in saṃsāra, just as the lost prince did. When one sees Buddha within oneself, it is like the lost prince becoming king again. The minister is like the lama who does the introduction; the marks of the sun and the moon on the prince's shoulders are like the clarity of one's mind; the marks of dice on the prince's thighs signify saṃsāra; consecrating the prince is like undertaking the preliminary practices; crowning the prince is like attaining the state of Buddhahood.

Human Face

Everyone, from the time he takes birth until death, does not part from his face, yet never sees it. Similarly, the mind as such is not hidden and is present in its natural state right from the beginning, but is not seen. It is seen only after a lama introduces one to it. Likewise, one needs a mirror if one wants to see one's face.

The Man Called 'Od-mdzes

There was a man named 'Od-mdzes. Some called him Apo 'Od-mdzes, others called him Anu 'Od-mdzes, still others called him

Uncle 'Od-mdzes, Cousin 'Od-mdzes, bZo-'o 'Od-mdzes, Physician 'Od-mdzes, Younger Brother 'Od-mdzes, and so forth. Although he was seen and called differently, his identity remained the same. Similarly, one might call the mind the Buddha, sentient beings, nirvāṇa, saṃsāra, the basis, path or result and so forth, but the mind as such never goes beyond its very identity.

The Mustard Seed and the Oil

All types of mustard seed, no matter whether they are big, small, good or bad, contain oil. All living beings, no matter whether they are tall, short, good-natured or bad, have the Buddha-mind in them. Just as oil is produced when it is pressed out and refined, Buddhahood is attained when the self is identified through practice.

Flame in the Lamp-pot

The lamp-pot is [like] one's physical body. The flame is [like] one's consciousness. Just as the flame shines from the lamp-pot's rim etc., the rays of mind in the middle of the heart shine forth from the five sense doors.

Imprisoned King

In one land, there were two kings. Each king had an equal number of subjects—three internal ministers, five external ministers, sixty-one attendants and eighty-four thousand soldiers. A fight broke out between the two kings, and the one who was good never managed to defeat the other one, who was bad. Therefore, one of the good king's ministers said, "Today we will wait in a narrow pass. The one coming in the front of their army will be the king himself. Our king should ambush and arrest him. Similarly, our three and five ministers, sixty-one attendants and eighty-four thousand soldiers should ambush and arrest theirs. We will be the winners this time." This having been done, the bad king, his ministers, attendants, army and his people came under the good king's rule and the land became free from enemies. This is the example.

Here the two kings are [like] the wisdom of awareness and ignorance; their three ministers are [like] the three Buddha bodies and the three poisons; their five ministers are [like] the five wisdoms and the five poisons; their sixty-one attendants are [like] the sixty-one pure wisdoms and the sixty-one afflictive emotions; and their eighty-four thousand armies are [like] the eighty-four thousand pure wisdoms and the eighty-four thousand afflictive emotions. Furthermore, the king of ignorance-oriented discursive thoughts is subdued by the king of self-aware wisdom; and the host of soldiers of afflictive emotions come to their end. Thereafter one finds no enemies in that direction. This is the implied meaning.

Thus end the stories which illustrate meanings through similes. Understanding the similes' implied meaning, the signs, one should practise in a way that reveals their ultimate meaning.

APPENDIX II

Index of Lamas

On p.76 there is a reference to the following:
bKa' babs su Bru Zhu'i gong ma kun
gTer ston gShen Gyer rMa dByil
Lo pan gS
hen brgyad
mKhas pa mi bzhi
gDung brgyud bcu gsum
Bla ma che drug

Index of Texts

Drang don p. 91, 99
mDo p. 86, 107
lDe mig p. 91
'Bum p. 86, 88, 94
rTsa rgyud p. 86
mDzod p. 106
rDzogs chen p. 112
rDzogs śhen snyan rgyud p. 113
Zhal chems p. 86
Ye phyi mo'i bon skor p. 105
Lung drug p. 90, 94, 99, 100, 107, 109, 111, 113
gShen rab 'da' dga' chi drod p. 95
Sems lung p. 69, 70
gSal byed p. 100
gSung rab p. 104, 107

The following texts are quoted on pp. 115-116, but the passage in which they are mentioned is only to be found in the *A khrid* text from sTod Tre-pa-dgon, being absent from the two other texts at the disposal of the editors:
Khod spungs kyi sgrub skor 'khrul pa rtsad gcod p. 116
mDo sgyu ma gtan 'bebs p. 116
'Bum p. 116
gSas mkhar tho tho rdzogs dgu rim p. 116
gSas mkhar ye rdzogs mchog go rgyud p. 115
Yongs rdzogs p. 115

APPENDIX III

Glossary of Technical Terms

DGE SBYOR. 'spiritual realization' seems to have a rather general application; it can refer to (limited) realization on any given stage in the process of liberation.

'CHAR TSHUL. 'mode of arising (of mental sensation)' is cut off through the observance of correct gaze and posture, 'stability' having been obtained; the 'confrontation' (*ngo sprod pa*) is precisely with the '*char tshul*, i.e. with the psychic experiences during meditation.

RTAGS, ZIN RTAGS. 'sign of spiritual progress' should result from meditation; eight internal signs; various external signs.

THUN. 'meditation'(?) regarded as a process taking place during a certain length of time. *thun skor* 'a session of meditation' (regarded as a completed process). *thun bar* 'interval between sessions of meditation'. *thun tshad* 'length of a session of meditation'. *thun sgom* 'periodical meditation' (contrasted to *ngang sgom* and *klong sgom*).

DRAN THAG. 'string of recollection' ('stream of consciousness') is cut off once the mind is equipoised; the *dran thag* which subsequently arises and which would seem to be of a different order ('neither meditation nor non-meditation') is extended uninterruptedly.

DRI MA MED PA'I YE SHES. 'stainless wisdom', the final stage, follows the 'casting off of defilements created by the intellect'.

RNAM PAR MI RTOG PA'I TING NGE 'DZIN 'samādhi void of discursiveness' produced spontaneously when the fivefold posture is assumed without conscious effort.

'BOG 'DON. 'procuring of benefit', probably a general term signifying the obtaining of the benefit, i.e. the further spiritual progress, connected with the attainment of a given spiritual condition; preceded by the acquiring of 'stability'.

DMIGS RTEN. 'visualization support' defined as *thig le, lha sku, A, g.yung drung*; serves as support for meditation (*bsgom*).

RTSAL. 'reflective power', identified with 'consciousness' (*shes pa*); dependent on 'mind' (*rig pa*); brought to rest; is the third of the triad *ma* 'the Mother' (the 'basis', the Unconditioned), *bu* 'the Son' (the mind, *rig pa*), and *rtsal*.

ZHI GNAS. three stages are enumerated:

a. *blos byas kyi zhi gnas*

b. *rang bzhin gyi zhi gnas*

c. *thar thug gi zhi gnas* which is united with 'supreme insight' (*lhag mthong*).

RANG 'BYUNG GI YE SHES. 'spontaneous wisdom', the first stage towards the confrontation with the Void, the psyche (*sems*) having been seen to be identical with the Void.

RIG PA. 'mind' (Skt. *citta*) is dependent on the 'gaze'; is made 'one-pointed'; is concentrated on a sound (*HŪM* etc.); internal and external signs of its having been brought under control; its being grasped causes the 'mild wind' to enter the *avadhūtī*; is equipoised on the Void; becomes 'without support'; regarded explicitly as psychic fluid; characterized as the 'Son' and thus second in the triad *ma, bu, rtsal*.

SHES PA. 'consciousness', assumes its 'natural state' as a result of correct posture and gaze (conscious effort), becomes 'luminous and unblinking'; 'courage arises therein as a result of the mind reaching 'stability'; its 'pure and impure aspects' (*dangs snyigs*) are separated; identified with 'reflective-power' (*rtsal*).

SEMS. 'psyche' in a more general sense than *rig pa* or *shes pa*; cf. the expression *sems phyogs kyi bstan pa* = *rdzogs chen*, identified with the Void/the sky.

APPENDIX IV

An Outline of the Original Text

Man ngag khrid kyi rim pa lag len thun mtshams dang bcas pa (p. 64-117 in A-TRI THUN-TSHAM CHO-NA DAN CHA-LAK CHE SHUK-SO)

I. *sngon 'gro (rgyud ma smin pa smin par byed pa sngon 'gro'i gdams pa)* p. 65-78 (original text)

1. *zhen pa bzlog pa'i thabs su mi rtag pa sgom pa* p. 65-67 (session 1)
2. *sems bskyed cing skyabs su 'gro ba* p. 67-71 (session 2)

   (a) *sems bskyed pa* p. 67-69
   (b) *skyabs su 'gro ba* p. 69-70
   (c) *sdig pa bshags pa* p. 70-71

3. *bsod nams kyi tshogs bsags pa* p. 71-75 (session 3)
4. *gsol ba gdab cing byin rlabs zhu ba* p. 75-78 (session 4)

II. *dngos gzhi (smin pa grol bar byed pa dngos gzhi'i gdams pa* p. 79-100

1. *mtshan bcas la sems bzung* p. 79-84 (session 5)

   (a) *lus gnad* p. 79
   (b) *lta stangs* p. 79-80
   (c) *dam tshig* p. 80-84

2. *mtshan med (mnyam par bzhag pa)* p. 84-91 (session 6)

   (a) *mnyam bzhag gnas cha ru nyams su blang pa* p. 84-88

      i. *bca' ba lus kyi gnad* p. 84-85
      ii. *lta stangs dbang po'i gnad* p. 85
      iii. *bzhag pa sems kyi gnad* p. 85-87
      iv. *srung ba dam tshig gi gnad* p. 87-88

   (b) *mnyams bzhag bog 'don du nyams su blangs pa* p. 88-91 (session 7)

      i. *lta stangs dmigs pa'i gnad* p. 88-91

ii. *'char tshul dge sbyor gyi gnad* p. 89-90
iii. *ngo sprod thabs lam gyi gnad* p. 90-91

3. *gnas lugs kyi don la ngo sprod pa* p. 91-100

(a) *rang 'byung gi ye shes ngos bzung* p. 91-95 (session 8)

i. *sgom sul gyi gdams pa dngos* p. 91-93
ii. *de la ngo sprad pa* p. 93-95

(b) *blos byas kyi dri ma dang bral* p. 95-98 (session 9)

i. *'jogs* p. 95-96
ii. *bshig* p. 96-97
iii. *skyong* p. 97-98

(c) *dri med pa'i ye shes lam du bslang pa* p. 98-100 (session 10)

i. *lus lha sku* p. 98
ii. *ngag zlas brjod* p. 98
iii. *yid ye shes* p. 98
iv. *sna tshogs thabs kyi 'khrul 'khor* p. 99-100

III. *mthar phyin pa (grol ba mthar phyin par byed pa'i khrid)* p. 100-115

1. *nub mo bag chags gtod la mnan pa* p. 101-104 (session 11)

(a) *bzung ba* p. 101-103
(b) *sbyang pa* p. 103
(c) *spel ba* p. 103-104
(d) *ar la gtad pa* p. 104

2. *nyin mo snang ba la rtsal sbyangs pa* p. 104-106 (session 12)
3. *nang nub rtog pa lam du bslang ba* p. 106-109 (session 13)
4. *rgyun du rang ngo sprad pa* p. 109-115 (session 14)

(a) *snang ba sems su ngo sprad pa* p. 109-111
(b) *sems mtha' bral du ngo sprad pa* p. 111-112
(c) *mtha' bral sku gsum du ngo sprad pa* p. 112-115 (session 15)

Conclusion p. 115
Colophon p. 115
Passage to be inserted on p.101, p. 115-117.

NOTES

Preface

1. "Bonpo Studies. The A Khrid System of Meditation", *Kailash. A Journal of Himalayan Studies*, vol.1, no.1 (Kathmandu 1973), pp. 19-50; no.4, pp. 248-332.
2. D.L.Snellgrove, *The Nine Ways of Bon. Excerpts from* gZi-brjid *edited and translated by...*,London Oriental Series, vol. 18, London (Oxford University Press), 1967, pp. 226-255. The Great Perfection is here presented as the ninth and final 'way' (*theg pa*) of Bon.
3. The most important study of the Buddhist tradition of *rdzogs chen* is Samten G. Karmay, *The Great Perfection. A Philosophical and Meditative Teaching of Tibetan Buddhism*, Leiden (E.J. Brill), 1988. Another interesting study is Franz-Karl Erhard, *"Flügelschläge des Garuda". Literar- und ideengeschichtliche Bemerkungen zu einer Liedersammlung des rDzogs-chen*, Tibetan and Indo-Tibetan Studies 3, Stuttgart (Franz Steiner), 1990, a detailed study of a collection of spiritual songs by Zhabs-dkar Tshogs-drug rang-grol (1781-1851). An important text for the Buddhist tradition of the Great Perfection is the *Man ngag lta ba'i phreng ba,* which is attributed to Padmasambhava, and translated into Italian by Guiseppe Baroetto, *L'insegnamento esterico di Padmasambhava. La collana delle visioni*, Arcidosso (Shang Shung Editizioni), 1990. A recent publication which contains a selection of *rdzogs chen* texts in translation is Jean-Luc Achard, *Les testaments de Vajradhara et des poreurs-de-science*, Paris (Les Deux Océans), 1995. Another work by J-L. Achard is in the press (1996): *Le Pic es Visions—Etude sur deux techniques contemplatives des traditions rNying-ma-pa et Bonpo de la Grande Perfection*. The numerous publications by Namkhai Norbu, an accomplished master of the Great Perfection, must also be mentioned, especially his spiritual autobiography, edited by J. Shane, *The Crystal and the Way of Light: Sutra, Tantra, and Dzogchen*, New York, 1986 (reprinted London(Arcana), 1993), and *Dzogchen. The self-perfected State*, edited by A. Clemente, London (Arcana), 1989. The only entry on the Great Perfection in a general work reference is, to the best of my

knowledge, my contribution to Paul Poupard (ed.), *Dictionnaire des religions*, 2 vols., Paris (Presses Universitaires de France), 1993 (3rd edition), "MEDITATION tibétaine de la Grande Perfection (Dzokchen)", pp. 1287-1288.

4. Samten G. Karmey (*sic*), "A General Introduction to the History and Doctrines of Bon", *Memoirs of the Research Department of the Toyo Bunko*, No.33, Tokyo (The Toyo Bunko), 1975, pp. 171-218. For further information on the Bon religion, the reader is referred to Per Kvaerne, *The Bon Religion of Tibet. The Iconography of a Living Tradition*, London (Serindia Publications), 1995.
5. Giacomella Orofino, *Sacred Tibetan Teachings on Death and Liberation. Texts from the Most Ancient Traditions of Tibet*, Bridport, Dorset (UK) (Prism Press) and Lindfield, NSW (Australia) (Unity Press), 1990.

Introduction and Text

1. This article has previously appeared in *Early Ch'an in China and Tibet* (ed. Whalen Lai and Lewis R. Lancaster), Berkeley Buddhist Studies Series 1983; and is reprinted here with minor changes and corrections, as an introduction for this book.
2. Guenther 1975 p.xvii adopts the translation "absolute completeness".
3. The Chinese dossier has been studied by Paul Demiéville (Demiéville 1952); the Tibetan sources have been studied by Tucci 1958. The *Bhāvanākrama* of Kamalaśīla, summing up the 'Indian' point of view, has been studied by Tucci 1958 and 1971 (with further references). See also Imaeda 1975 (with references to all previous works dealing with the debate).
4. See Demiéville 1970 and Imaeda 1975.
5. For some examples of such accusations, see Karmay 1975 pp. 214-15 and 1975 p. 152; Stein 1971 p. 9, 1972 p. 23. Other writers have criticized it for being "nothing but a blend of the doctrines of the Mu-stegs-pa (*tīrthika*) in India and that of the Bonpo in Tibet," Karmay 1975 p. 155.
6. Tucci 1958 pp. 21, 45, 60; 1970 p. 27.
7. Concerning Vairocana, see Tucci 1958 and Karmay 1975. The reference to "the statue of Vairocana" is probably to the deity (rNam-snang), as the Tibetan monk is, as far as I know, always styled Bai-ro (ca-na) etc. On the subject of gter-ma literature in

general, see Tucci 1948 p. 727, and 1970 pp. 52-53; Neumaier 1969, and Kvaerne 1974 pp. 18-40.

8. Texts are numbered according to Kvaerne 1974.
9. Concerning sNang-bzher lod-po, see Snellgrove/Richardson 1968 pp. 103-4 and Karmay 1972 pp. 97-99.
10. Chandra, Lokesh, (ed), *History and Doctrine of Bon-po Niṣpanna-yoga*, Śatapiṭaka Series vol. 73, reproducing a xyl. from the monastery of Sman-ri in Tibet; and Bonpo Monastic Foundation, Dolanji, H.P., 1974, reproducing a ms. from Dolpo. For further references, see Kvaerne 1974 pp. 109-11. The collection of biographies is entitled *rDzogs pa chen po Zhang zhung snyan rgyud kyi brgyud pa'i bla ma'i rnam thar* (Chandra 1968 pp. 1-130).
11. Neumaier 1970 p. 133 states that the Bonpos follow the Nyingmapas in basing their rDzogs-chen doctrines on the writings of Klong-chen rab-'byams-pa (1308-1364), but does not give any source for this statement which is clearly erroneous, the Bonpo rDzogs-chen being founded on texts which are, beyond all doubt, considerably older, and which in some cases (as the one discussed in this book) may be dated with a high degree of certainty.
12. Three versions of his biography are available: 1) *rTogs ldan nyams brgyud kyi rnam thar rin chen phring* (sic) *ba*, published Delhi 1967 (see Kvaerne 1973 pp. 19-22), pp. 8-14, translated Kvaerne 1973 pp. 29-36; 2) *Man ngag rin po che akhrid kyi bla ma brgyud pa'i rnam thar pad ma dkar po'i phreng ba*, composed by Shar-rdza bKra-shis rgyal-mtshan (1859-1935), concerning whom see Kvaerne 1973, xyl. 45 fols., preserved in the École Française d'Extrême-Orient (EFEOT. 0306), fol. 2a3-4b2 (a versified version of the preceding); 3) *Dam pa ri khrod pa'i rnam thar*, written by an otherwise unknown 'Dul-seng, ms. 10 fols., reproduced pp. 326-344 in Tenzin Namdak (ed.), *Sources for a History of Bon*, Dolanji 1972.
13. dGe-sbyor is an important term, having a wide field of application, meaning something like "success in meditation." Stein 1972 p. 430 translates it "(la véritable) vertu en méditation."
14. His biography is found in *rTogs ldan nyams brgyud*... pp. 14-19, translated Kvaerne 1973 pp. 36-41, and in *Man ngag rin po che* ... fol. 4b2-6b3 (see n. 12).
15. His biography is found in *rTogs ldan nyams brgyud*... pp. 39-42, translated Kvaerne 1973 pp. 41-44, and in *Man ngag rin po che*...

fol.14b3-16a3, finally in *Rdzogs pa chen po Zhang zhung snyan rgyud kyi brgyud pa'i bla ma'i rnam thar*, pp.98-104 (Chandra 1968).

16. Published in the same volume as the *rTogs-ldan nyams brgyud...* (A-*tri thun-tsham cho-na dan cha-lak che shuk-so*, Delhi 1967), pp. 64-117. Of its fifteen 'periods', nos. 5-10 have been translated in Kvaerne 1973 pp. 247-332. Three commentaries to it are available: 1) *Ngo sprod rin chen gsal 'debs rgyab skyor gyi gdams pa*, likewise by Bru-chen rGyal-ba g.yung-drung, pp. 117-85 in the same volume; 2) *Man ngag rin po che a khrid thun mtshams bco lnga pa'i sngon 'gro'i bsags sbyangs skor gyi sgom rim thar myur bgrod*, xyl. 18 fols., EFEO T.0278; commenting on the first part of the text (the *sngon 'gro*); 3) *Man ngag rin po che a khrid thun mtshams bco lnga pa'i dngos gzhi'i yang tig rdzogs pa chen po sku gsum rang shar*, xyl. 44 fols., EFEOT. 0302, commenting on the second part (the *dngos gzhi*). The latter two texts are written by Shar-rdza bKra-shis rgyal-mtshan (see n. 12).
17. See n. 16.
18. See n. 16.
19. Text and translation in Kvaerne 1973 pp. 252-319. References are to the Delhi edition of the text (relevant passages may thus be easily localized in Kvaerne 1973).
20. A dot, a swastika, etc. may also be used (p.80). Attention may also be focused on syllables like *hūṃ hri, hū hūṃ, hi hiṅ*, etc. which are described as "non-sexed" (*ma ning*). This may either imply that the sounds are neuter, without any significant meaning, or, on the contrary, that they represent ultimate truth, cf. *Sādhanāmālā* vol.2 p. 505 where *napuṃsaka* (= *ma ning*) is explained as the union of *śūnyatā* and *karuṇā*.
21. See *Visuddhimagga* 8 (3) (Nyanatiloka's translation, Konstanz 1952, p. 326).
22. See also Karmay 1975 p. 154.
23. This fact is stressed by Tucci 1958 p. 102. The similarity—both in doctrine and terminology—between Ch'an and the Indian siddhas was pointed out by Watts 1957 pp. 78-79. However, as pointed out by Stein 1971 pp. 5-6, Ch'an is earlier than the Indian siddhas, so that a parallel development is more probable than a direct influence.
24. Concerning the *smyon-pa*, see Stein 1972, particularly pp. 8-10. Stein stresses (p. 10) that the *smyon-pa* were not generally characterized by amoral behavior.

25. *mTshan bcas,* 'that which has attributes,' is, presumably, everything which can be perceived or become the object of conceptions. In this text, however, it seems to refer more specifically to the *dmigs rten,* 'visualization-support' which is the initial object of meditation. It is contrasted to *mtshan med,* 'that which is without attributes,' i.e. the Void, Unconditioned, which is the object and foundation of subsequent meditation. A better translation of *mtshan med* would perhaps be 'that which transcends attributes', cf. Ishihama 1989: 1602: *nimitta-niḥsaraṇam animittam—mtshan ma las 'byin pa ni mtshan ma med pa'o.*
26. To find a satisfactory translation of *mnyam pa bzhag pa* is not easy. 'Equipoise' has also been employed by Lessing and Wayman in mKhas grub rje's *Fundamentals of the Buddhist Tantras* (The Hague 1968).
27. 'Surrounding' is, strictly speaking, too imprecise a translation of *tho skor* which actually means 'the area surrounding the *mtshams tho*'; the *mtshams tho* is a small wooden post placed near the opening of the mtshams and indicating that it is occupied; it is decorated with wooden painted boards showing the four *lokapālas* and surmounted by a juniper twig.
28. *lTa stangs - dṛṣṭi,* 'gaze'; dealt with in detail and thus translated by Snellgrove 1959: vol I, pp. 84, 85. Note however that in our text *lta stangs* has no thaumaturgical connotations, being simply the correct way of holding the eyes in order to obtain the desired degree of spiritual concentration.
29. It is not clear to me in what way the subject-matter of c) has any connection with a 'vow' (*dam tshig*). Cf. section 6 where a 'vow' is likewise given as the heading of the last of four subdivisions.
30. *Gan bub,* opposite. of *gan rkyal,* "lying on the back"; cf. *kha bub* "inverted, tilted" (Jäschke p. 393).
31. The precise meaning of *gnad du 'gro* is not clear to me; perhaps it is more of a technical term than is suggested by the tentative translation 'concentrate intensely'. Cf. p. 91 where it occurs in a very similar passage: *lus gnad ni gong ltar cha lugs lnga ldan du bca' la khrims kyis bsgrim ste / gnad du 'gro bar bya /.* Cf. also the expressions *gnad du zin* (p. 81), *gnad du 'chun* (p. 79), and *gnad du bsnun* (p. 87, 95) which all seem to mean 'concentrate'.
32. I do not understand *khrom bu.*
33. This spelling does not seem to be a mere scribe's error for *dGongs mdzod* as it recurs on p. 86. Likewise the foreword to

the *Thun tsham* gives the transcription *'dGongs mdzad'*.

34. I.e. supporting the spear on the shield in order to take a steady aim.
35. *'Byams pa*, 'vacancy' cf. *Dag yig* p. 88,1.4: *'byam pa stong pa'i brda*. This statement is perhaps confirmed by the personal name *sTong 'byams dGra bla skyabs*. *'Byams pa*, 'mental vacancy', is a state which, like *ldengs pa* (cf. infra), should be avoided, cf. *Gyab skyor* p. 160,1.2: *tha mar skyong ma shes na gzhug tu 'byams pa bya ba 'ong*.. "If, finally, you do not know how to retain, there will, in the end, be mental vacancy."
36. The prayer-formula in question is: *a oṃ hūm a a dkar sa le 'od a yang oṃ 'du*.
37. *bsgom pas* is corrected to *bsgom pa'i*.
38. *Lung gnad*, 'control'.
39. Cf. *dred mo*, "one who had gone astray from religious life" (Das, p. 657); *gred* is presumably a misspelling.
40. The translation is tentative.
41. I follow the explanation suggested by Samten Gyaltsen Karmay.
42. According to Samten Gyaltsen Karmay *re dogs 'dzin pa* simply means 'hope or fear', but *'dzin pa* might be construed with *rtog dpyod* and *snyam byed* as well.
43. Here and elsewhere I have translated *don* by 'reality'. *Artha* (=*don*) seems to have precisely this meaning when it is opposed to *ruta* in several passages of the *Laṅkāvatārasūtra* (ed. B. Nanjio, 1923, p. 154, p. 197—I thank Professor Nils Simonsson for indicating these passages), as well as in the expression *bla med theg pa chen po'i don*. In some connections I have employed Snellgrove's rendering, "substance"—cf. n. 58.
44. The translation is tentative as the text is evidently corrupt.
45. I.e. becoming conscious of the contemplation as something objective. The same passage (with *bzhag* instead of *zhog*) occurs on p. 95 where it is stated to be a quotation from the *gShen rab 'da' dga' chi drod*.
46. I have translated *bun ne* twice, *skyi sha* being a *dvandva* compound. Cf. (')*bun pa*, 'to itch' (Jä. p. 393,2).
47. *Drog* is clearly a misspelling for *brod*, 'joy'.
48. I have translated *ngo sprod* by 'confrontation'. After the disciple has had a certain number of psychic experiences (*'char tshul*), he is supposed to relate them to his lama. The lama will then inform him as to the meaning and importance of the

various experiences. This instruction is called *ngo sprod.*

49. *Thabs* ("means".) is identified with *lam* "the Path", which belongs to the triad *gzhi, lam, 'bras bu,* "the Foundation (i.e. the *ālayavijñāna*, the Void, etc.), the Path (the means of identifying one's consciousness with the foundation, i.e. meditation etc.) and the fruit (the achievement of this identification.)"
50. The text erroneously has *spong* for *spor*, 'elevate'; cf. *ngar bskyed* (p. 89,1.4).
51. The 'illusory-body' is the physical body; the 'brightness' is another way of expressing bodily health and well-being.
52. The various explanations of *phyod de* serve to illustrate the general vagueness of meaning of this type of adjective/adverb. Snellgrove translates 'blank, colorless' (Snellgrove 1967: p. 302, following the explanation of Lobpon Tenzin Namdak); the same interpretation is found in *Gangs can bod kyi brda skad ming gzhi gsal bar ston pa'i bstan bcos* (1966, no place of publication indicated) p. 90: *phyod de sa le ba*. G. Uray, however, makes the following remark regarding *phyad de phyod de*: "adv. descriptive of uncertainty of movement (cf. Cl. T. *phyad phyod* 'id.', *phyad phyad* 'awkward gambols')" (G. Uray "The Suffix-E in Tibetan", *AOH*, vol. III, fasc. 3, p. 235). This interpretation is supported by another Bonpo dictionary, *Dag yig* p. 80,1.4: *phyod de glo bur.*
53. For *bun ne* cf. n. 46; further, *bun bun—rdog rdog* (Ch. gr. p. 562), 'piecemeal, dispersed' (Das p. 874). *Long long,* 'being in pieces, in fragments' (Jäschke: p. 544), *bun long,* 'whirling up and down, troubled, impure' (id. p. 369).
54. For *'thas pa*, cf. *rTogs ldan nyams brgyud kyi rnam thar rin chen phreng ba, Kailash*, vol.I, no.l. 1973 p.1.18: *dge sbyor thas pas bshig pa'am.*
55. I presume that *ltengs pa* is an error for *ldengs pa; ldeng* is explained as *g-yo* (*Gangs can bod kyi brda skad*...p. 77), 'unrest, instability'. According to Samten Gyaltsen Karmay, however, *ldeng pa* means 'to lose oneself in trance' and is a state which should be avoided. Cf. Bru-chen's own commentary (*rGyab skyor*) p. 160 1.12 *bar du bshigs ma shes na bzhag thog tu ldengs nas 'gro:* "If, intermediately, you do not know how to dissolve, you will, after equipoising (your mind), enter a state of stupor."
56. *'Dral* is a variant form of *ral*, cf. the *rGyab skyor* p. 172 1.15: *rig pa'i rgya phyogs med nas ral te/*
57. I have followed Samten Gyaltsen Karmay's explanation of *tol*;

cf. however *tol skyes shes—mthar phyin par shes pa* (Ch. gr. p. 335), *tol ba—gtol ba'am nges pa la'ang* (id). Cf. *gtol med* 'not known, dubious' (Jäschke: p. 210).

58. *Don*—this term is difficult to translate; its exact meaning in this context is not clear to me. Snellgrove translates *don* in the expression *dpe don rtags* by 'substance' (Snellgrove 1967: p. 251,1.3). In the expression *bla med theg pa chen po'i don* (id. p. 250 1.27 et seq.) he likewise translates as "the substance of the great Supreme Vehicle", cf. n. 43.
59. The syntactic function of *gnas pa* and *bde ba* seems uncertain.
60. The translation of this sentence is tentative. *tshang stang* is Zhang-zhung for "fire". Cf. the various techniques of producing the 'internal heat' (*gtum mo*). For *gnad bdun* in connection with the body, see Das, p. 748.
61. A 'psychic body' in which the three principal veins all reach the top of the head has, as far as I know, not been attested elsewhere. Normally only the central channel reaches the top of the head, the other two each ending in a nostril.
62. Cf. p. 112: *sems rang 'byung gi gShen lha / sku gsum rdzogs pa'i Sangs rgyas rang 'byung Rig pa'i rgyal po ye shes gnas lugs don gyi Sangs rgyas de...* and Snellgrove 1967: p. 228 1.13: *thog mar gzhi yi gnas tshul ni / ....'khor 'das ma srid gong rol du / thog mar Rig pa'i rgyal po snga /*
63. *Li shig* 'wind' (Zhang-zhung) cf. *Zhang zhung Tibetan Dictionary*, edited by Eric Haarh (The *Zhang-zhung Language*, Acta Jutlandica XL, vol. 1), which lists *li* and *le* as rlung (p. 40-41).
64. The Zhang-zhung term for 'moon', *zla ri*, is employed; the 'lunar fashion' means gradually increasing and decreasing, like the waxing and the waning of the moon.
65. I am not certain of the adverb (?) *dus kyis*.
66. The 'wind' should circulate continuously and rhythmically; if it is lost control of so that there is an interruption, it is said that 'the horse escapes', cf. the poem in which Milarepa likens his mind (*sems*) to a horse: *zur gsum snying gi bdu rtse na / sems kyi rta pho rlung ltar phyo /* (*Mi la ras pa'i rnam mthar*, ed. de Jong, The Hague 1959, p. 140, 1.24-25).
67. There appears to be an abrupt syntactical break in the text at this point.
68. The point of these two comparisons is, according to ST, that the sensation of the arising of spontaneous wisdom cannot be

expressed in words. Cf. Snellgrove 1959: (vol. I, p. 114) where the same two similes are used, likewise to describe the arising of a certain kind of knowledge. The expressions used are: *kumārāsuratam—gzhon nu'i dga' ba*, and *mūrkhasya svapnam—lkug pa'i rmi lam* (vol. II, p. 84-85 śloka 70). I think **kumāryā suraṭam*—both in the light of the present text and for reasons of symmetry, cf. *mūrkhasya svapnam*—is to be understood as a subjective, not objective, genitive.

69. Zhang-zhung Sad-ne-ga'u is mentioned in *rDzogs pa chen po zhang zhung snyan rgyud*....fol. 8b 1.5-9a 1.1. (Chandra 1968).

70. These three stages are, in fact, of fundamental importance. I am indebted to Samten Gyaltsen Karmay for the following table of corresponding terms:

A. *'jog pa*	B. *bshigs pa*	C. *skyong pa*
mnyam bzhag	*rjes thob/rjes shes*	*mnyam rjes dbyer med*
nyams	*rtogs pa*	*nyams rtogs zung 'jug*
zhi gnas	*lhag mthong*	*zhi lhag zung 'brel*
shes rab	*thabs*	*thabs shes zung 'brel*
lta ba	*spyod pa*	*lta spyod zung 'brel*
stong pa	*gsal ba*	*gsal stong gnyis med*

71. The disciple in question is sGom chen 'bar ba.

72. The phrase *bzang bdo sgom mkhan la cer gyis ltas te* is unclear to me.

73. I.e. one enters a state of permanent meditation, *ngang sgom*, in which all actions of daily life are performed while in meditation. This state is finally succeeded by one in which one's meditation becomes one with the Void (*klong sgom*). Cf. the *rGyab skyor* p. 168 1.20-21 where they are listed:

ting nge 'dzin gyi thun sgom dang/
sems dpa'i ngang sgom dang/
rtogs pa'i klong sgom gsum mo/

74. *'Khrul 'khor* (Skt. *yantra*) means 'yogic posture', of which there are 35 in the *A Khrid* system (and 45 in the *sNyan rgyud* system). They are said to be described in a work entitled *A khrid 'khrul 'khor*. In the present subtitle, *'khrul 'khor* would not seem to mean 'yogic posture', but rather something like 'yogic device', 'spiritual exercise'.

75. *'Dres ma* is a noun, 'intermixing, accompanying'.

76. I am not certain whether *Bya cha dge spyod* is the name of a person or the technical term for a particular *samādhi*.

77. These are the 'pure' actions.

78. *Theg chen* does not in this connection signify Mahāyana in the sense of a historical movement. This also applies to the expression *theg pa chen po'i don* (n. 58).
79. By 'physical suffering', *pūja*, study etc. is meant (ST).
80. The lama's instructions (*gdams ngag*) are 'lion's milk' (*seng ge'i 'o ma*) which must be kept in a 'golden vessel' (*gser gyi snod*), i.e. entrusted only to a suitable pupil.
81. Gyer-mi, i.e. Gyer-mi Nyi-ma 'od-zer, as mentioned in the *bstan rtsis of Nyi-ma bstan-'dzin* (*NT*), 91:
"In the year Rab gyal, i.e. the Earth-Rat-Year, Gyer-mi Nyi-'od and the incarnation rMa-ston Srid-'dzin found the Treasure of Dvangs-ra khyung-rdzong (1108)."
82. The spelling dGongs-mdzad occurs twice in the text instead of the normal spelling *mdzod*. A short biography of dGongs-mdzod ri-khrod-pa is found on p. 8-14 of *rTogs ldan nyams brgyud kyi rnam thar rin chen phreng ba* translated in "*Bonpo Studies: The A khrid system of Meditation*. Part I." Kailash, Vol. 1, No. 1, 1973. pp. 19-50. He lived from 1038 to 1096.
83. 'Gro-mgon refers to 'Gro-mgon bDud-rtsi, alias 'A-zha bDud-rtsi rgyal-mtshan, whose biography is given on p. 28-30 of *rTogs ldan nyams rgyud kyi rnam thar rin chen phreng ba*. He lived in the twelfth century.
84. 'Dul-ba rin-po-che alias Bru-zha 'Dul-ba-g.yung-drung (or 'Dul-ba rgyal-mtshan) preceded rGyal-ba g.yung-drung (1242-1290) in the spiritual lineage of *A khrid*, and must consequently have lived in the first half of the thirteenth century. His biography is given on p.35-39 of *rTogs ldan nyams rgyud kyi rnam thar rin chen phreng ba*.
85. Ne-gu, identical with sPe-Ne-gu, chapter 21 of *rGyal rabs bon gyi 'byung gnas*.
86. I.e. Me-nyag Ne-rgyung mKhar-bu, one of the Eight Great Translators (the full list is given on p.1 (marked p. 127) of the Introduction to *mDzod phug*, publ. by Tenzin Namdak, Delhi 1966.
87. In the work *mDzod phug*, Tha mir thad ge precedes the Eight Great Translators in the spiritual lineage of the doctrine of *mDzod phug*. On p. 2, line 18 of Part II of the same volume his name is given as *Da mi thad ge*.
88. Bla chen: identical with Dran pa nam mkha', who lived in the eighth century. He is mentioned as a disciple of

Padmasambhava in *rGyal po'i bka'i thang yig*, ch. 10. fol. 30a, 5 et seq., translated by H. Hoffman in *The Religions of Tibet*, London 1961.

89. Li-shu, i.e. sNya-chen Li-shu stag-ring, seems to be an important figure in the history of the Bonpos. According to *NT* 30 he was born in 1691 B.C., i.e. he comes in the same class of semi-legendary siddhas as Dran-pa nam-mkha', Tshe-dbang rig-'dzin, and Padma mthong-grol, for whom similar dates of birth are given but who all seem to have been active around the eighth century A.D.

    NT 49: "In the Earth-Monkey Year, lord sNya chen Li shu went to Tibet from *rTags gzigs*, i.e Inner Zhang zhung, by means of his skill in magic, bringing 10,000 Bon texts (552 B.C.)" NT 55: "In the Earth-Ox Year....a demon having entered the heart of the king...the sun of the Doctine was made to set.....having hid the Five Secret Treasures and the 1,700 subsidiary Treasures.....Li shu.....went to the Heavenly Sphere (749 A.D.)."

90. A short biography of Zhang-zhung Sad-ne-ga'u is found in Chandra 1968: fol. 16.5-17.1.

[illegible] ch. 14 fol. 30a.5 [illegible], translated by H. Hoffmann in The Religions of Tibet, London 19[illegible]

[illegible] is said to be an important figure in the history of the Bonpos. According to [illegible] Hoffmann, p. [illegible], he comes in the same class of semi-legendary [illegible] [illegible] [illegible] [illegible] [illegible] seem to have been [illegible] A.D.

[illegible] In the Earth Monkey Year [illegible] went to Tibet from [illegible] by means of [illegible] 10,000 Bon texts (552 B.C.) [illegible] In the Earth Ox Year [illegible] demons having [illegible] the heart of the king, the sun of the Dharma was made to [illegible] and the [illegible] secret [illegible] the 1,700 [illegible] Treasures [illegible] went to the Heavenly Sphere (?).

90. A short biography of [illegible] is found in Chandra [illegible] vol. 16, 5.17(?)

BIBLIOGRAPHY

Works in Foreign Languages

Bhattacharya, Benoytosh (ed), *S dhanam l* , Gaekwad's Oriental Series, Nos. XXVI & XLI, Baroda 1925-1928.

Das, Sarat Chandra, *Tibetan-English Dictionary with Sanskrit Synonyms*, Motilal Banarsidass, 1970.

Demiéville. *Le Concile de Lhasa*. Une controverse sur le quiétisme entre bouddhistes de l'Inde et de la China au VIIIe siècle de l'ère chrétienne, Bibliothèque de l'Institut des Hautes Études Chinoises vol. VII, Paris 1952.

——. *Recents travaux sur Touen-houang*. T'oung Pao vol. XLI (1970), pp. 1-95.

Guenther, H.V. *Kindly Bent to Ease Us, Part I*. Emeryville, Ca., 1975.

Imaeda, Y. "Documents tibétains de Touen-houang concernant le concile du Tibet". Journal Asiatique 1975, pp. 125-46.

Ishihama, Yumikoto, and Yoichi Fukuda (eds), *A New Critical Edition of the Mah vyutpatti: Sanskrit-Tibetan-Mongolian Dictionary of Buddhist Terminology*, Studia Tibetica No. 16, The Toyo Bunko, 1989.

Jäschke, H.A., *A Tibetan-English Dictionary*, Routledge & Kegan Paul Ltd., Broadway House, 68-74 Carter Lane, E.C. London, 1965.

Karmay, S.G. *The Treasury of Good Sayings: A Tibetan History of Bon*. London Oriental Series, vol. 26, London 1972.

——. *A General Introduction to the History and Doctrines of Bon*. Memoirs of the Research Department of the Toyo Bunko No. 33, Tokyo 1975, pp. 171-218.

——. *A Discussion of the Doctrinal Position of rDzogs-chen from the 10th to the 13th Centuries*. Journal Asiatique 1975, pp. 47-56.

——. *Annuaire de l'E.P.H.E. Section des Sciences Religieuses*. tome 82, Paris 1975 pp. 53-57.

Kvaerne, P. *A Chronological Table of the Bon-po, The bstan-rcis of Ñi-ma bstan-'jin*. Acta Orientalia, vol. 33, (1971), pp. 205-79.

——."Bonpo Studies. The A-khrid System of Meditation," Kailash, vol. 1 (1973), pp. 19-50, 247-332.

——. Review of: S.G. Karmay, *The Treasury of Good Sayings*. (Karmay 1972), Acta Orientalia vol. 35 (1973), pp. 273-79.

——. *The Canon of the Tibetan Bonpos*. Indo-Iranian Journal, vol. 16 (1974), pp. 18-56, 96-144.

Lalou, M. "Document tibétain sur l'expansion du Dhyāna chinois". Journal Asiatique 1939, pp. 505-23.

Neumaier, E. *Einige Aspekte der gTer-ma-Literatur der rÑiṅ-ma-pa-Schule*. Zeitschrift der Deutschen Morgenländischen Gesellschaft, Suppl. I, 1969. pp. 849-62.

——. "bKa'-brgyad raṅ-byuṅ-raṅ-śar, ein rJogs-C'en-Tantra," Zeitschrift der Deutschen Morgenländischen Gesellschaft, vol. 120, l (1970), pp. 131-63.

Snellgrove. D.L and H.E. Richardson. *A Cultural History of Tibet*. London 1968.

Snellgrove, D.L. *The Nine Ways of Bon*. London Oriental Series, vol. 18, London 1967.

——. *The Hevajra Tantra*, London Oriental Series, Volume 6, London Oxford University Press, 1959.

Stein, R.A. *Illumination subite ou saisie simultanée. Note sur la terminologie chinoise et tibétaine*. Revue de l'Histoire des Religions, vol. CLXXIX, 1, (1971), pp. 3-30.

——. *Vie et chants de 'Brug-pa kun-legs le yogin*. Paris 1972.

Tucci, G. *Tibetan Painted Scrolls*. Rome 1948.

——. *Minor Buddhist Texts, Part II*. Serie Orientale Roma vol. IX, 2, Rome 1958.

——. *Die Religionen Tibets*, in: Tucci/Heissig, *Die Religionen Tibets und der Mongolei*. Die Religionen der Menschheit Band 20, Stuttgart 1970.

——. *Minor Buddhist Texts, Part III*. Serie Orientale Roma vol.XLIII, Rome 1971.

Watts, A. *The Way of Zen*. New York 1957.

Works in Tibetan

Gangs can bod kyi brda skad ming gzhi gsal bar ston pa'i bstan bcos (1966)

rGyab skyor / "Ngo sprod rin chen gsal 'debs rgyab skyor gyi gdams pa," *A-tri thun-tsham cho-na dan cha-lak che shuk-so*, The Tibetan Bonpo Foundation, Delhi 1967, pp.117-184.

"rGyal rab bon gyi 'byung gnas," *Three Sources for a History of Bon*, published by Khedup Gyatsho, Tibetan Bonpo Monastic Centre, Dholanji, Via Solan, (H.P.) India 1974, pp.1-196.

"rTogs ldan nyams brgyud kyi rnam thar rin chen phreng ba," *A-tri thun-tsham cho-na dan cha-lak che shuk-so.* The Tibetan Bonpo Foundation, Delhi 1967, pp.5-63.

Dag yig/ *Gangs can bod kyi brda sprod dpag bsam ljon pa'i sne ma,* published by Sangye Tenzin Jongdong, Kalimpong 1960.

Chandra, Lokesh (ed), *The History and Doctrine of Bonpo Nispanna-yoga,* Satapitaka Series No. 73, International Academy of Indian Culture, New Delhi 1968.

"Man ngag rin po che a khrid kyi bla ma brgyud pa'i rnam thar pad ma dkar po'i phreng ba," *rDzogs pa chen po sku gsum rang shar gyi khrid gdams skor,* Published by Khedup Gyatsho, Tibetan Bonpo Monastic Centre, Dolanji, P.O. Oachghat, (Via Solan) H.P. 1974, pp.1-114.

Nyi-ma bstan-'dzin, "Sangs rgyas kyi bstan rtsis ngo mtshar nor bu'i phreng ba," *Tibetan Zhang zhung Dictionary,* Tibetan Bonpo Foundation, New Delhi 1965.

mDzog phug/ Srid pa'i mdzod phug ces bya ba bzhugs so, published by Tenzin Namdak, Delhi 1966.

Sādhana-mālā of the Panchen Lama, reproduced by Lokesh Chandra, International Academy of Indian Culture, New Delhi 1974, Parts I & II.

(p.64)མན་ངག་ཁྲིད་ཀྱི་རིམ་པ་ལག་ལེན་ཐུན་མཚམས་དང་བཅས་པ་བཞུགས་སོ།།

བླ་མ་བཀའ་དྲིན་ཅན་ལ་ཕྱག་འཚལ་ལོ། བླ་མ་རིག་འཛིན་གྲུབ་ཐོབ་རྣམས་ལ། རིག་པ་ཐབས་དང་རྡོ་འཕྲུལ་གྱིས་བརྒྱུད་པའི་མན་ངག་ཁྲིད་པར་ཡང་རྩེ་འདུས་པའི་ལྷ་དགོངས། ཚིག་ལྷུགས་པ་རུ་བཤད་པ། དོན་མཛུབ་ཚུགས་སུ་བསྟན་པ། གདམས་ངག་བརྡའ་ཐབས་སུ་འབོག་པ། ལག་ལེན་ཅར་ཕོག་ཏུ་བདེག་པ། ཡེ་ཤེས་གཅེར་མཐོང་དུ་གཙོར་(སྒྲོར་)བ། སེམས་ཐུག་ཕྲད་དུ་སྤྲོད་པ། དོན་གྱི་རྩ་བ་ནས་འཛིན་པ། ཚིག་གི་མདོ་འགག་ལ་འཇུ་བ། རིག་པ་རྐྱང་འདེད་དུ་འདེད་པ། སངས་རྒྱས་བཙན་ཐབས་སུ་བསྒྲུབས་པའི་གདམས་པ། རིན་པོ་ཆེ་མན་ངག་ཁྲིད་ཀྱི་རིམ་པ་ལ་གསུམ་སྟེ། རྒྱུད་མ་སྨིན་པ་སྨིན་པར་བྱེད་པ་སྔོན་འགྲོའི་གདམས་པ་དང་། སྨིན་པ་གྲོལ་(p.65)བར་བྱེད་པ་དངོས་གཞིའི་གདམས་པ་དང་། གྲོལ་བ་མཐར་ཕྱིན་པ་བྱེད་པ་རྗེས་ཀྱི་བྱ་བའོ། དང་པོ་ལ་བཞི་སྟེ། ཞེན་པ་ལྡོག་པའི་ཐབས་སུ་མི་རྟག་པ་སྒོམ་པ་དང་། ཡམ་སྒོ་དབྱེ་བའི་ཐབས་སུ་སྐྱབས་སེམས་ལ་འཇུག་པ་དང་། ཚོགས་གཉིས་རྫོགས་པའི་ཐབས་སུ་མཎྜལ་འབུལ་བ་དང་། བྱིན་རླབས་འཇུག་པའི་ཐབས་སུ་གསོལ་བ་འདེབས་པའོ། དང་པོ་ལ། ལུས་ཆ་ལུགས་ལྷུ་ལྷན་ནམ་ཅོག་པུ་བྱས་ལ། གློ་བུར་དུ་ཕཊ་ཅེས་ལུང་ལྟར། ཞེན་པ་རང་ལོག་གི་ཏིང་འཛིན་སྐྱེ་ཤ་བུན་ནེ་བ་ཞིག་ཡུན་རིང་དུ་བསྒོམས་པའི་རྗེས་ལ་བསམ་སྟེ། ང་ང་ཟེར་བའི་བར་དོའི་རྣམ་ཤེས་འཁྲུམས་པོ་ཤ་ཁྲག་རུས་པའི་སྤྲུབས་སུ་བཙུགས། སྐྱེ་དཀར་བུབ་གཅིག་གིས་(སྲུགས་པའི་)བཏུམས་པ་འདི་ཡང་། སྡུག་བསྔལ་མི་གཙང་བའི་ཁང་བུ། རོ་ཡི་རང་བཞིན་ཀེང་རུས་ཀྱི་ཐོ་ཡོར། ཆུ་རྒྱུས་ཀྱི་དྲྭ་བ། དུར་ཁྲོད་ཀྱི་རྣམ་པ། བསམ་ན་ཡ་ང་བ། དཔྱད་ན་སྐྱི་འདེག་པ། འདི་ལ་ལྟོས་དང་ཨ་ཙ་མ་ན། འདི་ལ་གསོ་བསྲུལ་ལ་འབད། བཙའ་རྗེ་ལ་རིམས། གོས་རྒྱན་གྱིས་སྤྲས་ངེས་ངེས་ཧྲག་ཧྲག་པོར་རེ་ཡང་། དུས་ད་ལྟ་ན་ཚའི་རྟེན་གཞི། སྡུག་བསྔལ་གྱི་རྒྱ་མཚོ། མཐར་ཐུག་གི་རུས་གཞོབ་སྟར་གང་ངམ། བམ་རུལ་བུབས་གཅིག་གམ། འབུ་དོང་གང་ངམ། བྱ་གཅན་ཟན་གྱིས་གཏོར་རྒྱུ་ཞིག་ཡིན་ན་ཨ་ཙ་མ། གནམ་ལ་ཐྭ་ཐིམ། ས་ལ་ཞག་ཐིམ། མ་བསྒྲིགས་པའི་དུས་ཀྱིས་སླེབས་པའི་ཚོ། འཆི་བའི་དུས་མ་ངེས། གནས་མ་ངེས། རྐྱེན་

མ་ངེས། ཅིས་ཀྱང་འཆི་བར་ངེས། གང་གིས་ཀྱང་སྡོང་མི་ཐེབས། ནམ་འཆི་ཆ་མེད་པ་ཡིན་
ན་ཡང་། ཤི་བའི་དུས་སུ་བསགས་པའི་ནོར། འགྲོགས་པའི་གྲོགས། འབྲེལ་བའི་གཉེན། བརྩིགས་
པའི་ཡུལ་མཁར། བཟའ་པའི་ཟས་(p.66)གོན་པའི་གོས། དེ་སོགས་འཇིག་རྟེན་སྣང་བ་གང་
གིས་ཀྱང་གྲོགས་སམ་ཕན་པ་མེད། སྡོང་པ་མེད་པའི་སྟེང་དུ། སླར་ལ་ཆགས་ཞེན་སྡུག་བསྔལ་
བསྐྱེད་ནས། ཕྱིར་སླུ་བར་བྱེད་ངེས་ན་ཡང་། རང་གཅིག་པུ་ཆ་མེད་ཡུལ་དུ་རྒྱུས་མེད་ལག་
སྟོང་སྟྲིན་མོར་འཁྱམས། རྟེན་མེད་ད་བུར་བུད། ཟ་འདྲེ་གཤེན་མས་ཁྲིད། སྡུག་བསྔལ་ཉམས་
སུ་མྱོང་། རང་ལས་རང་ལ་སྨིན་པའི་དུས་སུ། རེ་ས་བླ་མ་ཡིད་དམ། བསམ་པ་ཡང་དག་པའི་
དོན་མ་ཡིན་པ་མེད་ལ། གཞན་ཡང་ཚེ་རབས་ནས་ད་ལྟའི་བར་ལུས་ཅི་ཙམ་ཞིག་བླངས་པ་ལ་
ད་འབྲས་བུ་ཅི་བྱུང་བསམ་ གནས་ཅི་ཙམ་ཞིག་འཁྱམས་པའི། ད་ན་བརྟན་ས་ཅི་ཟིན་བསམ།
ལས་ཅི་ཙམ་ཞིག་སྤྱད་པ་ལ་ད་སྙིང་པོ་ཅི་བྱུང་བསམ། སྤྱོང་ཚད་ཅི་ཙམ་གྱིས་མནར་པས་ད་ཉེས་
པ་ཅི་བྱུང་བསམ། ད་རུང་ཡང་སྐྱེས་མཐའ་འཆི་བས། མི་ཤི་ཆེ་ཐར་དུ་ མི་ལུས་པར་ནི་གོ
བསགས་མཐའ་འཛད་པས་ཟས་ནོར་སྒྲུ་མར་ནི་མཁྱེན། འདུས་མཐའ་འབྲལ་བས་དགྲ་གཉེན་
སླུ་བྲིད་དུ་ནི་ཤེས། ཚེ་ལ་བསོལ་འདེབས་སྔོན་དུ་མེད་པར་ནི་རིག འདི་ཡི་ལོ་བདེ་ཟླ་བདེ་ལ་
དུས་གཏན་གྱི་འདུན་མ་འཆུག་པར་ནི་རྟོགས། ལར་ན་ཤེས་བཞིན་རིག་བཞིན་རང་གིས་རང་
སླུ་བ་སྙམ་དུ་བསམ། གཞན་ཡང་འདི་ལྟར་སྣང་བའི་འགྱུར་ཚུལ། ཆགས་གནས་འཇིག་སྟོང་
ལོ་ཟླ་ཞག་གྲངས་དར་ཙམ་ཡུད་ཙམ་ཡན་ཆོད་ལ་བསམ། སེམས་ཅན་གཞན་དག་གི་འགྱུར་ཚུལ་
སྐྱིད་སྡུག་ཕྱུག་དབུལ་དྲག་ཞན་སྐྱེ་འཆི་བཟང་ངན་ཐམས་ཅད་ལ་བསམ། རང་གི་ཡང་སྡོད་པའི་
གནས། འགྲོགས་པའི་གྲོགས། བྱེད་པའི་ལས། བཟའ་བའི་ཟས། གོན་པའི་གོས། འགྲོ་བའི་
ལམ་ལས་སོགས་ཀྱི་འཕོ་ཚུལ་འགྱུར་ཚུལ་ལ་བསམ། དེ་ལྟར་རྒྱུན་དུ་མི་རྟགས་རྒྱུད་ལ་(p.67)ཁྱིལ་
ན། རང་ལ་རང་ཡ་ང་བའམ། སྐྱེ་འཇིག་པའམ། ཧལ་པའམ། ཞེན་པ་གཏིང་ནས་ལོག་པ་
འབྱུང་། ཅི་རིགས་ཀུན་ལ་ཡང་འཁོར་བའི་སྣང་ཚུལ་རྒྱུ་འབྲས་ཡིན་ལུགས་ཤེས་པས་ཅི་བྱེད་
སྙམས་པའི་རིག་པ་སྣ་ཁ་འགྱུར་ཙམ་མི་འབྱུང་མི་སྲིད་དོ། དེ་ལྟར་བྱུང་ན་མི་རྟག་པའི་རྣལ་སྦྱོར་
ལ་འབྱོངས་པ་སྟེ། སྣང་བ་ཐམས་ཅད་སྒྲུ་མར་འཆར། བདེན་ཞེན་གྱི་འཕྲི་བ་ཆོད། འཁོར་བ་
ལ་བློ་ལྡོག འཇིག་རྟེན་གྱི་བྱ་བ་ལ་སྙིང་པོ་མེད་པར་རྟོགས། དགྲ་གཉེན་གྱི་རུ་འདྲེ་སྤོངས།

ཆགས་ཞེན་གྱི་མདུད་པ་གྲོལ། ཡང་དག་པའི་དོན་རང་ཤུགས་ཀྱི་དྲན་ཏེ། གྲོས་ཀྱི་འདྲི་ས་བླ་མ་དམ་པ། བློ་རྩེ་གཏན་ས་གཡུང་དྲུང་གི་བོན། ལུས་ངག་གི་བྱ་རྒྱུ་ཐེག་ཆེན་གྱི་དགེ་སྦྱོར། འདུག་པའི་གནས་རི་ཁྲོད་ཀྱི་དགོན་པ་མིན་པ་ཡིད་ལ་མི་བྱེད་ལག་ལེན་ལ་མི་འདེབས་པ་ཞིག་འབྱུང་བ་ལགས་སྟེ། གྱེར་མིའི་གསུང་ལས། སྐྱེས་པའི་མི་ཤི་མི་སྲིད། ཤི་བས་མི་སྐྱེ་མི་སྲིད། སྐྱེས་པ་མི་འཁོར་མི་སྲིད། ལར་འཁོར་བ་ལ་བདེ་བ་མེད་པ་དེ་ཤེས་སམ་ཞེས་དང་། མི་རྟག་རྒྱུད་ལ་སྐྱེས་ནས་འཆི་བ་དྲན་གྱུར་ན། རན་ཆོ་ཕྱི་རབས་རྗེས་འཇུག་གཤེན་པོ་ཀུན། ཅེས་བླ་ཆེན་གསུངས་སོ། ལམ་སྣོར་འཇུག་པ་སྐྱུལ་འདེབས་ཞིག་འབྱུང་བ་ལགས་ཀྱི་ཐུན་མཚམས་ཞག་ལྔ་བདུན་ལ་སོགས་སུ་སྦྱོང་ཞིང་། ལུང་གི་དགོངས་པ་ལྟར་སྦྲོས་པ་སྟེ་དང་པོའོ།། བླ་མ་དམ་པ་རྣམས་ལ་ཕྱག་འཚལ་ལོ། གཉིས་པ་སེམས་བསྐྱེད་ཅིང་སྐྱབས་སུ་འགྲོ་བ་ལ་གསུམ་ཏེ། སེམས་བསྐྱེད་པ་དང་། སྐྱབས་སུ་འགྲོ་བ་དང་། སྡིག་པ་བཤགས་པའོ། དང་པོ་ལ་སྤྱིར་གྱི་ལམ་ཐམས་ཅད་ཀྱི་སྔོན་དུ་སྐྱབས་སེམས་འབྱུང་བ་བཞིན། བྱེ་བྲག་གདམས་པ་ཁྱད་(p.68)པར་ཅན་འདི་ལ་འཇུག་པར་བྱེད་པ་ལ་ཡང་དང་པོར་སེམས་བསྐྱེད་དེ། དེའི་ཚུལ་ནི། འདི་ལྟར་མཁའ་མཉམ་འགྲོ་དྲུག་གི་སེམས་ཅན་རྒྱ་ཆེ་ཞིང་གྲངས་མང་བ་དག་ཀྱང་། ངེས་པར་བསམ་ན་བདག་གི་ཕ་མ་བུ་གཉེན་དུ་མ་གྱུར་པ་གང་ཡང་མེད་དེ། བདག་གིས་ལུས་སྣ་ཚོགས་བླངས་པས་ཇི་སྙེད་སྲིད། གནས་མཐོ་དམན་ཀུན་དུ་བརྒྱུད་པའི་ཕྱིར་དང་། དེས་ན་དེ་དག་གི་དྲིན་གང་གིས་ཀྱང་མི་འཁོར་བ། སེམས་བསྐྱེད་པས་འཁོར་བས། དེས་ན་སེམས་བསྐྱེད་ཀྱི་ཕན་ཡོན་དྲན་པར་བྱས་ལ། ལུས་ཆ་ལུགས་ལྷ་ལྡན་ནམ། ཅོག་པུ་ལས་སོགས་དག་པའི་འདུག་སྟངས་བཅའ། སྤྱན་སྣིན་མཚམས་སུ་སྟུད་དེ། བདག་གི་དྲིན་ཅན་གྱི་ཕ་མ་ཁམས་གསུམ་གྱི་སེམས་ཅན་འདི་དག་འཁོར་བའི་རྒྱ་མཚོར་བརྒྱུད་ཅིང་འཁྱམས། ལས་དང་སྡུག་བསྔལ་ཅི་སྙེད་ལ་སྤྱོད། ཐར་པ་དང་བདེ་བའི་གོ་སྐབས་དར་ཙམ་ཡང་མེད་པ་འདི་སྙིང་རེ་རྗེ་ན། འདི་དག་གི་དོན་བདག་གིས་མི་བྱེད་ཁ་མེད་ཡིན་པས། ད་ལྟ་ནི་ཚུས་ཁྱེར་བ་མཉམ་པོ་བཞིན་རང་མ་སྨིན་པས་སྟོབས་དང་ནུས་པ་མེད། དེའི་ཕྱིར་འདི་དག་གི་དོན་དུ་དམིགས་ནས། སངས་རྒྱས་སྐྱབ་ཚུལ་རྣམས་ལས་ཁྱད་དུ་འཕགས་པའི་མན་ངག་འདིའི་སྒོར་ཞུ་ཏེ། སྣང་ཡོར་གྱི་ལུས་རྒྱ་འདིའི་སྟེང་དུ་སངས་རྒྱས་ཀྱི་དགོངས་པ་ཐོབ་པར་བྱས་ལ། འཁོར་བ་སྟོང་པ་ཙམ་གྱི་སེམས་ཅན་བདག་གི་ཐུགས་རྗེའི་སྟོབས་ཀྱིས་དྲང་བར་ཤོག། སེམས་

ཅན་གྱི་དོན་ལ་རིང་ཐུང་དང་སྔ་ཕྱི་ཡོད་པས། བདག་དུས་ད་ལྟ་ཉིད་དུ་སངས་རྒྱས་ཀྱི་འབྲས་བུ་ཐོབ་པར་གྱུར་ཅིག ཐོབ་ནས་ཀྱང་བདག་གི་ལུས་ངག་ཡིད་གསུམ་ཐམས་ཅད་སེམས་ཅན་གྱི་དོན་ཁོ་ནར་གྱུར་ཅིག སྨམ་པའི་བསམ་པ་ཁ་ཙམ་ཚིག་ཙམ་འལ་འོལ་(p.69)སབ་སོབ་མ་ཡིན་པ་ཞེ་ཐག་པ་ནས་གཏུན་ལ། གནད་དུ་བསྟུན་ཏེ། ངག་ཏུ་ཕྱོགས་བཅུ་ལས་སོགས་པའི་ཚིག་བཅད་(བཤད་)བྱ་སྟེ། སེམས་བསྐྱེད་སྟོན་དུ་མ་སོང་ཞིང་པའི་རྒྱུ་བརྗོད་འདྲ། སེམས་བསྐྱེད་དོན་དང་ལྡན་པའི་གཤེན་རབ་ནི། མཁའ་ལས་ཆར་འབབ་རྒྱ་མཚོའི་རྟ་མ་འདྲ། ཞེས་སེམས་ལུང་ལས་གསུངས་སོ། གཉིས་པ་སྐྱབས་སུ་འགྲོ་བ་ལ། ལུས་གནད་སྔར་བཞིན་ཐལ་མོ་སྦྱར་ཏེ། མདུན་གྱི་བར་སྣང་ལ་སེང་གེ་གླང་ཆེན་རྟ་འབྲུག་ཁྱུང་གི་ཁྲི་ཟུར་ནས་སྐྱོབས་ཆེན་གྱིད་ཀྱིས་འདེགས་ཤིང་། སྟེང་ཕྱོགས་ཉི་ཟླ་པད་མས་སྤྲས་པ་བཀྲ་ལ་གསལ་བའི་སྟེང་དུ། བདག་གི་རྩ་བའི་བླ་མ་དམ་པ་ཉིད་ཁྲི་གདན་གྱི་སྟེང་དུ་འོད་དུ་ཞུ་བས་ཀུན་བཟང་གཤེན་ལྷ་འོད་དཀར་ཞལ་གཅིག་ཕྱག་གཉིས་སྐུ་མདོག་དཀར་པོ། ཞི་རྒྱན་བཅུ་གསུམ་ཚངས་པའི་རྒྱལ་དགུ་དང་ལྡན་པ། གསལ་བའི་འོད་ཟེར་འཕྲོ་ཞིང་ཚད་མེད་ཀྱི་ཐུགས་རྗེས་གདུལ་བྱ་འདྲེན་པ། གཟི་བརྗིད་མདངས་དང་ལྡན་པས་གཞན་སྣང་ཟིལ་གྱིས་གནོན་པར་བསམ། དེ་ལ་རང་གི་བླ་མར་གྱུར་ཚད་ཐ་ན་ཀ་ཁ་བསླབས་པ་ཡན་ཆད་སྤྱན་དྲངས་ལ་བསྡིམས་གསུངས། དེའི་སྐུ་གསུང་ཐུགས་ལས་འོད་ཟེར་གྲངས་མེད་པ་འཕྲོས་པས། མི་མངོན་པའི་དབྱིངས་དང་། ཕྱོགས་བཅུའི་ཞིང་ཁམས་མཐའ་དག་ནས། ཡིད་དམ་ཕྱི་ནང་གི་ལྷ་ཚོགས་ཕྱོགས་བཅུའི་སངས་རྒྱས་དང་རྒྱལ་སྲས་སེམས་དཔའི་ཚོགས། སྲིད་ལྷུམ་མཁའ་འགྲོ། བླ་མ་བརྒྱུད་པ་དང་བཅས་པ་སྤྱན་དྲངས་ཏེ། གཙོ་བོའི་མདུན་གྱི་བར་སྣང་ལ་མེ་ཏོག་པད་མའི་གདན་ལ་སྐུ་གཞའ་འོད་ཀྱི་རྣམ་པར་ཡམ་མེ་བཞུགས་པར་བསྐྱེད། གཙོ་བོའི་རྒྱབ་ཕྱོགས་སུ་སྐུ་གསུང་ཐུགས་རྟེན་མཆོག་རྣམས་ཀྱང་བཀྲ་ཅིག་གི་འོད་ཕུང་ངེ་། རི་བྲག་གཏམས་པ་ལྟར་བཞུགས་(p.70)པར་བསམ། དེ་ནས་བདག་ལུས་བརྒྱ་ཕྲག་དུ་མར་གྱུར་ཏེ། དེ་དག་རེ་རེས་ཀྱང་ཁམས་གསུམ་གྱི་སེམས་ཅན་བསམ་གྱིས་མི་ཁྱབ་པའི་སྣ་དྲངས་ཏེ། ཐམས་ཅད་དད་མོས་གུས་པའི་སྒོ་ནས་སྐོར་བ་བྱེད། ལྷ་ཕྱག་འཚལ་སྐྱབས་སུ་འགྲོ་བར་བསམ་ལ། མོས་གུས་དུང་པར་བསྐྱེད་དེ། བདག་སོགས་སེམས་ཅན་ཐམས་ཅད་དུས་འདི་ནས་བཟུང་ནས་ཇི་སྲིད་སྙིང་པོ་མ་ཐོབ་ཀྱི་བར་དུ། ཡུལ་མཆོག་ཐུགས་རྗེ་ཅན་ཁྱེད་རྣམས་ལ་སྐྱབས་

སུ་མཆིའོ། རྐྱེན་ཕྱི་ནང་གི་བར་ཆོད་ཞི་བར་མཛད་དུ་གསོལ། ཚེ་འདི་ཕྱི་བར་དོ་གསུམ་གྱི་འཇིགས་པ་ལས་སྐྱོབ་ཏུ་གསོལ་ལོ། མགོན་མེད་བདག་ཅག་རྣམས་ཀྱི་སྐྱབས་དང་དཔུང་གཉེན་དམ་པར་མཛད་དུ་གསོལ། མཁྱེན་པའི་ཐུགས་རྗེ་དུས་རྣམ་པ་ཀུན་ཏུ་གཟིགས་སུ་གསོལ་ལོ། སྙམ་པའི་འདུ་ཤེས་ཞི་ཐག་པ་ནས་སྐྱིད་ལ། བདག་དང་ལ་སོགས་པའི་ཚིག་བཤད་བྱ། ལྷ་ཚོགས་ཐུགས་ལས་འོད་འཕྲོས་པར་ཆོད་བསལ་ལ་སྒྲིབ་པ་སྦྱངས། སྐྱབས་འོག་བཅུག་སྟེ་ཐུགས་རྗེས་འཛིན་པར་བསམ་སྟེ། གཡུང་དྲུང་གནས་བཞིར་སྐྱབས་སུ་སོང་བ་ན། སྡུང་བ་དམ་པའི་མཆོག་ཏུ་དེ་འགྱུར་རོ། ཅེས་སེམས་ལུང་ལས་གསུངས་སོ།། །།གསུམ་པ་བཤགས་པ་དེ་དག་གི་སྤྱན་སྔར་བདག་དང་སེམས་ཅན་ཀུན་གྱིས་ཚེ་རབས་དཔག་མེད་ནས་དུས་ད་ལྟའི་བར་དུ། མི་དགེ་སྡིག་པའི་ལས་ཚོགས་དངོས་སུ་བགྱིས་པ། བཞན་ལ་བསྐུལ་བ། ཡིད་རངས་ཤུལ་བ། ཕྲ་བ་ རགས་པ་ ཟིན་པ་མ་ཟིན་པ་ལས་སོགས་མདོར་ན་སྡིག་པའི་ལས་ཚོགས་སྔར་ཅི་བགྱིས་པ་ཐམས་ཅད་མ་ཤེས་པ་མ་གོ་བ་ མ་རིག་པ་ འཁྲུལ་པའི་རང་བཞིན་དུ་གྱུར་པ། མི་འཆབ་བོ། མི་སྦེད་དོ། ཤིན་ཏུ་གནོང་ངོ་། རབ་ཏུ་འགྱོད་དོ། བཤགས་པ་འབུལ་ལོ། བྱང་ཞིང་དག་པར་མཛད་དུ་གསོལ་ལོ། སྙམས་པའི་འདུ་ཤེས་(p.71)བཅོས་མ། མ་ཡིན་པ་ཤ་དང་རུས་པ་བྱེ་བ་ཙམ་བསྐྱེད་པས། ལྷ་ཚོགས་ཐུགས་ལས་འོད་ཟེར་ཆར་རྒྱུན་ལྟ་བུ་བདག་སོགས་སེམས་ཅན་གྱི་སྤྱི་གཙུག་ཏུ་ཐིམ་པས། བག་སྒྲིབ་ཐམས་ཅད་གཤང་ལམ་དང་རྐང་པའི་སེན་བར་ནས་མར་ནག་ནུར་གྱིས་བུད། དབང་པོའི་སྒོ་དང་སྤྱི་བོ་བ་སྤུའི་བུ་ག་ཀུན་ནས་ཐྲངས་པ་སྔོན་དམར་དུ་ཕྱུར་གྱིས་ཐོན་ནས་སྡིག་སྒྲིབ་ཐམས་ཅད་བྱང་བར་བསམ་སྟེ། གལ་ཏེ་འགྲོད་པ་དྲག་པོ་དག་ཕྱིས་སྐྱེས་ན། ལས་སྒྲིབ་མ་ལུས་འབྱོང་པར་ཐེ་ཚོམས་མེད་ཅེས་གསུངས་སོ། ད་ནི་དུས་འདི་ནས་བཟུང་ནས་གཡུང་དྲུང་སྙིང་པོའི་བར་དུ་རང་ཡང་སྡིག་ཚོགས་མི་དགེ་བའི་ལས་ཕྲ་ཞིང་ཕྲ་བ་ནས་སྤང་བར་བྱའོ། (འཛེམ་པར་བྱའོ།) དགེ་བ་ཕྱོགས་མེད་ལ་བློ་སྦྱང་ཞིང་སྤྱད་པར་བྱའོ། གཞན་ལ་ཡང་དེ་བཞིན་དུ་བསྐུལ་བར་བྱའོ། གང་ཞིག་དགེ་བ་ལ་སྤྱོད་ཅིང་སྒྲུབ་པ་མཐའ་དག་ཀྱང་ཤིན་ཏུ་ངོ་མཚར་ཞིང་ཡིད་རང་ངོ་སྙམས་པའི་བསམ་པ་བཟུང་། བདག་དང་འགྲོ་བ་ལས་སོགས་བྱ་སྟེ། རྗེས་སུ་ཡིད་རངས་དགེ་རྩ་བསམ་མི་ཁྱབ་ཅེས་གསུངས་སོ། རྗེས་སུ་དགེ་བ་དེ་དག་ལས་སོགས་སེམས་ཅན་ཀུན་གྱིས་དུས་གསུམ་དུ་བསགས་པའི་དགེ་རྩ་ཐམས་ཅད་བྱང་ཆུབ་ཏུ་བསྔོ་བ་ཚིག་བཤད་དང་བཅས་པ་བྱའོ། མན་

ངག་ཁྲིད་ཀྱི་རིམ་པ་ལས་སྔོན་འགྲོ་སྐྱབས་སེམས་ཀྱི་ཡན་ལག   རྟོགས་ལྡན་གོང་མའི་དགོངས་ཚུལ་ཞལ་གདམས་དང་བཅས་པ། འདུལ་བ་རིན་པོ་ཆེའི་གསུང་བཞིན་ཡེ་གེར་བཀོད་པ་འདི། ཞག་གྲངས་དགུའམ་བདུན་ལས་སོགས་སུ་སྦྱངས་ཏེ་ཐུན་མཚམས་གཉིས་པའོ།། །།བླ་མ་དམ་པ་རྣམས་ལ་ཕྱག་འཚལ་ལོ། གསུམ་པ་བསོད་ནམས་ཀྱི་ཚོགས་བསགས་པ་མ་འདལ་གྱི་ཁྲིད་ལ། སྤྱིར་འདུས་བྱས་ཀྱི་དགེ་རྩ་རྣམས་ཀྱི་ནང་ནས། མ་འདལ་འབུལ་བ་འདི་བསོད་(p.72)ནམས་ཀྱི་ཚོགས་རབ་ཏུ་ཆེ་བ་། ཀླུ་འབུམ་དང་། གསང་སྔར་བླ་ཆེན་པོ་ལས་སོགས་གོང་མ་ཀུན་གྱིས་གསུངས་པས། དེ་ལ་ཡང་དམིགས་རྟེན་རབ་གསེར་དངུལ་འབྲིང་ལིའམ་འཁར་བ། ཐ་མ་ཤིང་དང་ས་ལ་བཟོ་ནས་འབུལ་བ་ཡན་ཆོད་ལ་བཟོ་ནས། ཁ་བརྡར། རྟེན་འབྲེལ་མ་འཆུག་པ་ཞིག་དགོས་ཏེ། འོད་འདུ་མེད་ན་གཞན་སྣང་ཟིལ་གྱིས་མི་ནོན། སྙིང་གསོང་བྱུང་ན་བསོད་ནམས་འཕར་འབུབ་འོང་། སྤྱི་རིས་དང་སེར་ཁ་ཡོད་ན་ཚེ་ལ་བར་ཆོད་འབྱུང་། མཚོ་མེད་ན་ཐུགས་བཅུད་མི་ཡོན། ཆུ་ཞེང་ཚད་དང་མ་ལྡན་ན་ཞིང་ཁམས་མ་དག་པར་སྐྱེ་བས་དེ་དག་གི་བླང་དོར་ཤེས་པར་བྱས་ལ། ཡོན་མཆོད་གཉིས་ཀའི་བསམ་སྦྱོར་སེམས་བསྐྱེད་དང་ལྡན་པའི་ངང་ལས། རྒྱུ་དཔྱིབས་ཆག་ཚད་དངོས་པོ་དག་པར་བཞེངས་པ་དེ་ནི། ཐོད་པ་མཚན་ལྡན་ལྷར་བཅངས་པས་འདོད་པ་འགྲུབ་ཅིང་། མཆོག་ཐུན་མོང་གཉིས་ཀའི་ཡོན་ཏན་དངོས་གྲུབ་འབྱུང་བས། དེའི་རྒྱུན་དུ་རབ་ཀྱིས་རིན་ཆེན་འབྲིང་གི་འགྲོན་ཚོམས། ཐ་ན་འབྲུ་སྣ་ཚུན་ཆད་ལ་འཛོམས་པའི་ཚོམས་བྱ་བཅུ་བདུན་བྱ། རིན་ཆེན་མཆ་ཊལ་ཡིན་ན་སོར་བཞི་ཡན་ཆད་ཀྱང་རུང་ལ། ཤིང་དང་ས་ལ་མཐོ་གང་དང་ཁྲུ་གང་ལས་ཆུང་དུ་མི་ཉན་ཏེ་ཕྱི་རོལ་པ་དང་། མཚུངས་པར་གྱུར། གསུངས་པས་དེའི་བླང་དོར་ཤེས་པར་བྱས་ལ། འབུལ་བའི་དུས་སུ། དང་པོར་སེམས་བསྐྱེད་སྐྱབས་འགྲོ་སྡིག་བཤགས་ལས་སོགས་བྱ་ཞིང་། དེ་ནས་ཕྱི་སྟེ། སྡིག་སྒྲིབ་བྱང་བར་བསམ་ལ་བོན་ཉིད་ལ་སོགས་བྱ། ལེགས་པར་ཕྱིས་པས་གཟུགས་བཟང་ཤེས་པ་གསལ་དབང་པོ་རྣོ། མཐར་ལས་སྒྲིབ་བྱང་བར་གསུངས། དེ་ནས་ལག་དང་བྲལ་ན་ཚད་ལྟར་སྐྱེ་བས་མ་བྲལ་བར་བཀོད་དེ། ཧཱུྃ་རི་ཏེ་གར་མ་ལ་ཏོ་ཞེས་(p.73)དབུས་སུ་བཀོད། ཨ་ཡཾ་རཾ་མཾ་ཁཾ་བྲཱུྃ་ཤག་ས་ལེ་སང་ངེ་ཡེ་སྭཧཱ།.ཞེས་རེ་རེ་ལ་རེ་རེ་བརྗོད་ལ། རང་གི་མདུན་ཤར་ཡིན་པས་དེ་ནས་གཡས་བསྐོར་དུ་ཕྱོགས་བཞི་རུ་བཀོད། མཚམས་བརྒྱད་བཀོད། ཕྱོད་ཕུར་ས་ལེ་ཏ་ལོ་སེང་ཞེས་དབུས་སུ་བཞི་དགོད། དེ་

ལྷར་རྒྱན་དེ་དག་འདུས་མིན་འགྱུར་མིན་རིག་མིན་ཆད་པ་མིན་པའི། སྨོན་ཡོན་བསམ་ལ་མཛེས་ཤིང་འཚམས་པར་བྱ་སྟེ། དབུས་སུ་ཉེ་ན་དབང་པོ་མི་ཚང་། མཐར་ཉེ་ན་མཐའ་འཁོབ་ཏུ་སྐྱོང་། བར་ན་ཆེ་ཆུང་ཞོར་ན་འཁོར་བཟང་ངན་ཅན་འབྱུང་ཞེས་གསུངས་སོ། དེ་ནས་བཀོད་པའི་རྗེས་ལ་འབུལ་ཏེ། དང་པོར་མདུན་གྱི་ནམ་མཁའ་ལ། སེང་གླང་རྟ་འབྲུག་ཁྱུང་ཉི་ཟླ་པད་མའི་གདན་སྟེང་དུ་རྩ་བའི་བླ་མ་ཡི་དམ་གྱི་རྣམ་པ་ཅན། བརྒྱུད་པའི་བླ་མ་དེ་ཡི་སྟེང་ན་ཡར་མཐོ་བརྩེགས་སུ་བཞུགས་པ། རྒྱབ་ཕྱོགས་སུ་སྐུ་གསུང་ཐུགས་ཀྱི་རྟེན། མདུན་ཕྱོགས་སུ་ཕྱོགས་བཅུའི་སངས་རྒྱས། ཡིད་དམ་ལྷ་ཚོགས་རིག་འཛིན་སེམས་དཔའ། ཆོད་ལྷམ་མཁའ་འགྲོ། དམ་ཅན་སྲུང་མ་དང་བཅས་པ་བསམ་གྱིས་མི་ཁྱབ་པ། ནམ་མཁའ་བར་སྣང་གང་བ་ཙམ་སྤྲིན་ཚོགས་གཏིབས་པའམ། སྐར་ཚོགས་བཀྲམ་པ་ལྟར་བཀྲ་ལ་གསལ་བར་བསྐྱེད། དེ་ནས་མཎྜལ་ནི། ས་གཞི་ཐམས་ཅད་རིན་པོ་ཆེའི་གསེར་གྱི་བྱེ་མ་བདལ་བའི་རང་བཞིན་ལ། དབུས་སུ་རི་རྒྱལ་མཆོག་རབ་ལ་གསེར་གྱི་རི་བདུན་རོལ་པའི་མཚོ་བདུན་གྱིས་བསྐོར་བ། དེའི་མཐར་གླིང་ཆེན་བཞི། ཕྲ་མོ་བརྒྱད་ཀྱིས་ཕྱོགས་མཚམས་བརྒྱད་ནས་བསྐོར་བ། དེ་དག་གི་མཐའ་ལྕགས་རི་ཆེན་པོ་གཅིག་གིས་འཁོར་ཞིང་། ཞིང་ཁམས་རྣམ་པར་དག་པ་དེའི་ནང་དུ་མཆོད་པའི་སྤྲིན་ཚོགས་དཔག་ཏུ་མེད་པ། བཀྲ་ཤིས་རྟགས་(p.74)བརྒྱད། རིན་པོ་ཆེའི་ནོར་བདུན། རིན་པོ་ཆེའི་གསེར་གྱི་མེ་ཏོག གཡུ་ཡི་མེ་ཏོག མཛེས་དགུའི་གཟུགས། སྙན་དགུའི་སྒྲ། ཞིམ་དགུའི་དྲི། བདའ་དགུའི་རོ། འཇམ་དགུའི་རེག འཐད་དགུའི་ཡོན། ལྷའི་ན་བཟའ། འགྲོ་མགྱོགས། སྟོབས་ཆེན། ལྷ་ན་སྡུག མེ་ཏོག་པད་མ་གེ་སར་འབུམ་དང་བཅས་པ་ལྷ་མིའི་མཆོད་སྤྲིན་ཡོངས་སྤྱོད་བསམ་གྱིས་མི་ཁྱབ་པས་ཞིང་ཁམས་གང་སྟེ། དེ་ནས་བདག་ལུས་ལྷའི་བུ་མཛེས་ཤིང་ཡིད་དུ་འོང་བ་རྒྱན་སྣ་ཚོགས་ཀྱིས་བརྒྱན་པ་གྲངས་མེད་པར་གྱུར་པ་དེ་དག ཚང་རྒྱུང་གི་ཞིང་ཁམས་ཆེན་པོའི་ནང་དུ་ཁྱབ་པར་འཕྲོས་ཏེ། དེ་དག་རེ་རེས་ཀྱང་ས་སྙིར་རེའི་སྐྱེ་འགུལ་(དགུ) སེམས་ཅན་བསམ་གྱིས་མི་ཁྱབ་པ་བསྐྱུལ་བཏབ་སྣ་དྲངས་ཏེ། ཐམས་ཅད་ཀྱང་ལུས་རང་རང་དང་བཏུན་པའི་རྒྱན་སྣ་ཚོགས་ཀྱིས་སྤྲས་ཏེ། གར་སྟབས་སུ་བསྒྱུར་ཅིག་དགའ་དད་མོས་པའི་སྟོབས་དང་ཆས་པ། མཆོད་པའི་རྫས་སྣ་ཚོགས་པ་ལག་ན་ཐོག་སྟེ། །སྙན་པའི་དབྱངས་ཀྱི་རང་སྒྲ་དི་རི་རི་མཆོད་པ་འབུལ་བའི་ལས་བྱེད་པར་བསམ། དེ་ལྟར་བསྐྱེད་པའི་ཞིང་ཁམས་མཆོད་སྤྲིན་དང་

བཅས་པ་ཐམས་ཅད། མཁའ་ལ་བསྐྱེད་པའི་སྐྱབས་ཡུལ་དམ་པ་རྣམས་ལ་ཞེན་པ་དང་། ཆགས་པ་མེད་པའི་སྒོ་ནས་ཡིད་ཀྱིས་མཆོད་པ་ཕུལ་ཏེ། ཐུགས་རྗེ་ཆེན་པོས་བྱིན་གྱིས་རློབས་ལ་བཞེས་སུ་གསོལ། བདག་སོགས་སེམས་ཅན་ཐམས་ཅད་ལ་གནས་ལུགས་ཐེག་པ་ཆེན་པོའི་ཉམས་རྟོགས་ཐུན་མོང་མ་ཡིན་པ་ད་ལྟ་ཉིད་དུ་རྒྱུད་ལ་སྐྱེ་བར་མཛད་དུ་གསོལ། ཕྱི་ནང་བར་ཆོད་ཞི་ཞིང་ལས་སྒྲིབ་ཐམས་ཅད་དག་པར་མཛད་དུ་གསོལ་ལོ། སྙམས་པའི་(p.75)འདུ་ཤེས་བསྐྱེད་དེ་ཞིང་ཁམས་ལས་སོགས་པའི་ཚིག་བཤད་ཀྱིས་དབུལ། མཆོད་ཡུལ་དང་མཎྜལ་ཐམས་ཅད་བྱེ་བ་ཕྲག་བརྒྱར་སྤྲུལ་གསུངས་པ་ནི་བློ་སྟོབས་རྒྱ་ཆེ་ཆུང་དང་སྦྱར་རོ། དེ་ནས་སྨྲ་ངན་མི་འདའ་ལས་སོགས་པས་གསོལ་བ་བཏབ། བདག་གི་ལུས་སྐྱུ་ལས་སོགས་པས་སྨོན་ལམ་བཏབ། རྗེས་སུ་དགེ་བ་བྱང་ཆུབ་ཏུ་བསྔོ་ཞིང་། བསྡུ་ན་མཐའ་ནས་གཡོན་བསྐོར་དུ་མ་འཁྲུགས་པར་བླང་ལ། བོན་ཉིད་སེམས་ཉིད་ལས་སོགས་པའི་ཚིག་བཤད་བྱ། ལྷ་ཚོགས་ཐམས་ཅད་གཙོ་བོ་ལ་ཐིམ། དེ་འོད་དུ་ཞུ་བས་བདག་སོགས་ལ་ཐིམ། ཞིང་ཁམས་མཆོད་སྤྲིན་དང་བཅས་པ་ནམ་མཁའི་ངང་བཞིན་མེད་པར་བསམ། ཡང་དབུས་ཀྱི་རྒྱན་མ་བླང་པ་ལ། སྐྱབས་སེམས་སྡིག་བཤགས་བྱ། དབུས་ཀྱི་རྒྱན་བླངས་མ་ཐག་ཏུ་ཕྱི། ཡང་བཀོད་པ་གོང་ལྟར་ཉིན་བརྒྱ་མཚན་བརྒྱ་ལས་སོགས་ཅི་རིགས་སུ་འབུལ། གཞི་ཁྲིད་དུས་སུ་བཅུ་བཅོ་ལྔ་ལས་སོགས་སུ་སྦྱང་ཞིང་། མ་འདལ་མེད་པ་དང་ནང་སྤྱ་ནུབ་ཕྱིའི་དུས་སུ་འདི་ལྟར་ཀྱི་སྣང་བ་ལ་ཧེན་ལ་འབུལ་ལོ། བསོད་ནམས་སོགས་པ་མ་འདལ་ཀྱི་ཁྲིད་གོང་མའི་གསུང་ལས་སྦྲིས་ཤིང་བསྒྲགས་པ་སྟེ་ཐུན་མཚམས་གསུམ་པའོ།། །།བླ་མ་དམ་པ་རྣམས་ལ་ཕྱག་འཚལ་ལོ། བཞི་པ་གསོལ་བ་གདབ་ཅིང་བྱིན་རླབས་ཞུ་བ། གོང་མ་ཀུན་གྱིས་སྐྱབས་སེམས་མ་འདལ་ཀྱི་ཞུགས་ལ་འདོགས་པ་ལས། ཡོགས་པའི་ཐུན་མཚམས་སུ་མི་མཛད་ཀྱང་། འགྲོ་མགོན་གྱིས། འོ་མ་མར་གྱི་རྒྱུ་ཡིན་ཡང་། མ་བཤིག་ན་མར་མི་འབྱུང་། ལྕགས་རྡོ་ལྕགས་ཀྱི་རྒྱུ་སྟེ་གཞུ་བཏུལ་མ་བྱས་ན་རྡོ་དང་ཅི་ཁྱད། དད་མོས་བྱིན་རླབས་ཀྱི་རྒྱུ་སྟེ། གསོལ་བ་མ་བཏབ་ན་རྒྱུད་ལ་གར་འཇུག ཅེས་དང་། འདུལ་བ་རིན་པོ་ཆེའི་(p.76)ཞལ་ནས། ལས་དང་པོའི་དགེ་སྦྱོར་བ་ཕལ་ཆེར་དད་པ་མོས་གུས་ལ་བརྟེན་ནས་སྐྱེ་བ་ཡིན། དེ་ལ་གསོལ་བ་འདེབས་པ་གལ་ཆེ་གསུངས་པས། དེའི་ལག་ལེན་ལ། བདག་ཉིད་ཐ་མལ་གྱི་ལུས་ཀྱི་སྤྱི་གཙུག་ཏུ་སེང་གླང་རྟ་འབྲུག་ཁྱུང་ཉི་ཟླ་པད་མའི་གདན་སྟེང་དུ། རྩ་བའི་བླ་མ་རྫོགས་སྐུ་གཤེན་ལྷའི་ཆ་

ལུགས་ཏེ། ཡིད་དམ་གྱི་རྣམ་པ་ཅན་ལ་བླ་མར་གྱུར་ཚད་སྙིམས། དེའི་སྐུ་གཤེན་རབ་གསུང་ཐོན་ཐུགས་སངས་རྒྱས་ཡིན་པས། ཡུལ་མཆོག་བཞི་ཚང་ཞེས་ཆེ་དབང་གིས་གསུངས། དེའི་སྙིང་ན་ཡར་མཐོ་རྩེགས་སུ་རྫོགས་ལྡན་ཉམས་བརྒྱུད་ཀྱི་བླ་མ་བརྒྱུད་དང་། བཀའ་བབས་བྲུ་ཞུའི་གོང་མ་ཀུན་དང་། གཏེར་སྟོན་གཤེན་གྱེར་ཟླ་དབྱིལ། ཡོ་པཙ་གཤེན་བརྒྱུད། མཁས་པ་མི་བཞི། གདུང་བརྒྱུད་བཅུ་གསུམ། བླ་མ་ཆེ་དྲུག བདེར་གཤེགས་དགོངས་བརྒྱུད་ཏེ། དེ་ཡང་འོག་མིན་ན་བཞུགས་པའི་ཀུན་ཏུ་བཟང་པོ་ནས། རང་གི་རྩ་བའི་བླ་མའི་བར་གྱི་བརྒྱུད་པ་རྣམས་ཀྱང་གཟི་མདངས་བརྗིད་དང་བཅས་པ། གསལ་བའི་འོད་ཟེར་ཕྱོགས་བཅུར་འཕྲོ་ཞིང་། ཚད་མེད་ཐུགས་རྗེས་གདུལ་བྱ་འདྲེན་པ། གསལ་ལ་རང་བཞིན་མེད་པ། གཞན་འོད་ཀྱིས་རྣམ་པར་བསྐྱེད། ཕྱི་རིམ་གྱི་བར་སྣང་ལ། ཡི་དམ་ལྷ་ཚོགས་ཕྱོགས་བཅུའི་སངས་རྒྱས་དང་རིག་འཛིན་སེམས་དཔའི་ཚོགས། རང་གང་མོས་ཕྱོགས་ཀྱི་བླ་མ་དང་བཅས་པ་བསྐྱེད། དེའི་ཕྱི་རིམ་དུ་བསྟན་པ་བསྲུང་པའི་དམ་ཅན་རྣམས་བར་ཆོད་ཕྲིན་ཟློག་པའི་ཚུལ་དུ་བཞུགས་པར་བསྐྱེད། དེ་དག་ལ་བདག་གིས་གཙོར་བྱས་ཁམས་གསུམ་གྱི་སེམས་ཅན་ས་གཞི་གང་བ་ཙམ་གྱིས་གུས་པས་ཕྱག་འཚལ་ཞིང་མོས་གུས་དུང་བ་བསྐྱེད་དེ། བདག་སོགས་ལས་ངན་གྱི་སེམས་ཅན་རྣམས་ཀྱི་(p.77)ཕྲིན་ངན་གྱི་བར་ཆོད་ཞི་བ་དང་། ལས་ངན་གྱི་སྡིག་སྒྲིབ་དག་པར་མཛད་དུ་གསོལ་ལོ། ཐུགས་རྗེ་ཅན་ཁྱེད་རྣམས་མ་གཏོགས་པའི་རེ་ས་མེད་དོ། སྐྱོས་ས་མེད་དོ། ཐུགས་རྗེས་གཟིགས། བར་ཆོད་སེལ་ལམ་སྣ་དྲོངས། བྱིན་གྱིས་རློབས། སྨམས་པ་ཞི་ཐག་པ་ནས་གནད་དུ་བསྣུན། བློ་ཐག་ཐད་ཀྱིས་བཅད། བློ་རྩེ་ཡིངས་ཀྱིས་བཀལ་བས། ཡུལ་མཆོག་རྣམས་ཀྱིས་ཅི་ལྟ་བ་བཞིན་མཁྱེན་ནས། དེ་དག་གི་ཐུགས་ལས་འོད་ཟེར་གྲངས་མེད་པ་འཕྲོ་འཕྲོ་འཁྲོས་པས་ཐམས་ཅད་ཆུ་རྒྱུན་དུ་གྱུར་ཏེ། བདག་སོགས་སེམས་ཅན་རྣམས་ཀྱི་བག་སྒྲིབ་ཐམས་ཅད་དུས་སྐད་གཅིག་མ་ལ། བ་མོ་ལ་ཉི་མ་ཕོག་པ་ལྟར་སྦྱངས། ཁྱད་པར་དུ་ཀུན་བཟང་ཐུགས་ལས་ཆུ་རྒྱུན་པའི་རིམ་པ་ལྟར་བརྒྱུད་དེ། བླ་མའི་ཐུགས་ཀ་ནས་བདག་ལ་ཐིམ།

སེམས་ཅན་རྣམས་ལ་འཁྲོས་པས། ལས་སྒྲིབ་ཐམས་ཅད་སྦྱངས། ནང་མི་གཙང་པའི་རྫས་དང་བྲལ། ཕྱི་གདོས་བཅས་ཀྱི་དངོས་པོ་ཐམས་ཅད་བཅོམ། དག་པ་གཞན་འོད་ལས་གྲུབ་པའི་ལུས་སུ་ལམ་ ལམ་གྱུར་པར་བསྐྱེད། དེའི་ངང་ལས་ཡང་མོས་གུས་དུངས་དུངས་པ་བསྐྱེད་དེ། དམ་

པ་ཕྲིད་རྣམས་ཀྱི་ནང་ལྷ་དགོངས་དང་ཉམས་རྟོགས། ཕྱི་འགྲོ་དོན་གྱི་འཕྲིན་ལས་མཛད་ཚུལ། ཐབས་དང་ཐུགས་རྗེས། མཁྱེན་པ་དང་བརྩེ་བ་ལས་སོགས་ཏེ། དོན་ལ་སྐུ་གསུང་ཐུགས་ཀྱི་ཡོན་ཏན་ཅི་མངའ་བ་ཐམས་ཅད་དུས་ད་ལྟ་ཉིད་དུ་བདག་ལ་བསྟུལ་དུ་གསོལ་ལོ། རྒྱུད་སྨིན་པ་དང་གྲོལ་བ་དང་རྟོགས་པར་མཛད་དུ་གསོལ་ལོ། སྐམས་པས་བ་སྤུ་གཡོ་བ་མཆི་མ་འཆོར་བ་ཙམ་གནད་དུ་བསྣུན་པས། ཡང་བྱིན་བརླབས་ཀྱི་རྒྱུན་ཆུ་གོང་ལྟར་རིམ་པ་བཞིན་བབས་པ། བླ་མའི་ཐུགས་ཁ་ནས་བདག་ལ་(p.78)ཐིམ། ཀུན་ལ་འཁྲོས་པས་ཤེལ་བུམ་དུ་ཆུ་བླུག་པའམ། (སློ་དཀར་ལ་མར་བླུག་པ་ལྟར་གྱུར་ཏེ།) དེ་དག་གི་ཡོན་ཏན་ཅི་མངའ་བ་ཐམས་ཅད་ད་ལྟ་ཉིད་དུ་གསོལ་ལོ།། །།ཤེས་པ་བུན་ནེ་བའི་ངང་ནས་མོས་གུས་དུངས་དུངས་བ་བསྐྱེད་ཅིང་། བདག་ཅི་ལྟ་བར་སེམས་ཅན་ཀུན་གྱིས་ཀྱང་སོ་སོའི་རང་སྐྲ་དང་བཅས་ཏེ། གསོལ་བ་ཝུར་ཝུར་འདེབས་པར་བསམ་ལ། བརྒྱུད་པའི་གསོལ་འདེབས་ལ་འབད། འཇོག་དུས་ཐམས་ཅད་འོད་དུ་ཞུ་ནས་བརྒྱུད་པ་རྣམས་ལ་ཐིམས། དེ་དག་ཡས་མར་འོད་དུ་ཞུ་ནས་བླ་མ་ལ་ཐིམས། དེ་ཁྲི་གདན་དང་བཅས་པ་འོད་དུ་ཞུ་ནས་བདག་སོགས་སེམས་ཅན་ལ་ཐིམ་པས། སྐུ་གསུམ་ཐུགས་ཀྱི་དངོས་གྲུབ་ཐོབ་པར་བསམ་ལ། རྗེས་སུ་བྱང་ཆུབ་ཏུ་བསྔོ་བའོ། དེ་ཡང་སྔ་དགོང་གསོལ་བ་འདེབས་པར་འབད་ཅིང་། གུང་དུས་མ་འདལ་སྐྱབས་སེམས་ལས་སོགས། བྱ་ཆ་གཞན་ཡང་ཅི་རིགས་སུ་བྱའོ། དེ་ལྟར་ཉམས་སུ་བླངས་པས། རབ་ལ་བྱིན་རླབས་ཀྱི་སྟོབས་ཀྱིས་དགེ་སྦྱོར་རང་འབབས་སུ་འཆར་བ་ཡང་ཡོད་ལ། དེ་ཙམ་མ་ནུས་ཀྱང་འཁོར་བ་ལ་བློ་ལྡོག ཐར་པ་ལ་བྲོད་པ་བསྐྱེད། སྣང་བ་ཐམས་ཅད་བན་བུན་དུ་འཆར་ཏེ། འདུ་འབྲལ་མེད་པ་མོས་གུས་བསྐྱེད་ནས། ཐང་ལྷོད་མེད་པར་གསོལ་བ་འདེབས་པ་འདི། ཁོ་བོའི་དཀར་པོ་གཅིག་ཐུབ་ཀྱི་གདམས་པ་བྱ་བ་ཡིན་པས། བདེན་ནམ་བརྫུན་ནམ་ཉམས་སུ་ལོངས་དང་། ཐེ་ཚོམ་མི་དགོས། ཉམས་ང་མི་དགོས། དྲོད་རྟགས་འཕྲུལ་འཕྲུལ་ལ་འབྱུང་བ་ལགས་སོ། དེ་ནས་སྤྱིར་ནི་འབྲས་བུ་ལ་མ་སླེབས་ཀྱི་བར་དུ་འདི་དང་འབྲེལ་དགོས་ཀྱང་། གཞི་ཁྲིད་ཀྱི་དུས་སུ་ཟླ་བའམ། བཅུ་བཅོ་ལྔ་ལས་སོགས་སུ་སྦྱོང་ངོ་། མོས་འདུན་གསོལ་འདེབས་ཀྱི་ཐུན་མཚམས། གོང་མའི་གསུང་བཞིན་སྦྲོས་པ་སྐྱེ་བཞི་པའོ།། །།བླ་མ་དམ་པ་རྣམས་(p.79)ལ་ཕྱག་འཚལ་ལོ། གཉིས་པ་རྒྱུད་སྨིན་པ་གྲོལ་བར་བྱེད་པ་ལ་གསུམ་སྟེ། མཚན་བཅས་ལ་སེམས་བཟུང་པ་དང་། མཚན་མེད་མཉམ་པར་བཞག་པ་དང་། གནས་

ལུགས་ཀྱི་དོན་ལ་ངོ་སྤྲོད་པའོ། དང་པོ་ལ། སྤྱི་དོན་དང་པོ་ནམ་མཁའ་གསལ་མ་ཁད་སློབ་མ་རྣམས་ཁྲུས་ནས་བཏོན། འདུག་ས་བདེ་བ་ལ་བཞག་ལ། མོས་གུས་བསྐྱེད་དེ་གསོལ་བ་འདེབས་སུ་བཞུག མདུན་དུ་གཏོར་མའི་རྟེར་མཐིང་ཤོག་ལ། ཨ་བྲིས་པ་ཤིང་མཐོ་དམན་རན་པ་ལ་བསྐྱོན་ཏེ་བཙུག་ལ། ཐོ་སྐར་དུ་མི་ཁྲིའི་ཀུ་ཅོ་ལས་སོགས་མེད་པ་ཤིན་ཏུ་དབེན་ཞིང་འགོལ་བར་བྱས་ལ། རྫས་ཁྲིད་བྱ་བ་ལ་གསུམ་ཏེ། ལུས་གནད་དང་། ལྷ་སྔངས་དང་། དམ་ཚིག་གོ དང་པོ་ལ་ཆ་ལུགས་ལྷ་ལྡན་དུ་བཅའ་སྟེ། ཞབས་གཡས་ཀྱིས་གཡོན་མནན་ཏེ། སྐྱིལ་ཀྲུང་དུ་བཅའ། ཕྱག་མཐེབ་ཆེན་གྱིས་སྲིན་མཛུབ་མནན་ཏེ། མཉམ་བཞག་ཏུ་བཅའ་སྣལ་ཚིགས་མ་བཙུས་མ་རྟེན་པ། ཡ་ཡོ་གན་བུབ་དུ་མ་སོང་པར་བྱས་ལ། ངང་པོར་སེང་གེས་སྒྲང་སྟེ། དཔུང་མགོ་གཟེང་བྱ། འཁྲིན་པ་ཅུང་ཙམ་བཀུག་ལ་སྣ་འཛིང་དྲང་ཐག་གེས་སྲུངས། མིག་གྱེན་ལྷ་ཐུར་ལྷ་མ་ཡིན་པ་ཐད་ཀྱིས་ཨ་ལ་ཧྲིག་གེ་གཟེར། འདི་ཡི་དུས་སུ་ལུས་ཁྲིམས་ཀྱི་བསྒྲིམས་ལ་རྒྱུན་གྱིས་བཙུན་ཏེ་གནད་དུ་འགྲོ་བར་བྱ། ལུས་འགལ་འགྱུལ་ཡ་ཡོ་བཅའ་གཙུ། མིག་སླབ་སླེབ་འབྱེད་འཛུམ་མི་བྱ། ཁ་རྒྱུ་སྣ་རྒྱུ་མིག་རྒྱུ་ཐམས་ཅད་རང་འབབས་སུ་འཁོར་བཞུག་སྟེ། ལུས་གནད་དེའི་ཡོན་ཏན་གྱིས་འདུ་བ་ཆ་སྙོམས། ཤེས་པ་རང་ས་ཟིན། རུས་ཚིག་ཁྲིམ་བུ་སྡེམས། རྩ་རླུང་ཐིག་ལེ་ཐམས་ཅད་གནད་དུ་འཆུན་པའི་ཡོན་ཏན་ཡོད་དོ། གཉིས་པ་ལྷ་སྔངས་ལ། རིག་པ་མིག་དང་བསྟུན་ཏེ། དེ་ཡང་དགོངས་(p.80)མཛོད་ཆེན་པོས། ཏ་ཙང་སྒྲད་ན་ཡུལ་འཛིན་དུ་འགྲོ། བཙུམས་ན་ཁྱིང་འཐིབས་སུ་འགྲོ་གསུངས་པས། ཏད་དེ་ཧྲིག་གེ་བ་ལ་གྱེན་ལྷ་ཐུར་ལྷ་གཡས་ལྷ་གཡོན་ལྷ་མ་ཡིན་པ། ཐད་དུ་འབྱེད་བཙུམ་མེད་པར་ཨ་ལ། ཕུབ་ཐོག་ཏུ་མདུང་སྒྲིལ་བའམ། ཁབ་མིག་ཏུ་སྐུད་པ་འཛུད་པའམ། འབེན་ལ་མདའ་འཕེན་པ་ལྟར། སྤྱི་བསམ་ཕྱིས་མོན། ཟློ་བུར་གྱིས་རྟོག་སྤྲོད་བཟང་ངན་གྱི་བསམ་དྲན་གེས་ཀྱང་མ་གཡོས་པར་བྱ་ལ། རིག་པ་རྩེ་གཅིག་ཏུ་ཁྲིམས་ཀྱིས་སྒྲིམས། རྒྱུན་གྱིས་བཙུན་ལ་བུག་པ་འབུག་པ་ལྟར་ཐུར་རེ་བྲེང་ངེ་བ་ལ། མདུན་ཤེང་ལྟར་དྲང་སེང་ངེ་བ། གཞུ་རྒྱུད་ལྟར་ཕྲ་ཐང་ངེ་བ། རོ་ལྟར་ཏད་དེ་བ། མ་ཡེངས་པ་མ་དྲན་པ། མ་བརྗེད་པ་མ་འབྱམས་པ། མ་བསམ་བ་ལ། སྐད་གཅིག་ཙམ་ཡང་གཡེལ་བ་མེད་པར་ལྟའོ། གསུམ་པ་དེའི་དུས་སུ་མིག་མི་འགུལ། རྗེ་མ་མི་གཡོ། ལུས་མི་འགུལ། མཆིལ་མ་མི་མིད། བློ་མི་ལྷུ། རྒྱུ་གསུམ་རང་འབབས་སུ་བཏངས། ཐུན་ཚད་ཀྱང་དང་པོ་ས་ལེ་འོད་འཕྲིང་

སྐོར་གཉིས་བརྒྱ་ཙམ་འདྲེན་ཡུན་ལ་ཐུན་སྐོར་རེ་ལ། དེ་ནས་ཕྱི་ཐུན་ནས་སུམ་བརྒྱ་ལས་སོགས་ཐུན་ཐང་འགྱུར་གྱི་ཇེ་རིང་ཇེ་རིང་ལ་བསྲིངས་ཏེ། རྟགས་མ་བྱུང་བར་དུ་གཙུན་ལ་བསྒོམ་དུ་བཞུག རྒྱུན་དུ་བསྒོམ་པས་དམིགས་རྟེན་ནི། ཐིག་ལེ་ཧྲཱ་སྐུ་ཨ་གཡུང་དྲུང་ལས་སོགས་གང་བདེ་ལ་གཏད་དུ་བཞུག་གོ དེ་ཡང་རབ་ལ་གཏད་མ་ཐག་ཏུ་ཟིན་རྟགས་ཚང་པ་ཡང་འབྱུང་ལ། ཅི་རིགས་ཀྱིས་ཞག་གཉིས་གསུམ་རྒྱུན་ཆད་ལ་ཟིན་པ་ཤས་ཆེ་སྟེ། གབ་པ་ལས། ཞག་གསུམ་གྲོ་དང་བཞི་དགོངས་པའི་ལུང་གནན་གསུངས་པ་འང་དོན་དེའོ། སྔ་ཐུན་གྱི་ཐུན་ཀུན་ལ་ཡང་(p.81)ཡང་ཁྲིད་ཅིང་ལྟ་བ་དང་འཚོས་ས་གནད་ཆེ། དེ་ལྟར་བྱས་ཀྱང་ཟིན་དཀའ་ན། ས་མཐོ་ཕྱོགས་སུ་ཟླ་གམ་གྲལ་བྱ། མང་ན་གྲལ་མདུན་རྒྱབ་རིམ་པ་མང་དུ་འཆར་བཙུགས་ཏེ། ལུས་གནད་སྔར་བཞིན་ལ་མིག་བར་སྣང་ལ་གཟེར། རིག་པ་སྒྲ་ལ་མ་ཡེངས་པར་གཏད་དུ་བཙུག་གོ་ཧཱུྃ་ཧྲི་འམ། ཧཱུྃ་ཧཱུྃ་ངམ། ཏེ་ཏེང་ལས་སོགས་མ་ཉེང་གི་སྒྲ་སྐད་གང་རུང་ལ། བརྒྱ་ཡན་ཆད་སྟོང་ཕྱིན་ཆད་ཅི་རིགས་སུ་འདྲེན་དུ་བཙུག་པས་ཟིན་རྟགས་མི་འབྱུང་མི་སྲིད་ཅིང་། གཞན་ཡང་སྒྲ་ཁྲིད་འདི་གྲེད་པོའི་རིགས་ཡོང་བ་དང་། ཀན་གོན་དང་ཀུན་གཞི་འཛམ་པའི་རིགས་རྣམས་ལ་མཆོག་ཏུ་བསྔགས་པར་སྣང་ངོ་། ཟིན་རྟགས་མང་ཡང་བསྡུས་ན་ནང་དང་ཕྱིའི་ཟིན་རྟགས་གཉིས་སུ་འདུས། ནང་དུ་རིག་པ་གནད་དུ་ཟིན་པའི་རྟགས་བརྒྱད་འབྱུང་སྟེ། རུས་སྦལ་འཁར་གཞོང་དུ་བཙུགས་པ་ལྟ་བུ་འཁྲུབ་མི་ནུས་པ་དང་། ཕྲེའུ་ཕྲུག་ལ་སེར་བུ་ཕོག་པ་ལྟ་འདར་ཆུང་སི་ལི་བ་ལ་རིག་པ་ཐེང་ངེ་བ་དང་། ཀུན་འབྱམ་བདལ་པ་ལྟ་བུ་ལུས་སེམས་གཉིས་ཀ་མེར་རེ་ལྷེམ་མེ་བ་ལ་གནས་པ་དང་། མི་ལྕུགས་བཏབ་པ་ལྟ་བུ་རེས་ཟིན་རེས་མི་ཟིན་པ་ཐུན་རེ་ལ་ཡང་བསྐྱོལ་མར་ཁྲིག་ཁྲིག་འོང་བ་དང་། ལྕུགས་སྦུབས་ནས་ཆུ་དྲངས་པ་ལྟ་བུ་རིག་པ་འཕྲ་ལ་དྭང་བ་ཐུར་རེ་བྲེང་ངེ་བ་ལ་རྩེ་གཅིག་ཏུ་གནས་པ་དང་། བུང་བ་རྩི་ལ་ཆགས་པ་ལྟ་བུ་རྫས་ལ་འབྲལ་མི་ཕོད་པ། བཏང་གིས་མི་ཐོང་བ་གཟེར་བཏབ་པ་ལྟར་འབྱུར་བ་དང་། རྒྱ་མཚོ་ལ་ཉ་འཕྱོ་བ་ལྟར་གང་ལ་ཡང་ཐོགས་པ་མེད་པར་ཕྱམ་ཕྱམ་འགྲོ་བ་བཞིན་དུ་རྩེ་གཅིག་ལས་མི་འདའ་བ་དང་། རྩེ་ཤིང་ལ་རླུང་འཕྱོ་བ་ལྟར་རིག་པ་སྤྲབ་ཕྱམ་ཕྱམ་སྣང་ཡུལ་ལ་ཞེན་ཆགས་(p.82)མེད་པ་འབྱུང་སྟེ། དེ་ཡང་རྟགས་རྣམས་ལ་ལ་ལ་ཚང་པར་འབྱུང་བ་ཡང་ཡོད། རེ་རེ་གཉིས་གཉིས་ལས་མི་འབྱུང་བ་ཡང་ཡོད། དེའི་དུས་སུ་ཕྱི་རྟགས་སུ་རབ་ལ་ལུས་གཡོ་འགུལ་མེད་པ་འབྱུང་། ཅི་རིགས་ལ་ངུ་རྒོད་འཁྲབ་

རྒྱུག་སྐྱིང་ཤུགས་འོང་བ་དང་། བཞིན་ཡོག་གིས་འགྱུར་བ་དང་། ཁ་མིག་མི་སྙུམ་པ་དང་། ལུས་སྒྲིད་པ། རྩལ་བ་ འདར་བ་ འགྲེལ་བ་ འབྱུང་སྐྱེ་རིག་པ་ཟིན་པས་འཛམ་རླུང་ཨ་བ་འདུ་ཧིར་ཚུད་པའི་རྟགས་ཡིན་གསུངས། གཞན་ཡང་ས་ཆུ་ཤས་ཆེ་ན། ཟིན་འཕྲི་སྐྱེ། རྗེས་ལ་གྲོགས་སུ་འོང་། མེ་རླུང་ཤ་ཆེ་ན་ཟིན་རྟགས་སྔ་སྐྱེ། རྗེས་ལ་གེགས་སུ་འགྱུར། དེ་ཡང་སྔོད་པའི་དུས་སུ་ཐུན་གྱི་མགོ་བཟང་ལ་ཞབས་ངན་ན། སྔར་བཏབ་ནས་གྲེད་པའི་རྟགས་ཡིན་པས་གདབ་པ་དཀའ་བས། མཚན་བཅས་ལ་ནན་ཏན་བྱེད་དུ་གཞུག མགོ་ངན་ལ་ཞབས་བཟང་བའམ། སྔ་མ་བས་ཕྱི་མ་ཀུན་ན་འཕར་ཏེ་བཟང་ལ་སོང་ན། བློ་གསར་པ་ཡིན་པས་གདབ་པ་སླ་བས་ཐབས་ལེགས་ཀྱིས་བརྟུན་ལ་མ་འགྲུས་པར་སྒོམ་དུ་གཞུག མཚན་བཅས་ལ་ཁྲིད་དུས་ངན་ཀྱང་མཚན་མེད་ལ་བཟང་ན་དབང་པོ་ཡང་རབ་ཡིན་པས་མཚན་བཅས་མི་དགོས། ཐམས་ཅད་ཀྱི་དུས་སུ་བཟང་ན་རྒྱུད་ལ་ཡོད་པའི་རྟགས་ཡིན། ཛས་མི་མཐོང་བའི་ནང་སྔ་ནུབ་ཕྱིའི་དུས་སུ་ཐམས་ཅད་ཀྱི་བྱེད་མཁན། ཉིས་པའི་རྩ་བ། གྱོད་ཀྱི་གཞི་མ། ལེགས་ཉེས་ཀྱིས་ཕུང་པོ། ཁོ་ཉིད་དུ་འདུག་པའི་ནང་དུ་ཁོ་རང་གི་ངོ་བོ་ལ་ལྷ་རུ་བཙུག་སྟེ། བྱུང་ས་ འགྲོ་ས་ གནས་ས་ ངོས་བཟུང་གཟུགས་དབྱིབས་ ལེགས་པར་རྩད་གཅོད་དུ་བཙུག་ལ་ཡང་ཡང་དྲི་ཞིང་སྐྱོན་ཡོན་གྱི་ཞུ་ཐུག་བྱ། ཕྱོགས་ཅམ་གོ་ཞིང་ནང་དུ་ཤར་པ་དང་། རྒྱལ་བུ་སྟོང་ཐུན་གྱི་དཔེ་ལྷ་བུ་ཞིག་ལ་བརྟེན་ནས། (p.83)བསྐལ་པར་འཁྲུམས་ཀྱང་སྟོར་བྲལ་མེད་པ་བཞིན་། གཅིག་ཀྱང་བདེ་སྡུག་གི་ཁྱད་པར་ཆེ་བར་ངོ་སྤྲད། སྐྱེས་བུའི་རང་བཞིན་ལ་བརྟེན་ནས་གར་ཡང་མ་སྤྲས་ལ་སུས་ཀྱང་མ་མཐོང་རྒྱུད་ལ་རང་ཆས་སུ་གནས་པར་ངོ་སྤྲད། སྐྱེས་བུ་འོད་མཛེས་ལ་བརྟེན་ནས་ངོ་བོ་གཅིག་ལ། མཐོང་སྣང་ཐ་དད་དུ་ཤར་ཀྱང་དོན་གཅིག་ལས་མ་འདས་པར་ངོ་སྤྲད། ཏིལ་དང་མར་ཁུ་ལ་བརྟེན་ནས་ཀུན་ལ་ཁྱབ་པར་གནས་ཀྱང་རང་གི་དགོས་ནོར་ཡིན་པར་ངོ་སྤྲད། བུམ་པ་མར་མེ་ལ་བརྟེན་ནས་ལུས་སེམས་རྟེན་འབྲེལ་བསྒྲིག་ཚུལ་དང་རིག་པའི་གནད་མིག་ལ་འཆར་བར་ངོ་སྤྲད། རྒྱལ་པོ་བཙོན་འཛིན་ལ་བརྟེན་ནས་ལེགས་ཉེས་ཀྱི་སྣང་དོར་དང་སེམས་འཛིན་གནད་དུ་ཆེ་བར་ངོ་སྤྲད་པ་དང་། དྲུག་པོ་འདི་ཉི་འདིའི་སྐབས་སུ་ལེགས་པར་བསིལ་ལ་བསྟན་ན་གནད་དུ་འགྲོ་བར་ཁོ་བོས་རྟོགས་སོ། གཞན་ཡང་ཛས་ཁྲིད་སྒྲ་ཁྲིད་སེམས་འཚོལ་ལས་སོགས་ཀྱིས་ཇི་ལྟར་ཁྲིད་ཀྱང་། རིག་པ་གནད་དུ་མ་ཟིན་ན་ལན་གཅིག་ཁྲིད་མ་ཐེབས་པ་ཡིན་པས་ཚོགས་སོག་སྐྲིབ་སྦྱོང་ཅི་རིགས་

པར་བྱ། བླ་མ་ཁྱད་པར་ཅན་ལ་དབང་ཞུ། དེ་ནས་གཞོད་གཞི་ནས་སྐྱུར་ལ་གདམས་པ་དཔོག ཅེས་གོང་མ་ཀུན་གྱིས་གསུངས་པའམ། ཡང་ན་སྐབས་སྐབས་སུ་མོས་གུས་བསྐྱེད་ལ་གསོལ་འདེབས་སུ་གཞུག་དམིགས་པ་སྤོ་བ་དང་། རླུང་གཟུན་པ་དང་། སྒྲ་སྐད་འཁྲུལ་འཁོར་རྣམས་གེག་སེལ་བཞིན་ཡོག་ལ་བརྩོན་འགྲུས་ཀྱིས་བསྐྱངས་པས་མི་ཟིན་མི་སྲིད་དེ། གྲུབ་ཆེན་གོང་མ་ཀུན་གྱི་ཞལ་ནས་བླ་མའི་བྱིན་རླབས་ཆེ་ཆུང་གདམས་པ་ཟབ་མི་ཟབ། སྟོན་ལུགས་བཟེ་མི་བཟེ། སློབ་མའི་དབང་པོ་རྣོ་རྟུལ། ཉེར་ལེན་ཆེ་ཆུང་། འབྱུང་བཞི་དར་རྒུད། དད་མོས་ཆེ་ཆུང་གིས་ཡུན་རིང་ཐུང་འབྱུང་མོད་ཀྱི། གང་ལ་ཡང་མི་ཐོབ་མི་སྲིད་གསུངས་པ་བཞིན། ཤས་(p.84)ཆེར་འདིའི་སྐབས་ནས་ཆ་ཕྱེད་(ཤན་ཕྱེད)པ་མང་། འགའ་ཟུང་གང་ཟག་གི་རིགས་མ་ངེས་པས་མཚན་མེད་དང་། རྩ་རླུང་དང་། ངོ་སྤྲོད་ལས་སོགས་དང་། གཞན་ཡང་བཟང་རྐྱེན་ངན་རྐྱེན་དོན་མེད་གཅིག་ལ་བརྟེན་ནས་དགེ་སྦྱོར་སྐྱེ་བ་ཡང་མང་པོ་ཡོང་བ་ལྟར་སྣང་བ་ནི་བདག་གིས་མྱོང་བའོ། དེས་ན་གདམས་པ་འདི་ནི་དམུ་རྗོད་གཡུང་དུ་འཕེབ་པ་ཡིན་པས། ལུང་ལས་གསུངས་པ་བཞིན་ཞག་གསུམ་ཊྲོས་བཞིའམ། རྟགས་མ་བྱུང་བར་སྒྲུང་ངོ་། མཚན་བཅས་སེམས་འཛིན་གྱིས་ཐུན་མཚམས་གོང་མའི་གསུངས་བཞིན་སྤྲོས་ཏེ་སྦྱར་བ་ལྔ་པའོ།། ||བླ་མ་དམ་པ་རྣམས་ལ་ཕྱག་འཚལ་ལོ། གཉིས་པ་མཚན་མེད་ལ་གཉིས་ཏེ། མཉམ་བཞག་གནས་ཆ་རུ་ཉམས་སུ་བླང་པ་དང་། ཐོག་འདོན་དུ་ཉམས་སུ་བླང་པའོ། དང་པོ་ལ་བཞི་སྟེ། བཅའ་བ་ལུས་ཀྱི་གནད། ལྟ་སྟངས་དབང་པོའི་གནད་དང་། བཞག་པ་སེམས་ཀྱི་གནད་དང་། སྲུང་བ་དམ་ཚིག་གི་གནད་དོ། དང་པོ་སྟན་བདེ་བའི་སྟེང་དུ་ལུས་རང་བཞིན་ཆ་ལུགས་ལྷ་ལྡན་གོང་དུ་བསྟན་པ་ལྟར་བྱ་སྟེ། ཆེད་དུ་ལུས་མི་སྒྲིམ། མི་གཟུན་མི་གློད་པར། རང་ས་རང་ཐོག་ཏུ་ཙམ་གྱིས་བཞག་སྟེ། མདོར་ན་ལུས་ལ་རྩོག་དཔྱོད་སྐམ་བྱེད་རེ་དོགས་འཛིན་པ་སྐད་ཙམ་ཡང་མེད་པར། རོ་ལྟར་ཡིངས་སེ་ཁྲིགས་སེ་ཡེ་རེ་བ་ལ་འཇོག་པ་ཡིན། དེ་ལྟར་བཞག་པས་འདུ་བ་ཆ་སྙོམས། རྩ་རླུང་ཐིག་ལེ་ཐམས་ཅད་རང་ས་འཛིན། ཤེས་པ་རྣལ་དུ་ཕེབས་ཏེ། རྣམ་པར་མི་རྟོག་པའི་ཏིང་འཛིན་རང་ཤུགས་ཀྱིས་བསྐྱེད་པ་ཡིན་ནོ། མདོར་ན་ཚེ་རབས་ནས་ད་ལྟའི་བར་ལུས་ཀྱི་བྱ་བྱེད་སྤྱོད་ལམ། འགྲོ་འདུག་དགག་མ་དག་ཅི་སྤྱོད་པ་ཐམས་ཅད་(p.85)རྩོལ་བཅས་སྡུག་བསྔལ་འབའ་ཞིག་ཏུ་སོང་བས། རྩ་སྒྲིགས། རླུང་བསྒྲུབ། འདུ་བ་འཁྲུགས། རིག་པ་གཡེངས་ནས་མི་རྟོག་པའི་ཏིང་འཛིན་སྐྱེ་བ་

ལ་གེགས་བྱས་པའི་ཕྱིར། ད་ནི་དམུས་ཤེས། འཇིཏ་ཤེས། སྨྲག་ཤེས་པར་བྱའོ། གཉིས་པ་ལྟ་སྟངས་ལ། ཁྲོ་བོ་དྲག་པོ་གྱེན་ལ་ལྟ་བ། ཞི་བ་བྱང་སེམས་ཐུར་ལ་ལྟ་བ། གཡས་ཐབས་ གཡོན་ཤེས་རབ་ཀྱི་ལྟ་སྟངས་མང་དུ་གསུངས་ཀྱང་། ད་རེས་སངས་རྒྱས་དང་སེམས་དཔའ་ཆེན་པོ་རྣམས་ཀྱིས་ཧིང་འཛིན་ཟབ་མོ་ལ་སློམས་པར་འཇོགས་དུས་ཀྱི་ལྟ་སྟངས་ཡིན་པས། ཐད་སོའི་བར་སྣང་སྟོང་པ་ལ་རིག་པ་མིག་དང་བསྟུན། མིཕ་འབྲས་དང་ཇི་མ་མི་སྐྱུལ་འབྱེད་འཛུམ་མི་བྱེད་པར་ཏད་དེ་ཐད་དྲང་ལ་ལྟ་སྟེ། འོད་ཟེར་དཔག་མེད་ཀྱི་ཞལ་ནས། ཕྱེད་པར་ལྟ་སྟངས་གནད་ཤེས་ན། ཡང་དག་དོན་རིག་འཁོར་བའི་ས་ལས་འཕགས། དེས་ན་ས་སེམས་དཔའི་ལྟ་སྟངས་བྱ། ཞེས་གསུངས་པས། ཡར་ལྟ་མར་ལྟ། ཕར་ལྟ་ཚུར་ལྟ་མ་ཡིན་པ་ཐད་སོར་ཏད་དེ་ཧྲིག་གེ་ཅེར་རེ་ལྟ་བའོ། གསུམ་པ་སེམས་ཀྱི་གནད་ལ་ཚེ་རབས་ནས་ད་ལྟའི་བར། བསམ་མནོ། རྟོག་དཔྱོད་བཟང་ངན་གྱི་དྲན་པ་ཅི་བསམ་ལ། ཐམས་ཅད་རྩོལ་བཅས་སྡུག་བསྔལ་གྱི་རྒྱུ་འབབ་ཞིག་ཏུ་སོང་བས། ད་ནི་དམུས་ཤེས་པར་བྱ་སྟེ། འདས་པའི་རྗེས་མི་བཅད། མ་འོངས་པའི་སྔོན་མི་བསུ། ད་ལྟར་ཀྱི་རིག་པ་སོ་མ་ལ་དངས་སེང་ངེ་བཞག་སྟེ། དོན་ལ་ཀུན་གཞི་མ་གཡོས་པའི་ཀློང་དུ་རིག་པ་མ་བཅོས་པར་འཇོག་སྟེ། དེ་ལ་འདོད་འདོད་ རེ་རེ་དང་ དགོས་དགོས་དང་། དྲངས་དྲངས་དང་ བསམ་བསམ་དང་། སྤྱོད་སྤྱོད་ཀྱིས་བསམ་དྲན་གཅིག་ཀྱང་མེད་པར་སྐྱེ་མེད་ཀྱི་སྟེང་(p.86)དུ་ཁྲོ་ཚོགས་ཀྱི་སྐྱུར། མཉམ་ཉིད་ཀྱི་ངང་དུ་ལྷན་གྱིས་བཞག་སྟེ་སློ་ལྷུ་རང་ཡན། རིག་པ་བརྟེན་མེད། འཛིན་པ་རང་གྲོལ། འགྱུ་བ་རང་སངས། མ་བཅོས་རང་ལུགས་ལ་འཇོག་སྟེ། དགོངས་མཛད་ཆེན་པོའི་ཞལ་ནས། མཚན་མེད་ཀྱི་སྟེང་དུ་མཉམ་པར་བཞག འབོལ་ལེ་བཞག ལྷོད་དེ་བཞག ཤིགས་སེ་བཞག་ཅེས་དང་། འབུམ་ལས་ཀྱང་མ་བཅོས་པའི་ཐེག་ལེ་གཅིག་ལ་བཞག་པར་བྱའོ། བཞག་ནས་ཀྱང་བཀའ་རྟགས་ཀྱི་ཕྱག་རྒྱ་དང་བཅས་སྟེ་ཨེ་མ་ཧོ། ཞེས་དང་། རྩ་རྒྱུད་ལས་བསྒོམས་པས་དབྱིངས་ཉིད་མི་རྟོགས་ཀྱིས། གསལ་ལ་དམིགས་མེད་ངང་ལ་ཞོག་ཅེས་དང་། ཀུན་བཟང་ཞལ་གདམས་ལས། སོ་མར་ཞོག རེ་དགོས་ཆོད། རྩོལ་བ་ཁྲོལ། གཅིག་ཏུ་སྡུས། དབྱིངས་སུ་དྲིལ། ངང་ལ་ཞོག་ཅེས་དང་། ཞལ་ཆེམས་ལས་དེར་གསལ་གྱི་དགོངས་པ་ལ་དེར་འཛིན་གྱི་ཤེས་པ་མེད་པར་ཞོག་ཅེས་དང་། མདོ་ལས་མི་ཡེངས་དོན་ལ་མི་རྟོག་ན། སྒོམ་པ་གཞི་གནས་དེ་ཉིད་ཡིན། མི་རྟོག་ཡོངས་ཁྱབ་གསལ་

ཉངས་ན། སྒོམ་པའི་དངོས་པོ་དེ་ཉིད་ཡིན། མི་ཆགས་རྟུལ་ཤུགས་མཁར་ལྷན་ན། བསྒོམ་པའི་འབྲས་བུ་དེ་ཉིད་ཡིན། ཞེས་སོགས། གཞན་ཡང་ངེས་ཤེས་སྐྱེ་བའི་ལུང་ཅི་རིགས་སུ་དྲངས་ཏེ་བཤད་ལ། དོན་དུ་རིག་པ་ཅི་ལ་ཡང་མི་བརྟེན་པར་རྟེན་མེད་ཅེར་རེ་བཞག གཟུང་འཛིན་གྱིས་མ་གཡོགས་པར་གཅེར་བུར་རྗེན་ནེ་བཞག རྣམ་རྟོག་གིས་མ་བསླད་པའི་ཀྱང་པར་ལྷང་ངེ་བཞག ང་བཞག་གིས་མ་བཅིངས་པ་རང་ལུགས་སུ་ལྷོད་དེ་བཞག་སྣམ་བྱེད་ཀྱིས་མ་རྟོག་པར་རྣལ་མར་ལྷང་ངེ་བཞག རབ་རིབ་ཀྱིས་མ་སྒྲིབས་པར་འོད་གསལ་དུ་ལམ་མེ་བཞག གྲངས་དང་བྲུན་དང་བཅད་དེ་(p.87)སྒོམ་དུ་གཞུག་གོ བཞི་པ་ལ། བྲུན་ཚད་ཆེ་ན་བྱིང་རྗོད་ཟིང་པོར་འགྲོ། ཆུང་ན་གནས་ཆ་མེད་ཅིང་རང་སོ་མི་ཟིན་པས། དང་པོ་ས་ལེ་འོད་བརྒྱ་རེ་ཙམ་ལ་བྲུན་སྐོར་རེ་བྱ་ཞིང་། ཕྱི་བྲུན་ཞག་རེ་ལ་བྲུན་བུན་ཐང་གིས་བསྲིང་སྟེ་ཇེ་རིང་ལ་བཏང་། ཇེ་ཞིག་ནས་ཞག་རེ་ལ་བྲུན་སྐོར་གསུམ་བཞིས་སྐྱོལ་བ་འབྱུང་གསུངས་ཏེ། ངང་ལ་ངང་གིས་སྒོམས་པ་གལ་ཆེའོ། ནེ་གུའི་ཞལ་ནས་ངན་གྱིས་མི་བྱ་བཟང་གྱིས་བྱ་ཞེས་པས་འཕྲོ་བཟང་དུས་སུ་བཅད་ལ་ངལ་གསོ། དང་པོ་བྲུན་བར་ཡངས་པ་ཙམ་བྱ། དེ་ནས་བྲུན་སྲིངས་ལ་ས་བྲུན་བར་ཇེ་ཐུང་དུ་སྟུད། བྲུན་བར་དུས་སུ་ཡང་མོས་གུས་སྙིང་རྗེ་མི་རྟག་པ་བསྒོམ་པ་རྣམས་གནད་དུ་བསྟུན། རྟོགས་པ་སྲིའུ་གསོ་བ་འདྲ་བས། ཉམས་གྲིབ་སྡིག་ནལ་ལས་སོ་ཏ་ལ་འཛེམས། སྤྱོད་ལམ་མོག་ཆག་གི་ནད་པ་དང་འདྲ་བས། མཆོང་རྒྱུགས་ཁུར་འགྲོས་ངལ་དུབ་ལས་སོགས་དྲག་ཤུལ་གྱི་ལས་མི་བྱ། སྨྲ་བརྗོད་ལྐུགས་པ་དང་འདྲ་བས། ཀུ་ཅོ་ཡོང་གཏམ་བཟླས་བརྗོད་གླེང་ཡངས་ཚིག་གཅིག་ཙམ་ཡང་མི་བརྗོད་ཅིང་། སྨྲ་བཅད། བསམ་དྲན་རོ་དང་འདྲ་བས། མི་གོན་མི་བསམ་མི་རྟོག་མི་དཔྱད། འགལ་རྐྱེན་སྤང་ཞིང་མཐུན་རྐྱེན་བསྟེན་ཏེ། མེ་དང་ཉི་མ་ལ་མི་བསྡད། ཆུང་དང་སེར་བུ་ལ་མི་ཕྱུར། ཆང་དང་སྟོ་ཧྲད་ལས་སོགས་འབྱུང་བ་འཁྲུག་ཅིང་བྱིང་འཐིབས་སྐྱེ་བས་ཟས་སྤངས། ཡེ་ཤེས་ཀྱི་འགྲིབ་པ་གང་གཉིས་ཀྱི་དུས་སུ་ཙུང་ཙམ་གློད་ལ་ངལ་གསོ། ཟས་གསོ་ཆ་མཉམ། མཆམས་དམ་དུ་བསྡམ། འཕེལ་བ་ལ་དགའ་བྲོད་མི་བསྐྱེད། འགྲིབ་པ་ལ་ཞུམ་སྡུད་མི་བྱེད། དོན་དུ་ཧྲིལ་གྱིས་དྲིལ་ནས་ལས་དང་པོ་བརྩོན་འགྲུས་ཁོ་ན་གཙོ་ཆེ་བས། སྐད་གཅིག་ཀྱང་གཡེལ་མ་གཞུག་པ་གལ་ཆེ། ཞུགས་ན་རང་གི་མངན་འཚང་བ་སྲུ་ཟིང་ངེ་བ་སྐྱེ་ཤ་བུན་ནེ་བསྲུང་སྟེ། ཉི་མའི་གུང་དང་(p.88)ནམ་གྱི་གུང་། བྱིང་འཐིབས་དུས་སུ་བསྒོམ་རྒྱུ་མིན། སྲོད་

དང་ཐོ་རངས་སྔ་དྲོ་དང་། ཕྱི་དྲོའི་དུས་སུ་ཉམས་སུ་བླང་། ལྷན་ཅན་ཡུལ་དུ་དབང་པོ་གསེང་། ཞེས་བླ་ཆེན་དང་། ལས་དང་པོ་པའི་ཉམས་ལེན་ལ་དྲོད་ཐེབས་བརྒྱ་དང་། དྲུ་ཐེབས་བརྒྱ་འབྱུང་ཞེས་རི་ཁྲོད་པའི་གསུངས་སོ། དེ་ལྟར་སྒོམ་པས། དང་པོར་བློས་བྱས་ཀྱི་གཞི་གནས་སྐྱེ། བར་དུ་རང་བཞིན་གྱི་ཞི་གནས་འཆར། ཐ་མ་མཐར་ཐུག་གི་ཞི་གནས་ལ་བརྟན་པ་ཐོབ་པ་འབྱུང་། དེས་ནས་གདམས་པ་འདི་ནི་དགེ་སྦྱོར་གྱི་འགྲམ་བཞི་ཡིན་པས་བརྟན་པ་ཐོབ་པར་བྱ། ཁྱད་པར་དུ་དགེ་སྦྱོར་འགོགས་པའི་དུས་སུ། བཙོ་ལྔ་ཉི་ཤུ། ཟླ་བ་ལས་སོགས་སུ་སྦྱང་དུ་གཞུག་གོ། མཚན་མེད་ལ་མཉམ་པར་བཞག་པས་ཐུན་མཚམས། བཀའ་དྲིན་ཅན་ལས་ཐོབ་པ་རྒྱས་པར་སྦྲིས་པ་སྙེ་དྲུག་པའོ།། །།བླ་མ་དམ་པ་རྣམས་ལ་ཕྱག་འཚལ་ལོ། གཉིས་པ་མཉམ་བཞག་འགོག་འདོན་དུ་ཉམས་སུ་བླངས་པ་ལ་གསུམ་སྟེ། ལྟ་སྟངས་དམིགས་པའི་གནད་དང་། འཆར་ཚུལ་དགེ་སྦྱོར་གྱི་གནད་དང་། ངོ་སྤྲོད་ཐབས་ལམ་གྱི་གནད་དོ། དང་པོ་ལ་འབུམ་ལས། རྒྱལ་མཚན་མཐོན་པའི་ཏིང་འཛིན་གྱིས་བཟུང་ནས། ཐར་པ་ཆེན་པོ་ཐོབ་པར་འགྱུར་ཅེས་དང་། བླ་ཆེན་གྱི་ཞལ་ནས། བྱ་ལ་གསོག་པ་མེད་ན་འཕུར་པའི་ཐབས་མེད། རྩལ་སྦྱོངས། ངར་སྐྱོང་། ཏུར་ཐོན། མདངས་ལ་ལྟོས་ཅེས་གསུངས་པ་དང་། རི་ཁྲོད་པའི་ཞལ་ནས་ཀྱང་། སེངས་ཏེར་གསེངས་ལ་ལྷུག་དེར་ཞོག   དགེ་སྦྱོར་གྱི་གནད་གཅིག་དེ་ན་གདའ་ ཞེས་གསུངས་པས། དེ་ལ་ལུས་གནད་གོང་ལྟར་བཅས་པའི་ངང་ནས། འོད་ཟེར་དཔག་མེད་ཀྱི་གསུང་ལྟར་མིག་(p.89)མ་བཙུམས་པའི་རྣལ་འབྱོར་དེ། རྣལ་འབྱོར་ཀུན་ལས་ཁྱད་དུ་(པར་)འཕགས། སེང་གེ་ལྟ་སྟངས་ཞེས་སུ་སྤྱོད་ཅེས་པས། རིག་པ་མིག་དང་བསྟུན་ཏེ། བར་སྣང་སྟོང་པ་ལ་ཏུར་གྱིས་གཏད་དེ། དབང་པོ་ལ་ཧྲིག་འདོན་རིག་པ་ལ་ངར་བསྐྱེད། སྒྱུ་ལུས་ལ་མདངས་ཕྱུངས་ཏེ། ཤེས་པ་ས་ལེ་ཧྲིག་གེ་བ། རྣམ་རྟོག་ཡ་ལེ་ཕྱོད་དེ་བ། སྣང་བ་བུན་ནེ་ལོང་ངེ་བ། ཕྱིའི་ཡུལ་ལ་མ་ཞེན། ནང་གི་སེམས་ལ་མི་དཔྱོད། གསལ་རིག་ངར་དང་ཆས་པ། གཏིང་གསལ་བཀྲག་དང་ཆས་པ། རྩ་བྲལ་དུ་ལྷག་གེ   རང་གསལ་དུ་ཡེར་རེ། རྟོག་མེད་དུ་ཟེན་ནེ། འཛིན་མེད་དུ་ཧྲིག་གེ   ཟང་ཐལ་དུ་སེང་ངེ། རང་ཤར་དུ་ཁྲོལ་ལེ། དེའི་ངང་ལ་རྒྱུན་ཆགས་སུ་གནས་པར་བྱ། ཐུན་ཚད་ཀྱང་ཇེ་རིང་ལ་སྲིང་སྟེ་གོང་ལྟར་སྒོམ་ཞིང་། ཁ་ཟས་སྤྱོད་ལམ་ལུས་ངག་ཡིད་གསུམ་གྱི་སྤྱོད་ཚུལ་འགལ་རྐྱེན་སྤང་བ། མཐུན་རྐྱེན་སྟེན་པ། ཐམས་ཅད་གོང་ལྟར་བྱ་ཞིང་རྒྱུན་དུ་གཡེལ་

བ་མེད་པར་ཉམས་སུ་བླང་ངོ་། གཉིས་པ་ལ། དེ་ལྟར་བསྐྱངས་པས་ཇི་ཞིག་ལ་ཕྱི་ནང་གི་འཆར་ཚུལ་ཐམས་ཅད་རང་བཞིན་གྱི་ཐད་ཀར་ཐད་ཐད་ཆོད་ཅིང་ཅི་བྱུས་ཀྱང་རིག་པ་རྩོལ་བྲལ་ལྷུགས་པ་ལས་མི་འདའ་བ་དང་། ཤེས་པ་ལ་བྱ་རྩོད་པོ་ནམ་འཕངས་གཙོད་པ་ལྟ་བུའི་དཔའ་འབྱུང་། འཐམས་པ་ ལྡེངས་པ་ བྲིང་བ་ རྨུག་པ་ལས་སོགས་པའི་སྐྱོན་ཐམས་ཅད་རང་གྲོལ་དུ་འགྲོ། དགེ་སྦྱོར་བ་ལ་བོག་གཅིག་ཆར་དུ་སྐྱེ། རིག་པའི་རྒྱ་ཕྱོགས་མེད་ནས་འདྲལ། རྟོགས་པའི་ཡེ་ཤེས་རང་བཞིན་གྱིས་འབར། ཏོལ་སྐྱེས་ཀྱི་དྲན་པས་འཁྱུབ་མི་ནུས། ཕྱི་ནང་གི་བར་ཆོད་རང་ཞིར་འགྲོ་བ་ལས་སོགས་པའི་ཕན་(p.90)ཡོན་ཉམས་སུ་བླངས་བ་དང་། གསལ་བ་འབྱུང་བས། གོང་གི་ཞི་གནས་ཀྱི་གཞི་ལེགས་པར་ཐིངས། དགེ་སྦྱོར་གྱི་འགྲམ་ཚུགས་པ་དང་། བོག་འདོན་པ་ལ་གདམས་པ་འདི་ཤིན་ཏུ་གཅེས་པ་ཡིན་ནོ། གསུམ་པ་སྤྲིན་དང་ལྷག་ཀླུང་མེད་པའི་ནམ་མཁའ་དངས་པ་ལ། གོང་གི་ལྟ་སྟངས་ལུས་གནད་འཆར་བཅུག་སྟེ། རིག་པ་བར་སྣང་ལ་གཏད་དེ། ནམ་མཁའ་དང་རིག་པ་ཁྲུག་གིས་འདྲེས། ཀད་ཀྱིས་འཐྲོད། དབྱེ་ཡིས་མི་ཕྱེད་པར་གྱུར་པའི་དུས་སུ། དཔེ་དོན་རྟགས་གསུམ་གྱི་སྒོ་ནས་ངོ་སྤྲད་དེ། གབ་པ་ལས་དཔེ་དོན་རྟགས་དང་གསུམ་དུ་མཉམ་པ་འདི། སྐལ་ལྡན་སེམས་ལ་གཉིས་མེད་དོན་དུ་སྒོམས་གསུངས་པས། དེའི་དུས་ན་ཕྱི་ནམ་མཁའ་ལ་དངོས་པོ་དབྱིབས་ཁ་དོག་མཐའ་དབུས་ཕྱོགས་མཚམས་མཚན་ཉིད་ངོས་བཟུང་གང་དུ་ཡང་མ་གྲུབ་པས་རྩ་བྲལ་དུ་སང་ངེ་། སྟོང་ཉིད་དུ་ཁྲོལ་ལེ་བ་འདི་དཔེ་ཡིན། ནང་དུ་བདག་གི་སེམས་ཟེར་བའི་རིག་རིག་པོ་སལ་སལ་པོ་འདི་ཡང་ཕྱི་ནང་དབྱེར་མེད་པར་གཅེར་གྱིས་མཐོང་། སལ་གྱིས་རྟོགས་པ་དེ་རྟགས་ཡིན། དེ་གཉིས་མཉམ་ཁ་དེ་བཅད། ནམ་མཁའ་ཅི་བཞིན་སེམས་ཉིད། སེམས་ཉིད་ཅི་བཞིན་ནམ་མཁའ་ཁྲུག་གི་འདྲེས། དབྱེ་ཡིས་མི་ཕྱེད་པ་གཉིས་མེད་མཉམ་པ་ཆེན་པོའི་ངང་ལས་རྒྱུན་ཆགས་སུ་གད་དེ་བ་དེ་ལ། (དོན་བོན་ཉིད) བོན་སྐུ་བྱ་སྟེ། དེ་ཡིས་མཚོན་ནས་ཡུལ་ཤེས་ཐམས་ཅད་ལ་སྦྱར་དུ་རུང་སྟེ། ལུང་དྲུག་ལས། སྣང་བ་སྣ་ཚོགས་འདི་ནི་ཀུན་ཏུ་བཟང་མོ་ལ། མཛད་སྤྱོད་ཐམས་ཅད་ཐབས་ཏེ་ཡབ། དེ་ལས་མ་གཡོས་པ་དེ་གཤེན་ལྷ་ཨང་གསུངས་པ་དག་དང་གནད་གཅིག་ཏུ་གོ་སྟེ། འགྲེལ་བ་ལས།. དཔེ་དོན་རྟགས་གསུམ་དུ་ཕྱེ་བ་ཡང་། (p.91)འཁོར་བའི་སེམས་ཅན་བཀྲི་དྲང་ཙམ་དུ་ཟད་གསུངས་སོ། དེ་ནས་གདམས་པ་འདི་འང་། དགེ་སྦྱོར་སྟོན་པའི་དུས་སུ་དགུའམ། བཅུ་གཅིག་བཅོ་ལྔ་ལས་སོགས་སུ་བསྐྱང་

དུ་གཞུག་ཅིང་། ཞི་གནས་ལྷག་མཐོང་ཟུང་འབྲེལ་དུ་བསྐྱེད་ཅིང་། ཐོག་འདོན་པའི་ཐུན་མཚམས། འགྲོ་མགོན་བླ་མའི་གསུངས་བཞིན་སྦྲོས་པ་སྟེ་བདུན་པའོ།། །།བླ་མ་དམ་པ་རྣམས་ལ་ཕྱག་འཚལ་ལོ། གསུམ་པ་གནས་ལུགས་ཀྱི་དོན་ལ་ངོ་སྤྲོད་པ་ལ་གསུམ་སྟེ། དང་པོ་རང་འབྱུང་གི་ཡེ་ཤེས་ངོས་བཟུང་། བར་དུ་གློས་བྲས་ཀྱི་དྲི་མ་དང་བྲལ། མཐར་དྲི་མེད་ཀྱི་ཡེ་ཤེས་ལམ་དུ་བསླང་པའོ། དང་པོ་ལ་གཉིས་ཏེ། སྒོམ་ཚུལ་གྱི་གདམས་པ་དངོས་དང་། དེ་ལ་ངོ་སྤྲོད་པའོ། དང་པོ་ལ་ལྡེ་མིག་ལས། གནས་པ་བདེ་བ་དབུས་མཐིང་རྩ་ལ་བཟུང་ཞེས་དང་། དྲང་དོན་ལས། གསང་བ་རྩ་དང་རླུང་དང་ཐིག་ལེ་ལ། རིག་པ་སེམས་ཀྱི་འགྲོ་ལྡོག་སྒོམ་པ་སྐྱབས་ཀྱི་རབ་ཅེས་དང་། བླ་ཆེན་གྱི་ཞལ་ནས་རང་ལུས་ཤེལ་གྱི་སྦྲུ་གུ་ལ། རྩ་གསུམ་འཁོར་ལོ་རྩ་འདབ་བས་ཀྲུས། གཞལ་ཡས་འོད་ཀྱི་ཁང་བུ་ལ། ནང་རླུང་ཕྱི་རུ་མདའ་ལྟར་འཕངས། ཕྱི་རླུང་ནང་དུ་གཞུ་ལྟར་དགུག བར་རླུང་གནས་སུ་ཞོ་ལྟར་བསྐྱུག དེ་ཡིས་སྒོམ་པའི་རྩལ་གསུམ་རྫོགས། ཞེས་གསུངས་པས། དེ་ལ་ལུས་གནད་ནི་གོང་ལྟར་ཆ་ལུགས་ལྔ་ལྡན་དུ་བཅའ་ལ་ཁྲིམས་ཀྱིས་བསྒྲིམ་སྟེ། གནད་དུ་འགྲོ་བར་བྱེད། ཡང་ན་ཚངས་སྟང་གི་གནད་བདུན་བཅའ་ཡང་གསུངས། དམིགས་པའི་སྒོམ་ལུགས་ནི། ཁོང་པའི་ནང་ནས་ཡར་རྩ་གསུམ་སྤྱི་བོར་སྦུགས་སྦུབས་བཅད་པ་འདྲ་བ་ལ། གསང་གནས་སུ་གཡས་གཡོན་གཉིས་ཡི་གེ་ཆའི་ཞབས་བཞིན་(p.92)དབུ་མ་ལ་ཡར་ཟུག་པ། སྦྲམ་འཕྲ་གཡས་གཡོན་མདའ་སྨྱུག་འབྲིང་པོ་ཙམ་ལ། དབུ་མ་དེ་བས་ཅུང་རགས་པ་ཙམ་དུ་བསྐྱེད། ཁ་དོག་ནི་གཡས་དཀར་གཡོན་དམར་དབུས་མཐིང་ཁའོ། སྤྱི་གཙུག་གི་གཡས་གཡོན་གྱི་ཐད་ཀྱི་བར་སྣང་ལ་ཨ་མ་གཉིས་བསམ། འོད་དུ་ཞུ་ནས་ཡབ་མཁའ་ལ་རིག་པའི་རྒྱལ་པོ་དང་། ཡུམ་སྐྱེས་ཀྱི་ཉི་མ་གཞའ་ཙམ་གཉིས་བསྐྱེད། དེ་གཉིས་ཞུ་སྟེ་དཀར་དམར་གྱི་ཐིག་ལེ་སྲན་འབྲུ་བཙོས་པ་ཙམ་དུ་གྱུར་ཏེ། རྩ་གཡས་གཡོན་གྱི་ཁ་ལ་ཆགས་པར་བསམ་ལ། རླུང་ལེན་གསུམ་ཕྱིར་སྤྱུར་བས་བག་སྒྲིབ་དང་བཅས་པ་ཐོན་པར་བསམ། དེ་ནས་རང་བབས་སུ་ཧྲུབ་སྟེ། འོག་རླུང་འཐེན། སྟེང་རླུང་མནན་ལ། རྩ་གཡས་གཡོན་གྱི་ཐིག་ལེ་ཞུགས་དབུ་མའི་ནང་དུ་ཚུད་དེ། སྟེང་འོག་གམ་གཅིག་ཏུ་བསྒྲིལ་ལ། སྤྱི་གཙུག་ཏུ་སླེབས་པ་དང་། རྩ་གཡས་གཡོན་ཁ་ལ་ཆགས་པར་བསམ་ལ། རླུང་མ་ཐུབ་ན་ཏལ་གྱིས་བཏང་། དེ་ནས་ཡང་ཐུབ་ལ་གོང་ལྟར་སྦྱང་། དེ་ལྟར་སྐོར་ལྡོག་ལན་གསུམ་ལྔ་བདུན་ནམ། བར་དུ་དགུ་བཅུ་གཅིག་བཅོ་ལྔ། ཐ་མ་བཅུ་བདུན་བཅུ་

དགུ་རྩ་གཅིག་ལས་སོགས་སུ་རྒྱུག་སྦྱོང་བྱ་སྟེ། ཡི་སེག་ནི་བླ་རིའི་ཚུལ་དུ་ཐུན་ནི་དུས་ཀྱིས་གོམས་པ་གཅེས་པ་ཡིན་གསུངས་པས། ཡང་བར་མ་སྟོང་བར་སྐོར་ཟློག་བྱ། རླུང་ཐུན་བཅུའམ། བཅོ་ལྔ་ཉི་ཤུ་ཙམ་སོང་བ་དང་། ཡར་སྲར་དུས་ཀྱི་ཐུགས་ཁའི་ཐད་ཙམ་དུ་སླེབས་པ་དང་། གར་སོང་ཚ་མེད་པར་བསམ་ལ། ཧའམ་ཕཊ་ཀྱིས་སྒྲ་འཚམས་ཕྱེད་ངེས་བཏབ་སྟེ། གནས་ལུགས་ཀྱི་ཐོག་ཏུ་ལྷོད་ཀྱིས་ཀློད་ལ་ལྷ་སྣངས་བཅས་སྟེ། དགེ་སྦྱོར་གྱི་སྟེང་དུ་ཧེ་ལྷར་གནས་པ་ཞིག་བཞག དགེ་སྦྱོར་ཐུན་སྐོར་(p.93)ཟླའམ་བཅུ་ཙམ་ཞིག་བསྒོམ། ཡང་སྔར་བཞིན་རྩ་རླུང་གི་དམིཏ་པ་གནད་དུ་བསྟུན་ཏེ། སྲོད་ཐོ་རངས་སྔ་དགོངས་དུས་རབ་ཏུ་ཡང་གཅུན་པ་གལ་ཆེའོ། དེ་ཡང་ལས་དང་པོའི་དུས་སུ་འཇམ་རླུང་ལ་སྦྱང་ཞིང་ཙུང་ཟད་འགྱོང་པ་དང་། རྩུབ་རླུང་ཐོག་ཆེ་བས་དེ་ལ་གཙོ་བོར་བྱ། རླུང་ཡང་ཧ་མ་ཤོར་བ་ལས་(སྲུར་)འགྱུར་དུ་བཟུང་། རྒྱུན་པར་ཧེན་ན་མ་ཞིང་གི་རླུང་ལ་ཁྲིལ་ཞིང་། སྲུར་བ་འཇུག་པ་མནན་པ་བཏང་བ་ཐམས་ཅད་ཀྱི་གནད་གོ་བར་བྱ་ལ། ཞི་དལ་གྱིས་བསླབ་ཅིང་གགས་སུ་མ་སོང་བ་གལ་ཆེ། གལ་ཏེ་སོང་ན་ཡང་བཅོས་ཤེས་པ་གལ་ཆེ་སྟེ། སྤྱིར་གྱི་གདམས་པ་འདི་ཐོག་དང་གེགས་གཉིས་ཀ་ཆེ་བར་ཤེས་པར་བྱའོ། གཉིས་པ་ལ་གོང་གི་ཐབས་ལམ་གྱི་དམིཏ་པ་སྐོར་གཅིག་སྒོམ་དུ་བཙུག་པའི་རྗེས་སུ་གནས་ལུགས་ཀྱི་ངང་ལ་སློབ་པས། དེའི་དུས་སུ་ཐབས་ལམ་ཟབ་མོ་དེ་ཡིས་ཤེས་པའི་དངས་སྙིགས་ཕྱེད་ནས། དེའི་སྐབས་དར་ཙམ་གཅིག་ལ། སྐན་རྒྱུད་ལས། སྙིགས་མ་ཀློང་དུ་ཐིམ་ནས་དངས་མ་འོད་དུ་གསལ། བློ་ཡིས་གཡང་ལུག་བུད་ནས་རིག་པ་གཅེར་བུར་འཆར། རྟོག་པའི་སྤྲིན་ཚོགས་སངས་ནས་ཡེ་ཤེས་སྒྲིབ་གཡོཊ་མེད་ཅིང་གསལ་བ་ལྟར། ཀུན་གྱི་རྒྱུད་ལ་རང་ཆས་གནས་པའི་ཉམས། རང་འབྱུང་གི་ཡེ་ཤེས་སྤྲིན་བར་ཉི་མ་ཙམ་ཞིག སྒྲིབ་མེད་ཟང་ཐལ་དུ་ལྷག་གེ་འཆར་ཏེ། དེའི་ཚུལ་ནི་སྔར་ཞེན་གྱི་བག་ཆགས་མ་དྲན་པ། ཕྱིས་འོངས་ཀྱི་སྔོན་མི་བསུ་བ། གློ་བུར་གྱི་དྲན་རྟོག་མ་གཡོས་པ། བྱིང་རྨུག་གི་དབང་དུ་མ་སོང་བ། རིག་པ་ཡུལ་དུ་མི་བྱེད་པ། ཚོགས་དྲུག་སྣ་ལྔའི་རྗེས་སུ་མི་འབྲང་བ། ཏིང་ངེ་འཛིན་གྱི་རོ་ལ་མི་ཆགས་པ། ད་ལྟའི་ཤེས་པ་རང་གསལ་འཛིན་མེད་ས་ལེ་བ། སྤྲོས་དགའ་དང་ཆས་པས་དངས་སིང་ངེ་བ། དེག་མས་(p.94)བུ་རམ་བཟོས་པའམ། ན་ཆུང་མས་བདེ་བ་མྱོང་བ་ལྟ་བུ་ཞིག་འཆར་བ་དེ་ལ། ལྷན་གཅིག་སྐྱེས་པའི་ཡེ་ཤེས་ཞེས་ཀྱང་བྱ། ཐེག་པ་ཆེན་པོ་དོན་གྱི་གནས་ལུགས་ཀྱང་ཟེར། དུས་གསུམ་སངས་རྒྱས་

ཀྱི་དགོངས་པ་ཡང་ཟེར། སེམས་རང་འབྱུང་གི་གཞིན་ལྷ་དཀར་པོ་ཡང་ཟེར་བས་བླ་མས་བསྟན་བསྟན་བཤད་བཤད་པ་རང་གིས་བསྒོམས་བསྒོམས་སྦྱངས་སྦྱངས་པས། འཆར་ལུའང་རེ་རེ་བ། མ་ཤར་ཀྱིས་ཀྱང་དགོས་དགོས་པའི་སྒྲོའི་ཆེ། གཡེར་པོ་ཆེ་དེ་དེ་ཁོ་ན་ཡིན་ནོ། ལོགས་ན་མེད་དོ། རྒྱུད་ལ་ཁོལ་གཅིག ཉམས་སུ་ལོངས་ཤིག དམར་ཐག་ཆོད་གཅིག དེ་ལྟར་དུ་ཡང་ལུང་དྲུག་ལས། དེ་ཡིན་དེ་ལ་ཆོར་ཏེ་ལྟོས། བལྟས་པས་མཐོང་བ་ཅང་ཡང་མེད། དེ་ཡིས་དེ་ཉིད་མཐོང་བ་ཡིན་ཅེས་དང་། ལེ་ཤུའི་གསུངས་ལས། འདི་ཀ་རང་ཀ་ཡིན་པ་ལ། མི་ཤེས་བྱ་བ་ཅི་ལ་ཟེར་ཅེས་དང་། འབུམ་ལས། རང་རིག་པའི་ཡེ་ཤེས་དེ་ནི་ཕྱི་ནས་ཀྱང་མི་འཆར། ནང་ནས་ཀྱང་མི་འཆར། རང་ལ་རང་འཆར་གསུངས་པ་རྣམས་ཀྱང་། དེ་ལྟར་རོ་ཞེས་སོགས་རྒྱས་པར་ངོ་སྤྲད་དོ། དེ་ནས་ཐབས་ལམ་གྱིས་བོག་འདོན་འདི་ནི་ཤེས་པའི་དངས་སྙིགས་འབྱེད། རང་འབྱུང་གི་ཡེ་ཤེས་མངོན་དུ་སྟོན། རིག་སྟོང་མ་བུ་འཕྲོད། ཉམས་རྟོགས་ཀྱི་བོགས་གཅིག་ཆར་དུ་སྐྱེ་བས་ཤིན་ཏུ་གལ་ཆེ་སྟེ། སད་ནི་གཙུ་ལ་ལོ་ཟླར་འབྱམས་ཐུབ་པའི་ཞི་གནས་སྐྱེས་ནས། སློབ་དཔོན་ནེ་གུ་ལ་ཞུས་པས། ཁྱོད་ཀྱི་དེ་ཞི་གནས་ལྷིངས་པོ་ཡིན། དེ་ལ་མཆོག་ཏུ་མ་འཛིན་པར་ངའི་ཨ་བ་སྦྲག་རྩོལ་གྱི་གདམས་པ་སྒོམས་དང་། ཕྱིས་དགེ་སྦྱོར་ཞིག་ཡོང་བར་འདུག་གསུངས་པ་བཞིན་བསྒོམས་པས། སྔར་གྱི་ཉམས་རྣམས་སྤྲུལ་ལྦུགས་(p.95)བཞིན་ཟེས་ནས་ཉམས་རྟོགས་བཟང་པོ་ཤར་བའི་ལོ་རྒྱུས་གསུངས། ལར་ཡང་ཐབས་ལམ་ཟབ་དགུ གཅེས་དགུ་མང་པོ་བས། རྩ་རླུང་གི་དམིགས་པ་སྐོར་རེ་བོག་ཆེ་བ་མྱུར་བར་ཉམས་སུ་མྱངས་པས། བུ་ཀུན་རྒྱུན་དུ་འདི་ཉེན་པ་གལ་ཆེ་བ་ཡིན། ཐེ་བྲག་འདི་སྐྱོང་བའི་དུས་སུ་བཙུ་བཅོ་ལྔ་ལས་སོགས་སུ་སྒོམ་དུ་གཞུག རང་འབྱུང་ཡེ་ཤེས་ངོས་འཛིན་གྱི་ཐུན་མཚམས་མཚན་ལྡན་གྱི་ཕྱག་ལེན་བཀོད་པ་སྟེ་བརྒྱད་པའོ།། །།བླ་མ་དམ་པ་རྣམས་ལ་ཕྱག་འཚལ་ལོ། གཉིས་པ་བར་དུ་གོམས་བྱས་ཀྱི་དྲི་མ་དང་བྲལ་བའི་ཐབས་ལ་བསླབ་པ་ལ། འཇོག་བཤིག་སྐྱོང་གསུམ་གནད་དུ་བསྟུན་པ་གལ་ཆེ་སྟེ། དང་པོ་བཞག་ཐབས་ལ། གཤེན་རབ་འདའ་དགའ་འཆི་དྲོད་ལས། དེར་གསལ་གྱི་དགོངས་པ་ལ་དེར་འཛིན་གྱི་ཤེས་པ་མེད་པར་བཞག སྒོ་ལྔ་རང་ཡན་དུ་བཞག རིག་པ་ཁྲབ་བདལ་དུ་བཞག ལུས་སེམས་བཅོས་མེད་དུ་བཞག་ཅེས་དང་། གབ་པ་ལས། སེམས་ཀྱི་ལམ་ནི་བཅོས་སུ་མེད་པ་བདེ་ཞེས་དང་། བླ་ཆེན་གྱི་གསུང་ལས། གང་སྣང་རང་ཤར་གྱི་སྤྱོད་ཡུལ།

ཐུག་ཕྲད་རང་སོར་བཞག འཛིན་ཆགས་ཞེན་མེད་ཀྱི་ཤེས་པ་རྒྱ་ཡན་ལྷུག་པར་བཞག གཟུང་འཛིན་དབྱེར་མེད་ཀྱི་ཤེས་པ་སྒོམ་མེད་ཡེངས་མེད་དུ་བཞག་ཅེས་དང་། རི་ཁྲོད་པ་ཡབ་སྲས་ཀྱི་ཞལ་ནས་ཀྱང་། མ་བཅོས་པའི་ངང་ལ་རང་ལུགས་སུ་ལྷུག་གེ་བཞག ལྷོད་དེ་བཞག འབོལ་ལེ་བཞག་ཤིགས་སེ་བཞག་ཅེས་དང་། དོན་དུ་མ་ཀུན་གཞི་ཡིན་ལུགས་ཀྱི་སྟེང་དུ་བུ་རིག་པ་ལ། བཅས་བཅོས་སྤྲོ་ཐོག་མེད་པ། རྩལ་བསམ་དྲན་གྱི་ཤེས་པ་(p.96)མ་གཡོས་པར་བྱ་སྟེ། རང་ས་རང་ཐོག་ཏུ་ཀད་དེ་འཇོག་པ་ཡིན་ཏེ། བླ་ཆེན་གྱིས་བརྩལ་བས་སྟོར། བལྟས་པས་འགྲིབ། བསྒོམ་པས་སྒྲད། བྱ་བྱེད་མང་ན་འཁོར་བར་འཁྲུམས་ཉེན་འདུག གསུང་པ་དང་གནད་གཅིག་པས། རྒྱུད་ལ་འཇོར་བ་བྱ་ཏེ། འཇོག་ཤེས་པ་གལ་ཆེའོ། གཉིས་པ་བར་དུ་བཤིགས་ཐབས་ལ། བཞག་ཐོག་དེ་ར་མ་ལྡིངས་པ་བྱས་ལ། རྗེས་ཀྱི་ཤེས་པ་ལ་བལྟ་དགོས་ཏེ། ཤིག་ཤིག་བཤིག་ཅིང་སྒོམ་ཡོད་ཐམས་ཅད་སྒོམ་མེད་དུ་བཤིག་ཅིང་། སྒོམ་མཁན་གྱི་དྲན་ཐག་ཐད་དེ་བཅད་ལ་ཡེངས་མེད་དུ་ཉམས་སུ་བླང་སྟེ། རྒྱུད་ལས། བསྒོམ་པས་སངས་རྒྱས་མི་རྙེད་ཀྱི། རང་འབྱུང་ཡེ་ཤེས་འཆར་དུ་ཆུག ཤར་བས་དབྱིངས་ཉིད་མི་རྟོགས་ཀྱི། གསལ་ལ་དམིགས་མེད་རང་བཞིན་ཞོག་ཅེས་དང་། ནེ་རྒྱུང་གི་གསུང་ལས། བསྒོམས་པས་གཏན་ལ་མི་ཕེབས་ཀྱི། སངས་གཞིའི་སྟེང་དུ་རང་བཞིན་ཞོག བཞག་པས་ཐ་མལ་གྱི་སར་གོལ་གྱི། དྲན་གསལ་གྱི་ཡེ་ཤེས་འཆར་དུ་ཆུག ཤར་བས་སྟོང་ཉིད་མི་འཛིན་གྱི། བསྒོམ་མེད་སྟེང་དུ་ཡེངས་མེད་སྟེན། ད་ལྟའི་ཤེས་པ་བྲེལ་བྲེལ་པོ། ཀློག་དཀྲོལ་ཤིག་ལ་ཅི་དགར་སྤྱོད། ཅེས་དང་། བླ་ཆེན་གྱི་གསུང་ལས། ཤེང་ཁྲུར་དང་འདྲ་སྟེ་ལྷོད་ཀྱིས་ཀློད། ཤིགས་ཀྱིས་ཤིག ཁྲོལ་གྱིས་དཀྲོལ། ཅེས་གུངས་པས། བར་དུ་བཤིག་ཤེས་པ་གལ་ཆེ། བླ་མ་ཁ་ཅིག་གི་ཞལ་ནས། སྒོམ་ཞི་གནས་ཐོག་ཏུ་ལྡིངས་པ་ཉི། དོན་གཉེར་ལམ་དུ་གཉིད་ཡོག་འདྲ། ཞེས་གསུངས་པ་དང་། ཏིང་ངེ་འཛིན་རོ་ལ་ཆགས་པ་ཉི་ནང་གི་བདུད། ཅེས་དང་། གབ་པ་ལས་ བསྒོམས་སོ་སྙམ་པའི་བསྒོམ་པ་དེས་ཀྱང་། ཀུན་གཞི་བྱང་ཆུབ་(p.97)སེམས་ལ་འགྲིབ་ཅེས་གསུང་པ། རྣམས་ཀྱང་དོན་དེ་ལ་མི་དགོངས་སམ། གསུམ་པ་ཐ་མར་བསྐྱངས་པ་ལ་ཡང་། བཤིག་པའི་རྗེས་ལ་ཆེད་དུ་མི་སྒོམ་པར། ངང་གིས་དྲན་ཐག་འཕྲུད་ལ་སྒོམ་མེད་ཡེངས་མེད་དུ་བསྐྱང་པར་བྱ་སྟེ། ཚིག་བཞག་ལས། སྒོམ་དུ་ཅི་ཡང་མེད་པ་ལ། ཡེངས་སུ་མེད་པའི་མན་ངག་གིས། རིག་པའི་རྒྱུན་ཡང་གསལ་བར་སྟོན། ཅེས་

དང་། དཔོན་གསས་ཐ་མི་ཐད་གེའི་གསུང་ལས། ཐམས་ཅད་ནས་ཐམས་ཅད་དུ་རྗེས་གདབ་ཀྱི་ཧེ་ཏུ་གཏེར་ལ་དོན་གསལ་བའི་གཏིང་ (ཧེང་) ཆེན་དང་མི་འབྲལ་བར་གཟེར་གདབ་ཅེས་དང་། བླ་ཆེན་གསུངས་ལས། ཀློད་དཀྲོལ་བཤིག་གསུམ་གྱི་རྗེས་ལ། སྒོམས་ཡེངས་མེད་རྟོག་འཛིན་མེད་པར་རྒྱུད་ལ་བརྟེན་ཅེས་པས། ངང་ལ་ངང་གིས་དྲན་ཐག་འཐུད་དེ། དུས་དང་རྣམ་པ་ཀུན་ཏུ་བསྐྱང་ངོ་། དེ་ཡང་ལས་དང་པོ་སྐྱེར་རེ་ལ་ཚང་བར་བྱེད་པའི་དུས་སུ། ལུས་གནད་ལྔ་སྡངས་མཉམ་བཞག་ལྟར་བཅའ་སྟེ། རིག་པ་མ་བཅོས་གནས་ལུགས་ཀྱི་སྟེང་དུ་འཛོག བར་དུ་བཤིག་སྟེ་བཟང་བརྗོད་བ་སྒོམ་མཁན་ལ་ཅེར་གྱིས་ལྟས་ཏེ། སྒོམ་ཡོད་སྒོམ་མེད་དུ་ཤིགས་ཀྱིས་བཤིག ཐ་མར་བསྐྱང་སྟེ་ཆེད་དུ་མི་སྒོམ། དྲན་པ་ཐག་པས་རིག་པ་ཐ་མལ་དུ་མ་ཤོར་བར་བྱ་སྟེ། སྒོམ་མེད་ཡེངས་མེད་འབྲལ་མེད་དུ་རྒྱུད་ལ་བསྟེན་ཏེ་བསྐྱང་། དེ་ཡང་དང་པོ་བཤིག་པ་ཐུང་ལ་འཛོག་པ་དང་སྐྱོང་བ་ཡུན་ཆ་མཉམ་ཙམ་བྱ། དེ་ནས་སྐྱོང་ཤེས་རྗེ་རིང་དུ་རྒྱུན་འཐུད་ལ་ཐ་མ་སྐྱོང་ཤེས་འབའ་ཞིག་ཏུ་གྱུར་པ་དང་། འཛོག་བཤིག་མི་དགོས་ཏེ། དེ་ཙམ་ན་ཐུན་སྒོམ་ཟད་སར་སྐྱོལ་བ་ཡིན། དེས་ན་ད་ལྟ་ཐུན་སྒོམ་དུས་ཀྱི་མཚན་མེད་ཀྱི་དངོས་གཞི་ཉམས་ལེན་གྱི་སྙིང་ཐིག་འདི་ཉིད་ཡིན་པས། དུས་རྣམས་ (p.98)ཀུན་གྱི་ཉམས་ལེན་ལ་གདམས་ངག་འདི་སྦྱོར་འདྲིམ་ཤེས་པར་བྱ་ཞིང་། ཕྱི་བྲག་ཏུ་འབོག་པའི་དུས་སུ་ནི་བཅུ་བཅོ་ལྔ་ལས་སོགས་སུ་བསྒོམ་དུ་གཞུག་གོ དྲི་མ་དང་བྲལ་བའི་ཐབས་ལ་བསླབ་པའི་ཐུན་མཚམས་དམ་པ་རིན་པོ་ཆེའི་གསུང་བཞིན། སྤྲོས་པ་སྟེ་དགུ་པའོ།།

།།བླ་མ་དམ་པ་རྣམས་ལ་ཕྱག་འཚལ་ལོ། གསུམ་པ་དྲི་མ་མེད་པའི་ཡེ་ཤེས་ལམ་དུ་བསླང་པ་ལ་བཞི་སྟེ། ལུས་ལྷ་སྐུ། ངག་བཟླས་བརྗོད། ཡིད་ཡེ་ཤེས། སྣ་ཚོགས་ཐབས་ཀྱི་འཁྲུལ་འཁོར་རོ། དང་པོ་ལ་གོང་གི་སྐྱོང་ཤེས་ཀྱི་སྟེང་ནས་ཡར་ལྷ་མར་ལྷ། ཕར་ཁྲུལ་ཚུར་ཁྲུལ། ཡ་ཡོ། གཅའ་གཙུ་སང་སིང་བྱས་ལ་བསྒྲི། མི་གནོད་ན་དལ་གྱིས་ལངས་ཏེ་དག་པའི་ཕྱག་སྐོར་ལ་བསྒྲི། དེ་ནས་དྲག་ཏུ་བཏང་ལ་བསྒྲི། དེ་ནས་ལུང་མ་བསྟན་བཟའ་བཟོ་མཆོང་རྒྱུགས་ལས་སོགས་བྱ་བྱེད་སྣ་ཚོགས་ལ་བསྒྲི། དེ་ནས་བདེག་བརྡུང་འཁྲི་ཚིག་ལས་སོགས་མ་དག་པ་ལ་བསྒྲི། དེ་དག་ཀུན་ཀྱང་འདྲེས་ནས་ལུས་ཀྱི་བྱ་བྱེད་སྤྱོད་ཚུལ་དག་མ་དག་ཐམས་ཅད་དགེ་སྦྱོར་གྱི་ངང་དུ་ལམ་དུ་སློང་བ་ཡིན་ནོ། གཉིས་པ་ལ་ཡང་དགེ་སྦྱོར་ངང་ནས་དག་པའི་སྙིང་པོ་སྐྱབས་སེམས་ཁ་ཐོན་མདོ་བློས། སྐད་དང་སྒྲ་དབྱངས་ཞི་དྲག་ཅི་རིགས་སུ་བྱས་ལ་བསྒྲི། མི་གནོད་

ན་ཡོང་གཏམ་གླེང་སྐད་ཀུ་རེ་དྲི་སྨད་ལས་སོགས་ལུང་མ་བསྟན་ཅི་རིགས་ལ་བསྔོ། དེ་ནས་ཀུ་ཅོ་ཚིག་རྩུབ་ཛུན་ཕྲ་ལས་སོགས་མ་དག་པ་རྣམས་ལ་ཡང་ཆེད་དུ་བསྔོ། དེ་དག་ཐམས་ཅད་ལམ་དུ་སློང་ན་ངག་དང་འདྲེས་མ་ཡིན། གསུམ་པ་ལ་ དགེ་སྦྱོར་གྱི་ངང་ནས་བདག་ལུས་ཡི་དམ་དུ་བསྐྱེད་ལ་བསྔོ། གཞན་ཡང་བྱ་ཆ་དགེ་སྦྱོད་ཀྱི་ཧིང་ངེ་འཛིན་དང་། སྔགས་ཕྱི་ནང་གི་བསྐྱེད་རིམ་ལས་སོགས་ལ་བསྔོ། དེ་ལ་འདྲེས་ནས་ལུང་མ་བསྟན་གྱི་བསམ་མནོ་རྟོག་དཔྱོད་སྣ་ཚོགས་ལ་བསྔོ། དེ་ནས་དུག་གསུམ་དུག་ལྔ་ལས་སོགས་(p.99)མ་དག་པ་ཀུན་ལ་བསྔོ། དེ་དག་ཐམས་ཅད་འདྲེས་ན་ཡིད་དང་དགེ་སྦྱོར་འདྲེས་པའོ། བཞི་པ་ལ་ བྲེད་སྐྲག་སྔངས་པ་དང་། འཐེ་ཏ་ཤེང་ཡ་ང་བ་དང་། སྐྱུག་བྲོ་ཞི་ལོག་པ། ན་ཞིང་ཚ་བ་དང་། འཁྲོ་ཞིང་འཚིག་པ་དང་། འཚེར་ཞིང་ངོ་ཚ་བ་དང་། ཞེན་ཅིང་ཆགས་པ་དང་། སྡུག་ཅིང་བསྔལ་བ་དང་། བདེ་ཞིང་སྐྱིད་པ་དང་། དེ་ལས་སོགས་པའི་སྐམ་བྱེད། ཁྲུ་འཁྲིག སོམ་ཉི། རེ་དོགས་ སྡུག་བསྔལ་ འགལ་སྐྱེན་ མི་འོས་མི་ཐང་པ་རྣམས་དང་། འཕྲུལ་ཟ་འཆག་འགྲོ་འདུག་བྱ་བྱེད་སྤྱོད་ལམ་རྣམས་ནས། མཐའ་ན་འཆི་བ་ཡན་ཆོད་ལ་རིག་པའི་གནད་མ་ཤོར་དྲན་འཛིན་གྱི་གཉེན་པོ་དང་མ་བྲལ་བ། དགེ་སྦྱོར་གྱི་ངང་ནས་ལམ་དུ་ཁྱེར། ཐད་དུ་གཅོད། ཐོག་ཏུ་འགེལ། ཕམ་རྒྱལ་སྒྲེ་བ་སྟེ། ལུང་དྲུག་ལས། རྟུལ་ཤུགས་ཆེན་པོ་སྤྱོད་ནུས་ན། བཟང་ངན་མེད་པར་སྤྱོད་པ། དེ་ནི་རྫོགས་ཆེན་སྟོད་དུ་བསྡུགས་ཞེས་དང་། མ་བཀག་ས་པ་དེ་སྤྱོད་པའོ། ཞེས་གསུང་པས་ཤེས་ཤིང་། དེ་དག་གི་ལམ་དུ་ཁྱེར་ཚུལ་ཀྱང་ཞི་དལ་གྱི་ཐབས་ལ་མཁས་པས། དལ་གྱིས་ངང་བསྲིང་ལ་བསྲེ་ཞིང་སོ་སོ་ཕྱེ་ནས་མཚན་མེད་ལ་ནན་ཏུར་བྱ། ལས་དང་པོ་སློ་གསུམ་སྣ་རེ་ནས་བསྔོ། རྫི་ཞིག་ནས་གསུམ་ཀ་ལ་དུས་མཉམ་སུ་བསྔོ། ཐོག་འགེལ་ཐད་ཆོད་དུ་བསྔོ། དེ་ཡང་དང་པོར་སོ་སོར་(ཡ)གྲུ་མ་བྲལ་བ། བསྔོ་ཐུབ་པ་ཙམ། བར་པའི་སྐབས་སུ་འདྲེས་ནས་མི་གནོད་པ་ཙམ། ཐ་མའི་སྐབས་སུ་གྲོགས་སུ་འཆར་བ་ཞིག་ཡིན་ཏེ། དྲང་དོན་ལས། སྣང་བ་གནོད་པའི་དུས་ན་ཕན་པའི་གྲོགས་སྟེན་ཏེ་ཞེས་དང་། སྣང་བ་ཕན་པའི་དུས་ན་ཐམས་ཅད་གྲོགས་སུ་འཆར། ཅེས་གསུང་པ་དང་། (p.100)གཞི་ཐེག་ཆེན་གྱི་ངང་ནས་(ཐམས་ཅད་)ལམ་དུ་ཁྱེར་ཐུབ་ན། ལུས་ངག་གི་བྱ་བྱེད། སྤྱོད་ལམ་དག་མ་དག་དགེ་མི་དགེ་བཟང་ངན་འབྲིང་གསུམ་ཅི་བྱས་པ་ཐམས་ཅད་དགེ་སྦྱོར་དུ་འགྲོ་སྟེ། གསལ་བྱེད་ལས། གཞི་མའི་དོན་ཞིག་རྟོགས་པ་ན། བསྐལ་པ་དུ་

མར་སྡིག་སྤྱོད་ཀྱང་། དགེ་མེད་སྡིག་དང་བྲལ་པ་ཡིན། ཞེས་དང་། ཐེག་པ་ཆེན་པོའི་དོན་དང་མ་འབྲེལ་ན་སྒོ་གསུམ་དག་པའི་དཀའ་སྤྱད་དུ་མ་སྤྱོད་ཀྱང་འབྲས་བུ་མི་ཐོབ་སྟེ། གཞི་མའི་དོན་ཞིག་མ་རྟོགས་ན། བསྐལ་པ་དུ་མར་དགེ་སྤྱད་ཀྱང་། དགེ་རྟོག་སྡིག་གིས་བཅིངས་པ་ཡིན། ཅེས་དང་། ལུང་དྲུག་ལས། ལུས་ཀྱི་སྡུག་བསྔལ་བྱང་ཆུབ་རྒྱུར་འདོད་པ། དེ་ལ་དེ་མིན་ཆུ་ལ་མར་ཅི་ཡང་། དགེ་སྡིག་གཉིས་མེད་སྡིག་ཉིད་བྱང་ཆུབ་ཡིན། ཞེས་དང་། གཞན་ལ་འདི་མེད་སྟོང་སྒྲོ་སྐྱོང་པ་ཡིན། འདི་ལ་གཞན་མེད་གསེར་གྱི་ཕྱིས་བུ་ཡིན། གསུངས་པ་རྣམས་ཀྱང་དོན་དེ་འདྲའི་དགོངས་པ་མཐོང་ཞིང་། དེས་ན་ལས་དང་པོ་དགེ་སྦྱོར་གྱི་འགྲམ་མ་ཐེང་བར་དུ་བཅས་བཅོས་དང་། སྒྲོ་བཀློག་མངས་ན་རྐང་པས་ས་མ་ཟིན་པར་ལག་པས་གར་བསྒྱུར་བ་དང་འདྲ་བས། ཁོ་རང་ལ་དྲིལ་གྱིས་འདྲིལ་བ་གལ་ཆེ། གཞི་ཐེང་པ་དང་། ལམ་དུ་ཁྱེར་མ་ཤེས་ན། ཆུ་ཕྲན་ཐན་པས་བསྐམས་པ་དང་འདྲ་སྟེ། རྐྱེན་མི་ཐུབ་པས་གདམས་པ་འདི་གཙོ་ཆེ་བ་ཡིན་པས། ཕྱིར་གྱིས་དུས་རྣམས་ཀུན་གྱི་ཉམས་ལེན་ལ། གཞི་ཁྲིད་ཀྱི་དུས་སུ་བཅུ་འམ་བཅོ་ལྔ་ལོགས་སུ་འབོག་གོ ཏྲེ་མེད་ཀྱི་ཡེ་ཤེས་ལམ་དུ་སླང་བའི་ཐུན་མཚམས། བླ་མ་དམ་པའི་གསུངས་བཞིན་བཀོད་པ་སྟེ་བཅུ་པའོ།། །།བླ་མ་དམ་པ་རྣམས་ལ་ཕྱག་འཚལ་ལོ། གསུམ་པ་གྲོལ་བ་མཐར་ཕྱིན་པར་བྱེད་པའི་ཁྲིད་ལ་བཞི་སྟེ། རྣབ་མོ་(p.101)བག་ཆགས་གཏོད་ལ་མནན་པ་དང་། ཉིན་མོ་སྣང་བ་ལ་རྩལ་སྦྱང་བ་དང་། ནང་རྣབ་རྟོག་པ་ལམ་དུ་སླང་བ་དང་། རྒྱུན་དུ་རིག་པ་རང་ངོ་སྤྲོད་པའོ། དང་པོ་ལ་བཞི་སྟེ། བཟུང་བ་དང་། སྦྱང་པ་དང་། སྲེལ་བ་དང་། ཨར་ལ་གཏད་པའོ། དང་པོ་ལ་སྟན་བདེ། སྟུས་མཐོ་བ་ལ་སངས་རྒྱས་ཀྱི་གཟིམས་ཚུལ་བྱ་སྟེ། གདན་སེང་གླང་རྟ་འབྲུག་ཁྱུང་ལྔ་ཉི་ཟླ་པད་མ། རང་བླ་མ་ཡི་དམ་གང་མོས་སུ་སྐྱེད་པ་ཞིག་སྡེམ། གཞི་མོས་གུས་སྙིང་རྗེ་ངང་ནས་ཨག་ཤོ་འཁོར་ལོའི་དབུས་སུ་རིག་པ་ཨའི་རང་བཞིན་འོད་ཟེར་གྱི་འཕྲོ་འདུ་དང་ལྡན་པས། རྩ་མིག་སྒྲུ་ལུས་འོད་དང་ཐིག་ལེས་གང་བར་བསམ་ཞིང་དྲན་པ་ཨ་ལ་གཏད་དེ། (ཕྱི་རུ་མི་སྤྲོ་ ནང་དུ་མི་སྡུ་) རིག་ལ་འདུ་འཕྲོའི་རྟོག་པ་སྐད་ཅམ་ཡང་མེད་པའི་སྟོང་ཉིད་ཀྱི་ངང་ནས་ཕྲིག་གེ་བ་ལ་ཉལ་བས།° རབ་ལ་གཉིད་དང་བསམ་གཏན་འདྲེས་ནས་གཉིད་དུ་ནི་སོང་། དྲན་པས་རྩིས་ནི་ཟིན། དགེ་སྦྱོར་དང་སྐད་གཅིག་ཅམ་ཡང་མ་བྲལ་བ་དེ་ལ། གཉིད་འཐུག་ན་འཐུག་པའི་འོད་གསལ། སྲབ་ན་སྲབ་པའི་འོད་གསལ་དུ་འཆར་ལ། འཁྲིང་མི་ལམ་གྱི་སྣང་བ་མི་ལམ་

ད་ངོ་ཤེས་པ་འབྱུང་། དེ་ཚེ་ཉམས་ལེན་དྲན་པའི་སྒོམ་པས་རྨི་ལམ་ཐ་མལ་རང་དགའི་འཁྲུལ་ཤེས་ཐམས་ཅད་ལམ་དུ་བསླངས་ནས། ཉིན་བས་ཀྱང་མཚན་དགེ་སྦྱོར་འཕེལ། ཐོག་ཀྱང་འགྱུར་གྱིས་ཆེ་བས་དྲན་ཐག་མི་བཅད་པར་ཉམས་སུ་ལེན་པ་གལ་ཆེའོ། ཐ་མས་ཀྱང་རྨི་ལམ་རང་ཁ་མར་ཤར་བའི་སྐབས་སུ་ངོ་ཤེས་ཉམས་ལེན་དྲན་པ་རེ་རེ་ཙམ་འབྱུང་། སྦྱངས་པས་ཇེ་རྒྱས་ལ་འཕེལ་ཞིང་མཐར་ལེགས་པར་ངོས་ཟིན་པ་འབྱུང་། གོང་ལྟར་སྦྱངས་པས་རབ་ཏུ་འགྲོའོ། མི་ཟིན་པའི་རྒྱུ་ནི་བླ་མ་ལ་གུས་པ་མ་ཆུང་(p.102)པ། གདམས་པ་ལ་ངེས་ཤེས་མ་སྐྱེས་པ། བརྩོན་འགྲུས་ཀྱི་ཉེར་ལེན་མི་ནུས་པ། རྣམ་རྟོག་གིས་རྒྱུད་དཀྲུགས་པ་གཞི་སེམས་ཀྱི་སྐྱོན་ཡིན་པས་སྤང་། འབྱུང་མ་མི་སྙམས་པའི་ཟས་ཟོས་པ་ངལ་དུབ་ཀྱི་ལས་བྱས་པ། ཕོ་མོའི་འདོད་སྲེད་ལ་སྤྱད་པ། འབྱུང་བའི་སྟོབས་ཆུད་པ་གཞི་ལུས་ཀྱི་སྐྱོན་ཡིན་པ་སྤངས། ལས་དང་པོ་མི་ཟིན་པ་ཤས་ཆེ་བའི་དུས་སུ། གཉིད་ལ་ཁད་དང་། པད་མ་ཐོག་གི་དུས་སུ་ཧིང་ངེ་འཛིན་ལ་ལེགས་པར་གཏུན་ཞིང་བག་ཡངས་ལ་མི་འཛོག་མ་གཉིད་པའི་རྟོག་པ་རགས་པ་འགག རྨི་ལམ་མ་ཤར་བའི་བར་དེར། གང་གི་རྟོག་པ་རབ་རིབ་བྱུང་བའི་དུས་དེ་ཀ་ལ་རྨི་ལམ་གྱི་མགོ་གཡོས་པར་ཤེས་པར་བྱས་ལ། མིག་མི་འབྱེད་འོག་ཆུང་ཙུང་ཙམ་བསྡམ། ཉམས་ལེན་དང་སྲེས་ལ་གང་ཟིན་པག་མེད་དུ་སྤྲུལ་པའི་ཟིན་པ་མྱུར་བར་འགྱུར་ལ། སྲོད་ཐོ་རངས་དང་། གཉིད་དུ་མ་སོང་བའི་སྐབས་ཐམས་ཅད་དུ་བླ་མ་ཡིད་དམ་མཁའ་འགྲོ་ལ་གསོལ་བ་བྱུན་བྱུན་པ་བཏབ་སྨྲུན་དྲངས་ཏེ་ལུས་ལ་སྟིམས་ལ། གཉིད་དང་བསམ་གཏན་འདྲེས་པར་བྱིན་གྱིས་བརླབ་ཏུ་གསོལ་ལོ་སྙམ་པ་ཡང་ཡང་བྱ། ཐུར་བས་གཉིད་སྲབ་ཅིང་། རྨི་ལམ་གསལ་པོ་དོད་པོ་མྱུར་པོ་རུ་སོང་ནས་རིག་པ་དངས་སྒྲིགས་ཕྱེད་ནས་ཟིན་ལ་ཁད་ཡིན་པས་བཤུར་གཅིག ཉིན་གྱི་དུས་ཀྱང་འདི་ལྟར་གྱི་སྣང་བ་འཇིག་རྟེན་གྱི་བྱ་བྱེད་ཐམས་ཅད་འདྲ་ཡང་རྨི་ལམ་དང་འདྲ། སྣང་ཡང་རྨི་ལམ་དུ་སྣང་། ཡིན་ཀྱང་རྨི་ལམ་དུ་ཡིན་ཏེ། རྨི་ལམ་ལ་ཡང་འདི་ཡིན། ཐུར་གྱི་བག་ཆགས་གང་གོམས་པས། གང་ཞེན་གང་འདྲིས་དང་། ཕྱིས་ཅི་འབྱུང་། གང་བྱེད་རྣམས་ཇི་ལྟ་བ་འམ། འོལ་འདྲ་ཕྱོགས་དོད་དོད་སལ་སལ་དུ་འཆར། (p.103)དེས་ན་འདི་ལྟར་སྣང་བ་ཀ་རྨི་ལམ། རྨི་ལམ་ཀ་སྣང་བ་ཡིན་ཏེ། སྐད་ཙམ་ཡུད་ཙམ་གྱི་དོན་བྱེད་ནི་རྨི་ལམ་སྣང་བས་ཀྱང་ནུས་ལ། མཐར་ཐུག་གི་བདེན་པ་ནི་འདི་ལྟར་གྱི་སྣང་བ་ལ་ཡང་མེད། སྐད་ཙམ་ཡུད་ཙམ་དུ་ནི་རྨི་ལམ་གྱི་སྣང་པ་ཡང་བདེན་པའི་ཕྱིར།

འདི་ཉིད་དབྱེར་མེད་རོ་གཅིག་གནད་གཅིག་ཏུ་གནས་པ་ལྟར་ཡང་ཡང་བསམ། འདྲིས་ཤིང་གོམས་པས་ཐམས་ཅད་རྨི་ལམ་སྒྱུ་མ་ལྟ་བུར་འཆར་རོ། གཉིས་པ་སྦྱོང་བ་ནི། རྨི་ལམ་ངོས་ཟིན་པའི་དུས་སུ། གཞི་ཉམས་ལེན་གྱི་ངང་ལས། ངའི་བག་ཆགས་ཀྱི་ཡིད་གཟུགས་འདི་གང་སྒྱུར་ཡིན་སྙམས་སུ་བསམ་ལ། ལུས་རྩ་ལག་ལྷ་གཙོ་འཁོར་དུ་སྐྱེད་ལ། སྣང་བ་ལྷ་དང་གཞལ་ཡས་སུ་བསྐྱེད་པས་གསལ་ལམ་གྱི་བྱུང་ཙམ་ན། ལྷ་ཚོགས་ཀ་ང་། ང་ཀ་ལྷ་ཚོགས། སྙམས་པའི་སྒྱུ་མ་རྨི་ལམ་གྱི་དྲན་འདུན་བྱས་ལ་སྟོང་ཉིད་ངང་ལས་ལྷོད་ཀྱིས་ལྷོད་ལ་བཞག ཡང་ཡང་དྲན་པར་བྱ། གཞན་ཡང་མེ་ཆུ་གཡང་གསུམ་ལས་མཆོང་པ། མཁའ་ལ་འཕུར་བ། དགྲ་ལ་སྡོ་བ། གཉེན་ལ་འཐབ་པ། ཁང་བ་རི་བྲག་ལ་ཟང་ཐལ་ལས་སོགས་ལ་ཐོགས་འགལ་གྱིས་ཆོད་དུ་སྦྱང་ཞིང་ཡ་ང་ཏིང་གིས་བྱུང་བ་དང་། སྒྱུ་མ་རྨི་ལམ་གྱི་དྲན་འདུན་བྱས་ལ་དགེ་སྦྱོར་ངང་ལ་གློད། ཡང་སྔར་ལྟར་ཡང་ཡང་དྲན་པར་བྱའོ། གསུམ་པ་སྤྲུལ་བ་ལ་ཉམས་ལེན་དང་ནས་སྣང་བ་འདི་རྨི་ལམ་ལུས་འདི་ཡིད་གཟུག། ཡིན་ནི་གཉིད་དུ་སོང་བ་ཡིན། འདི་ལ་ཇི་ལྟར་སྦྱངས་སྦྱངས་སྤྲུལ་སྤྲུལ་ཡིན་སྙམས་པ་ལས། ལུས་སེམས་ཕྲ་རག་གང་ཡིན་དུ་བསམ་དེ་ལ་བག་ཆགས་བརྟན་པ་བྱུང་ན་ དེ་བརྒྱ་སྟོང་ཁྲི་འབུམ་དུ་སྤྲུལ། དེ་བཞིན་འབྱུང་བཞི་ཕྲ་རག་རྣམས་ཀྱང་དེ་བཞིན། གཞན་ཡང་གང་ལ་འདུལ། (p.104)གར་འདོད། མེ་ལ་ཆུ་ རྡོ་ལ་གསེར་ལས་སོགས་དང་། སེམས་ཅན་གང་འདུལ། ཀླུ་ལ་ཁྱུང་། ཁྲི་ལ་སེང་གེ ཉོན་མོངས་གང་འདུལ། ཞེ་སྡང་ལ་གཙོ་མཆོག ལས་སོགས་དང་། དོན་ལ་བག་ཆགས་ཀྱི་ཡིད་གཟུགས་གང་དུ་ཡང་སྤྲུལ་ནུས་ཤིང་། ཡིད་ལ་དྲན་པ་ཙམ་གྱིས་འགྱུར་བ་དང་། འགྱུ་བྱེད་ཀྱིས་ཤེས་པ་གར་ཁྲིད་དུ་འགྲོ་ནུས་ཏེ། བསམ་པ་ཙམ་གྱིས་གནས་གང་འདོད་དུ་ཕྱིན་པ་དང་། འདི་ལྟར་གྱི་སྣང་བ་གང་དུ་ཡང་བསྒྱུར་དུ་བཏུབ་སྟེ། ཡིད་ལ་ཅི་ལྟར་བྱས་པ་ལྟར་འགྱུར་བ་དང་། གསུམ་བྱུང་ན། རྨི་ལམ་གྱི་འཁྲུལ་སྣང་ལམ་དུ་སློབས་པའོ། བཞི་པ་ལ་ཅི་ལྟར་བྱས་ཀྱང་མ་ཟིན་ན། དུས་གནད་སུ་གོང་མ་ལུས་གནད་ལྷ་ལྡན་ནམ་ཅོག་པུ། ཐབས་གནད་ལོངས་སྤྱོད་ཀྱི་འཕར་རྩ་བསྡམ་ཞིང་ཕྱི་ནང་གསལ་གདབ་རང་གི་ཏིང་འཛིན་གཙུན་པས་མི་ཟིན་མི་སྲིད་ཅིང་། འཕར་རྩ་བསྡམ་ཡུན་རིང་ན་རིག་པ་འཕོ་བའི་ཉེན་ཡོད་པས་ཆོད་ཟིན་པར་བྱ། ཡང་ན་ཉལ་དུས་ཤེ་ཐུན་གྱི་འཁོར་ལོ་ལ་གོང་ལྟར་གྱི་དམིགས་པ་གཙུན་པས་རྨི་ལམ་གྱི་བར་དོ་ཆོད་ (པ) ཀྱང་། བླ་ཆེན་དང་འགྲོ་མགོན་

མཐུན་པར་གསུངས་སོ། བསམ་གཏན་གཉིད་དང་བསྲེས་པའི་རྟགས་རབ་འབྲིང་ཐ་མ་གསུམ་མ་བྱུང་བར་ལ་སྦྱང་ཞིང་རིག་འཛིན་གྲུབ་ཆེན་རྣམས་ཀྱི་གསུངས་བཞིན་བཀོད་པ་སྟེ། བཅུ་གཅིག་པའོ།།

།།བླ་མ་དམ་པ་རྣམས་ལ་ཕྱག་འཚལ་ལོ། གཉིས་པ་ཉིན་མོ་སྣང་བ་ལ་རྩལ་སྦྱངས་པ་ལ། བླ་ཆེན་གྱི་གསུངས་ལས། རབ་ལ་བཐོང་གསས་སྒྲོན་མ་ནས་རྩལ་སྦྱངས། འབྲིང་པོ་དབང་པོ་སྒོ་གསུམ་ནས་རྩལ་སྦྱངས། ཐ་བ་བ་སྤྱིའི་བུ་ག་ནས་རྩལ་སྦྱངས། ཞེས་དང་། གསུང་རབ་ལས། གཟུགས་སེམས་ཀྱི་རང་(p.105)བཞིན་གསལ་བའི་ཡེ་ཤེས་ཀྱི་འབྲས་བུ་དེ་ནི་ཐོབ་པར་འགྱུར་རོ་ལས་སོགས་གསུངས་པ་དང་། ཡེ་ཕྱི་མོའི་བོན་སྐོར་ལས། དབང་པོ་ཡུལ་ལྷའི་རྗེས་སུ་མ་འབྲེང་བ། འབྲེངས་ཀྱང་རྣམ་པར་མ་ཕྱེ་བ། ཕྱི་ཡང་བདག་ཏུ་མ་བཟུངས། བཟུང་ཡང་བག་ཆགས་སུ་མ་ཞེན་པ། ཞེས་དང་། གབ་པ་ལས། ཉམས་ང་མེད་པར་རྩལ་སྦྱོང་། རེ་དོགས་མེད་པར་རྩེད་མོ་རྩེ། ལས་སོགས་དུ་མར་གསུངས་པས། ཚོཏ་དྲུག་སྒོ་ལྔའི་ཤེས་པ་ཐམས་ཅད་སྐད་ཅིག་ཙམ་ཡང་ཐ་མལ་དུ་མ་ཤོར་བར་རྩལ་སྦྱངས་ཏེ། སྒོ་ལྔའི་ཡུལ་གཟུགས་སྒྲ་དྲི་རོ་རེག་བྱ་ལས་སོཏ་ཅི་ཤར་བ་ཐམས་ཅད་ལ། རྟོགས་དཔྱོད་དང་བསམ་གཞིག་དང་། སྐམ་བྲེད་དང་བླང་དོར་ལས་སོགས་མེད་པར་མདོར་ན་རང་ཁ་མར་ཁ་ཟགས་སུ་སྐད་ཙམ་ཡང་མ་ཤོར་བར་བྱ་སྟེ། རབ་ལྟ་བའི་ངང་ནས་རང་ཤར་རང་གྲོལ་མཚོན་དང་དུ་ཁ་ཆར་བབ་པ་ལྟ་བུ། འབྲིང་སྒོམ་ཐོག་ནས་ཅེར་ལྟ་ཅེར་གྲོལ་སྟར་འདྲིས་ཀྱི་མི་དང་འཕྲད་པ་ལྟ་བུ། ཐ་མ་གཉེན་པོའི་དྲན་ཐག་ཐུགས་སྤྲུགས་ནས་ཆུ་འདྲེན་པ་ལྟ་བུའི་རྩལ་སྦྱངས་ཏེ། དེ་སྦྱོང་བ་ལ་(ཁོ་ཉིད་)ཁོང་གཉིས་ཀྱི་ངོ་བོ་ཡིན་ལུགས་འགྲོགས་ལུགས་འབྲེལ་ཚུལ་ཀྱུ་མཚན་ཤེས་དགོས་ཏེ། དེའི་ཚུལ་ནི། ནང་གི་འཛིན་མཁན་གྱི་ཤེས་པ་ལ་དཔྱད་ན་ཡང་བཀགས་པས་མི་ཁོག་པར་འཆར་བ། སྤངས་པས་མི་སྟོངས་པར་སྐྱེ་བ། ཐུག་ཕྲད་དུ་འཛིན་པ། འབྲལ་མེད་དུ་མཐུད་པ། མི་བསྡོད་པར་འགྲིམ་པ་ སྣ་ཚོགས་སུ་འགྱུར་བ་ཞིག་ཡིན་ལ། ཕྱི་ཚོགས་དྲུག་གི་སྣང་བ་འདི་ཡང་མ་བརྟགས་མ་དཔྱད་ན། ཡིན་ཡིན་པོ་གསལ་གསལ་པོ་དོད་དོད་པོ་ངེས་ངེས་པ་བདེན་(p.106)བདེན་པོ་ཅིག་སྣང་སྟེ། གཞིག་ཅིང་བརྟགས་ན་མི་རྟག་འགྱུར་བའི་རང་བཞིན་ཅན། བརྟགས་མི་བཟོད་དཔྱད་མི་བཟོད་པ། རྨི་ལམ་ལྟ་བུ་སྒྱུ་མ་ལྟ་བུ་བསླུ་བྲིད་ལྟ་བུ་ཅིར་ཡང་འཆར་ལ་གང་དུ་ཡང་མ་གྲུབ་པས་སེམས་ཀྱི་ཚོ་འཕྲུལ་ཡོ་(ལང་)ཡང་རང་རྩལ་ཏེ། དེས་ན་སྣང་བ་ཡང་སེམས་སེམས་ཀྱང་སྣང་བ་ཡིན་པས།

སྣང་སེམས་གཉིས་མེད་སྣང་ཙམ་ཉིད་ན་སྟོང་། སྟོང་ཙམ་ཉིད་ན་སྣང་བས་སྣང་སྟོང་གཉིས་མེད་མ་འགག་པར་ལྷག་ལྷག་ཤར་རང་བཞིན་མེད་པར་ཁྲོལ་ཁྲོལ་གྲོལ་བས། ཤར་གྲོལ་དུས་མཉམ་སྟེ། དེ་ཡང་རབ་ཀྱི་རང་ཤར་རང་གྲོལ། འབྲིང་གི་ཅེར་ལྷ་ཅེར་གྲོལ། ཐ་མ་དྲན་འཛིན་གྱི་གཉེན་པོའི་གཟུགས་མཐོང་སྟོང་སྒྲ་གྲགས་སྟོང་དྲི་ཚོར་སྟོང་རོ་མྱོང་སྟོང་རེག་གོན་སྟོང་པོན་དྲན་སྟོང་ལས་སོགས་ཐག་ཆད་ཆད་བཅད་ལ་ཉམས་སུ་བླང་སྟེ། མཛོད་ལས་ཁ་དོག་གསལ་སྤྱོད་དབང་པོའི་ཡུལ། ཁ་དོག་ཅི་གསལ་སེམས་ཀྱི་དབྱིངས་ཅེས་པའང་དོན་དེའོ། དེས་ན་ཚོགས་དྲུག་གི་སྣང་བ་འདི་དག་ཀྱང་། ངོང་ཆེད་དུ་རྩལ་སྦྱང་། འགྱིངས་ཙམ་གྱིས་མི་ཆོག་སྟེ། དེ་དག་གིས་མི་གནོད་པ་ཞིག་དགོས། བར་དུ་མི་གནོད་པ་ཙམ་གྱིས་ཀྱང་མི་ཆོག་སྟེ་གྲོགས་སུ་འཆར་བ་ཞིག་དགོས། ཐ་མར་གྲོགས་སུ་ཤར་བ་ཙམ་གྱིས་མི་ཆོག་སྟེ་གཉིས་མེད་དུ་རོ་མྱོང་བ་ཞིག་དགོས་པ་རྣམ་པ་ཀུན་ཏུ་བརྟེན་ཅིང་གཞི་ཁྲིད་ཀྱི་དུས་སུ་ལྡོ་བདུན་ལས་སོགས་སུ་འབོག་གོ སྣང་བ་ལ་རྩལ་སྦྱོང་གི་ཐུན་མཚམས་བླ་མའི་གསུངས་བཞིན་བཀོད་པ་སྟེ་བཅུ་གཉིས་པའོ།།

།།བླ་མ་དམ་པ་རྣམས་ལ་ཕྱག་འཚལ་ལོ། གསུམ་པ་ནང་ནུབ་རྟོག་པ་ལམ་དུ་(p.107)བསླང་བ་ལ། མདོ་ལས། མ་རིག་པ་ཉིད་རིག་ཙམ་ན། རིག་པའི་ཡེ་ཤེས་རང་ལ་འཆར། ཞེས་དང་། ལུང་དྲུག་ལས། དུག་ལྔ་སྤངས་ལོགས་ཡེ་ཤེས་མཚོན་དུ་མེད། ཅི་མ་སྤངས་པའི་སེམས་ཉིད་ཉག་གཅིག་མ། ཞེས་དང་། གསུང་རབ་ལས། ཡིད་བཞིན་གྱི་ནོར་བུ་རིན་པོ་ཆེ་ཚོལ་དུ་འགྲོ་བའི་ཚོང་པ་ལམ་དུ་ཞུགས་པ་ལ་དུག་ལྔའི་གནོད་པར་བྱེད་པའི་དགྲ་མང་བའི་སྐྱེས་བུ་དག་ཡེ་ཤེས་ལྔའི་གོ་ཆ་བགོ་བོར་བྱའོ། ལས་སོགས་གསུངས་པས། རྒྱུད་ལ་འཁྲུལ་པ་ཉོན་མོངས་རྣམ་རྟོག་ཕྲ་རགས་ཅི་གཡོས་ཀྱང་། ལྟ་བ་རྟོགས་པའི་རྩལ་དང་ལྡན་པས་རང་འབྱུང་རང་ཤར་རང་གྲོལ་གཉེན་པོ་བརྟེན་པའི་སྐམ་བྱེད་མེད། སྤང་བྱ་སྤོང་པའི་བློ་རྩོལ་ཟད་ཞིག་ཡིན་ཏེ། ལུང་དྲུག་ལས། རྒྱ་མཚོ་ཆེན་པོར་མ་གཡོས་པར་རླབས་ནི་མཚོའི་ངང་དུ་ཞི། ནམ་མཁའི་ངང་དུ་གཟའ་སྐར་ཞི། སེམས་ཉིད་ངང་དུ་སེམས་འབྱུང་ཞི། ཐམས་ཅད་ཞི་བ་(བདེ་)ཆེན་པོ་ ཐམས་ཅད་ལྷུན་གྲུབ་(བདེ་)ཆེན་པོ། ཞེས་གསུངས་པ་དང་མཐུན་ལ་དེ་ཙམ་གྱི་སྟོབས་མེད་པ་རྣམས་ཀྱིས་ཀྱང་རྟོག་པ་རང་ཁ་མར་མ་ཤོར་བ། ཁ་ཟགས་སུ་མ་འབྱམས་པ། མུ་ཡན་དུ་མ་འཕྲོས་པར་ཉམས་སུ་བླང་སྟེ། དེའི་གཉེན་པོ་བརྟེན་ཚུལ་ལ་ཡང་མཐའ་དག་སྤྱི་འབྱིན་(བྱིན་)དང་སོ་སོ་མགོ་གནོན་

གཉིས་སུ་གསུངས་ཀྱང་འོག་མ་ནི་སྣང་བྱ་ངོ་སྐལ་ལ་གཉེན་པོ་ཡང་ངོ་སྐལ་དུ་བརྟེན་པའི་ལུགས་ཏེ། ཞེ་སྡང་གི་གཉེན་པོར་བྱམས་པ་བསྒོམ་པ་ལྟ་བུའོ། འདིར་ནི་རྩ་བརྒྱ་ཐེར་ཁ་གཅིག་ལ་བཏང་བ་ལྟ་བུའམ། རོལ་བརྒྱ་ཤལ་ཡུག་གཅིག་(p.108)ལ་འབྱུང་བ་ལྟ་བུ་མཐའ་དག་སྤྱི་འབྱིན་གྱི་གཉེན་པོ་བསྟེན་ལུགས་ཏེ། ཧོལ་སྐྱེས་དྲན་པ་བྱེ་བ་སྨུ་མེད་པ་ཞིག་ཤར་ཀྱང་བདག་མེད་རྟོགས་པའི་ཤེས་རབ་གཅིག་གིས་འཇོམས་པ་འདི་ནི་ནད་བརྒྱ་སྨན་གཅིག་ལྟ་བུའི་གཉེན་པོའོ། དེ་ལ་ཡང་རབ་ཀྱིས་ཟིལ་གནོན་གྱི་གཉེན་པོ་མཆོག་ཐོག་ཏུ་ཁ་བ་བབ་པ་ལྟ་བུ་བརྟེན་ལ། རང་ཤར་རང་གྲོལ་དུ་ཉམས་སུ་བླང་། འབྲིང་གི་འབུར་འཇོམ་བ་མོ་ལ་ཉི་མ་ཡོག་པ་ལྟ་བུས་ཅེར་ལྟ་ཅེར་གྲོལ་དུ་ཉམས་སུ་བླང་། ཐ་མས་རྗེས་སློགས་སྐྱེས་བུ་ཞེ་སྡང་ཅན་ལ་གྲོས་ཐེབས་པ་ལྟ་བུ་ཉོན་མོངས་པ་རང་ཁ་མར་མ་སྤྱོད་པར་ཉམས་སུ་བླང་། ཡང་ན་རི་ཁྲོད་པ་ཆེན་པོའི་ཞལ་ནས། རབ་ཀྱིས་རྗེས་ཐོག་ནས་ངོས་ཟིན་པས་འཁྲུལ་པའི་གཡུལ་ངོ་བཟློག་པ་ཡིན། འབྲིང་གི་གྲིབ་ཐོག་ནས་ངོས་ཟིན་པས་འཁྲུལ་པ་ཁ་ཡན་མུ་འབྱམས་སུ་མི་འཚོར་པ་ཡིན། ཐ་མས་ཚེ་འཕྲུལ་གྱི་སྟེང་ནས་ངོས་ཟིན་པས་ཉོན་མོངས་པ་རང་ཁར་མི་སྤྱོད་པ་ཡིན། གསུངས་པ་དག་ཀྱང་དོན་གོང་མ་དང་དབྱེར་མེད་ཅིང་རྩལ་བཞིན་དུ་གོ་བདེ་བར་སྣང་ངོ་། གཞན་ཡང་དམ་པའི་ཞལ་ནས། རྟོག་པ་ཀུན་བུ་བཅོར་བ་ཡང་མི་སྟོད་དྭངས་སྙིགས་ཕྱེད་པ་ཡིན། ལས་དང་པོའི་དུས་སུ་ཧོལ་སྐྱེས་དྲན་པ་མང་བ་མ་ཡིན་ཏེ། རྒྱུ་དངས་པའི་སྲོག་ཆགས་དང་འདྲ་སྟེ་གསལ་བ་ཡིན། དེ་སྟ་ཕན་ཆད་ཉུང་བ་མིན་ཏེ། རྒྱུ་སློགས་པའི་སྲོག་ཆགས་དང་འདྲ་བས་ངོས་མ་ཟིན་པ་ཡིན། དེས་ན་དང་པོའི་དུས་སུ་རྟོགས་པ་ངོས་འཛིན་ལམ་དུ་སློང་ངོ་བོ་ལ་ལྟ། ཁྲུངས་བཅར་གཞི་རྩ་བཅད་འགྲོད་པས་ཞེ་ཁྲེལ་གདབ། ཕྱིས་མི་སྐྱེ་བའི་གོ་ཆ་གོན་ཅིང་དྲན་འཛིན་གྱི་གཉེན་པོ་དང་མ་བྲལ་བར་བྱེད་པ་ཤིན་ཏུ་གནད་ཆེ། བར་པའི་སྐབས་སུ་(p.109)ཆེད་དུ་སྤང་མི་དགོས་ཏེ། རང་བཞིན་གྱི་མཚོན་ཆའི་འཁོར་ལོ་ལྟར་རང་ཤར་རང་གྲོལ་འགྱུར་ལ། ཐ་མའི་སྐབས་སུ་ཅི་འཆར་ཡེ་ཤེས་སུ་ལྷག་ལྷག་ཤར་ནས་སྣང་གཉེན་རོ་གཅིག་གསེར་གླིང་དུ་ཕྱིན་པ་ལྟར་འགྱུར་རོ། ལུང་དྲུག་ལས་ཇེ་ཞི་ཇེ་ཞི་རྣམ་རྟོག་ཞི། ཇེ་གསལ་ཇེ་གསལ་ཡེ་ཤེས་གསལ། ཞེས་གསུངས་པས་དུས་རྣམ་ཀུན་ཏུ་ཉམས་སུ་བླང་ཞིང་། གཞི་ཁྲིད་ཀྱིས་དུས་སུ་ལྔ་བདུན་ལས་སོགས་སུ་བསྐྱང་དུ་གཞུག་གོ རྟོག་པ་ལམ་སློང་གི་ཐུན་མཚམས་བླ་མའི་གསུངས་བཞིན་སྦྱར་བ་སྟེ་བཅུ་གསུམ་པའོ།། །།བླ་མ་དམ

པ་རྣམས་ལ་ཕྱག་འཚལ་ལོ། བཞི་པ་རྒྱུན་དུ་རང་ངོ་སྤྲོད་པ་ལ། རི་ཁྲོད་པ་ཆེན་པོའི་ཞལ་ནས་སྤྱིར་སེམས་ཅན་སངས་རྒྱས་པ་ལ་བསྒོམ་དགོས། སྒོམ་པ་ལ་ལྟ་བ་རྟོགས། ལྟ་བ་རྟོགས་པ་ལ་ངོ་སྤྲོད་ཀྱི་མན་ངག་དགོས། ངོ་སྤྲད་པ་ཙམ་གྱི་མི་ཆོག་ཉམས་སུ་བླང་དགོས། ཉམས་སུ་བླངས་པ་ཙམ་གྱིས་མི་ཆོག་རྒྱུད་ལ་སྐྱེ་དགོས། དེ་སྐྱེས་པ་ཙམ་གྱིས་མི་ཆོག་དྲོད་རྟགས་འབྱུང་དགོས། དེ་བྱུང་བ་ཙམ་གྱིས་མི་ཆོག་འབྲས་བུ་མངོན་དུ་གྱུར་དགོས། དེ་མངོན་དུ་གྱུར་པ་ཙམ་གྱིས་མི་ཆོག་གཞན་དོན་རྒྱ་ཆེན་པོ་ནུས་དགོས་གསུངས་པས། དེ་ལ་ངོ་སྤྲོད་ཀྱི་མན་ངག་ལ་གསུམ་སྟེ། སྣང་བ་སེམས་སུ་ངོ་སྤྲད་པ། སེམས་མཐའ་བྲལ་དུ་ངོ་སྤྲད་པ། མཐའ་བྲལ་སྐུ་གསུམ་དུ་ངོ་སྤྲད་པའོ། དང་པོ་ལ་སེམས་ལ་མ་གཏོགས་གང་ཡང་མེད། ཐམས་ཅད་སེམས་ཀྱི་ཆོ་འཕྲུལ་ལོ། ཞེས་དང་སྣང་བ་ཐམས་ཅད་བྱང་ཆུབ་སེམས་སུ་ལུང་མནན་ལ་སྒོམ་ལས་སོགས་གསུངས་པས། འདི་ལྟར་གྱི་སྣང་བ་ཐམས་ཅད་སྣང་ཡང་སེམས་སུ་སྣང་སྟེ། སེམས་(p.110)སྟོང་པ་རྩ་བྲལ་དུ་རྟོགས་པ་ལ་སྣང་བ་ཡང་སྟོང་པ་རྩ་བྲལ་དུ་འཆར། སེམས་ལྷ་དང་གཞལ་ཡས་རྟོགས་པ་ལ་སྣང་བ་ཡང་ལྷ་དང་གཞལ་ཡས་དང་། དེ་བཞིན་དུ་སེམས་ལ་རང་དབང་ཐོབ་པས་སྣང་བ་ལ་ཡང་རང་དབང་ཐོབ་སྟེ་ས་གསེར་རྡོ་གཡུ་མི་ཆུ་ལས་སོགས་སུ་བསྒྱུར་ནུས་པ་རྟོགས་པའི་དུས་ན་ཡང་སྣང་སེམས་གནད་གཅིག་པར་འདུག མ་རྟོགས་པའི་དུས་སུ་ཡང་སྣང་བ་གཅིག་པོ་འདི་ལ་སེམས་དམྱལ་བའི་སྒྲུབས་སུ་ཞུགས་པའི་ཚེ། སྣང་བ་ཐམས་ཅད་ཡང་དམྱལ་སྣང་དུ་འཆར་ལ། སེམས་ཡི་དྭགས་ཀྱི་སྒྲུབས་སུ་ཞུགས་པའི་ཚེ་སྣང་བ་ཐམས་ཅད་ཀྱང་ཡི་དྭགས་ཀྱི་སྣང་བ་ལས་སོགས་རིགས་དྲུག་ཐམས་ཅད་ལ་རང་རང་གི་བག་ཆགས་ཀྱི་ཞེན་སྣངས་བཞིན་འཆར་ལུགས་དང་། ད་ལྟ་ཡང་ཡིད་ཤེས་འཁྲུལ་ན་རྨི་ལམ་བར་དོ་དང་གདོན་གྱིས་བརླབས་དུས་དང་སྨན་དང་ཟས་ཀྱིས་བསླད་དུ་ལས་སོགས་ལ། སྣང་བ་འདི་ཤ་ལོག་སྤྱི་ལོག་ཏུ་འཆར་ལུགས་དང། དབང་ཤེས་འཁྲུལ་པའི་ཚེ་ཟླ་གཉིས་དང་སེར་ཐག་པ་སྤྲུལ་འཛིན་གངས་རི་གསེར་ལྗོན་ཤིང་འགྲོ་སྣང་སྒྱུ་མའི་རྟ་གླང་ལས་སོགས་སུ་འཆར་ལུགས་ཀྱིས་ཀྱང་སེམས་ཀྱི་ཆོ་འཕྲུལ་ཕོ་ཡི་བྱེད་ལས་ཐམས་ཅད་ཕོ་ཡིས་གར་བསྒྱུར་ཞིག་ཏུ་འདུག་མོད། ཡིན་ཀྱང་སྣང་བ་འདི་ལས་སེམས་ལོགས་ན་མེད་དེ། རྒྱུ་མཚན་ཀྱང་སྣང་བ་ལ་སོ་སོར་འབྱེད་པ་བླང་དོར་བྱེད་པ་རྟོགས་དཔྱོད་གཏོང་བ་ཐམས་ཅད་བྱེད་མཁན་རང་རིག་ཏུ་འདུག་པ་ལ། སྣང་པ་ཡིས་ཚུར་བཀལ་མ་ཡིན་རིག་པས་

ཕར་བཟུང་དུ་འདུག་པས། དེས་ན་ཆོ་རབས་དཔག་མེད་ཀྱི་དུས་ན་སེམས་མ་རིག་པས་བསྒྲད་པའི་བློ་འཁྲུལ་པ་ལ་རྫུན་སྣང་དུ་ཤར་ནས་རིག་པ་བཅོལ་ཆུང་བྲིད་པས་ཁོ་ཉིད་དེའི་དབང་(p.111)དུ་སོར་བར་མངོན་ཏེ། མ་རིག་གཉིད་ཀྱིས་བསྒྲད་པའི་འགྲོ་བ་གང་ལ་གང་སྣང་དེ་ནི་རྫུན་ཏེ་སྒྱུ་མ་རྨི་ལམ་ལྟ་བུ་འདོད། ཅེས་དང་། ལུང་དྲུག་ལས། གཞི་རྩ་མེད་པའི་བོན་འདི་ལ། གང་ལྟར་བརྟགས་པ་དེ་ལྟར་སྣང་ རིགས་དྲུག་ཆུ་ལ་དྲུག་ཏུ་མཐོང་། ལས་སོགས་དུ་མ་གསུངས་པ་རྣམས་ཀྱིས་ཤེས་པས་སྣང་བ་ཐམས་ཅད་སེམས་སུ་ཐག་ཆོད་ཀྱིས་བཅད་ལ་དབྱེར་མེད་རོ་གཅིག་ཏུ་ཉམས་སུ་བླངས་པས། འཁྲུལ་སྣང་སེམས་སུ་གཏན་ལ་ཕེབས་པར་འགྱུར་རོ། གཉིས་པ་ལ་སེམས་བྱ་བའི་རིག་རིག་པོ་གསལ་གསལ་པོ་རྟེན་རྟེན་པོ་དོད་དོད་པོ་འདི་ཡང་ཡོད་དམ་བྱས་ན་གཟུགས་དབྱིབས་སུ་མ་གྲུབ་ཁ་དོག་ཏུ་མ་གྲུབ། ཆེ་ཚད་ཆུང་ཚད་ཀྱིས་གཞལ་དུ་མེད་པ་འདི་ཁོ་ན་ཞེས་སུས་ཀྱང་མ་བསྟན་པའི་མིག་གི་མ་མཐོང་ རྣ་བས་མ་ཐོས་སྣ་ཡིས་མ་ཚོར་ལྕེ་ཡིས་མ་མྱོང་ལུས་ཀྱིས་མ་སྤྱད། དོང་གང་ནས་མ་སྐྱེས། ཐ་མ་གང་དུ་ཡང་མི་འགག་བར་དུ་འདིར་གནས་ཀྱིས་ངོས་བཟུང་མེད་ལ། མེད་དམ་བྱས་ན་དུས་ད་ལྟ་ཡང་སོབ་སོབ་ཡའང་ཐལ་ལེ་ཁྲུག་གེ་སལ་ལེ་རྟེན་ནེ་འཐོལ་ལེ་ཤིགས་སེ་འདུག་ལ། གཞིགས་ན་སངས་རྒྱས་སེམས་ཅན་དག་མ་དག་ཕྱི་ནང་ཡུལ་ཤེས་ཅེས་ཅི་དང་ཅི་ཐམས་ཅད་སྐྱིད་མཁན་བྱེད་མཁན་ཐམས་ཅད་ཁོ་རང་སྟེ། བྱེད་པ་པོ་ཐམས་ཅད་རང་དུ་སྣང་བ་ལ། མཚན་ཉིད་གར་ཡང་མ་ངེས་པ་དང་། ཡོན་ཏན་ལྷུན་གྱིས་གྲུབ་པ་དང་མཐུན་པར་སྣང་ལ། སྣ་ཚོགས་སུ་འཆར་བ་རང་བཞིན་སྐྱེ་མེད་དུ་གནས་པ་དང་། རོལ་པ་འགག་མེད་དུ་འཆར་བ་དང་། ངོ་བོ་གཉིས་མེད་དུ་གནས་པ་དང་། མཚན་ཉིད་མཐའ་བྲལ་དུ་གནས་པ་ཏེ། སྨྲ་བསམ་བརྗོད་(p.112)མེད་མཐའ་བྲལ་ལ་བློ་འདས་དག་པ་པ་ཟང་ཐལ་དུ་དོན་ལ་གནས་པ་ལྟར་རྒྱུད་ལ་བཀལ་ལོ། གསུམ་པ་ལ་སེམས་རང་འབྱུང་གི་གཤེན་ལྷ། སྐུ་གསུམ་རྫོགས་པའི་སངས་རྒྱས་རང་འབྱུང་རིག་པའི་རྒྱལ་པོ་ཡེ་ཤེས་གནས་ལུགས་དོན་གྱི་སངས་རྒྱས་དེ་ཅི་འདྲ་ཞིག་ཡིན་ཡིན་གང་ན་གནས། ཇི་ཙམ་ན་མཐོང་ནམ་ཙམ་ན་མཇལ། ཇི་ལྟ་བུ་ཞིག་ཡོད་སེམས་ན། དུས་ད་ལྟའི་ཤེས་པ་སྔ་ཕྱིའི་རྟོག་པས་མ་བསླད་བྱིང་རྨུག་གི་དབང་དུ་མ་སོང་། ཚོགས་དྲུག་སྣ་ལྷའི་རྗེས་སུ་མ་འབྲང་བའི་རང་གསལ་འཛིན་མེད་དུ་ཧྲིག་གེ་བ་འདི་ཡིན་ཏེ། སྐྲ་བོ་ཆེ་དེ་ནི་གཡེར་པོ་ཆེ་འདི་ ཁ་བུག་ཏུ་བཤད་པ་དེ་འདི། འཕོངས་ཏུལ་ཏུལ་ཏུ་བསྒོམ་

པ་དེ་འདི། བཀྲ་བསམ་ཀྱང་འདི་ སྟོང་གཞིག་ཀྱང་འདི་ཡིན་ཏེ། དེ་ཡིན་དེ་ལ་ཆེར་གྲིས་ལྟོས་ཞེས་དང་། རང་ལ་གནས་བཞིན་དུ་འདི་བཙལ་ན། བསྐལ་པ་གསུམ་དུ་འདི་བཙལ་རྙེད་མི་འགྱུར། ཅེས་རྫོགས་ཆེན་ལས་གསུངས། དེ་ཡོད་ཚུལ་ཀྱང་ཆེ་བ་ཀུན་བཟང་ནས་ཆུང་བ་འཇག་མིག་གི་སྲིན་བུ་ཡན་ཆད་ལ། ཆེ་ཆུང་མང་ཉུང་བཟང་ངན་སྲབ་འབུག་མེད་པར་ཁྱབ་བྱེད་དུ་ཡོད་ལ་ ཁྱད་པར་དུ་ད་ལྟ་ཕྱི་སྒྲ་ལུས་ཀྱི་སྒྲུབས། ནང་ཙི་ཏའི་དབུས་གསང་བ་ཀུན་གཞིའི་ཀློང་ནས། སྐུ་གསུམ་དུ་ཁྲིང་ངེ་བཞུགས་ཏེ། དེ་ཡང་མ་ཀུན་གཞི་སྟོང་ཉིད་རྩ་བྲལ་དུ། དང་སེང་བ་འདི་བོན་སྐུ། བུ་རིག་པ་རང་གསལ་འཛིན་མེད་དུ་སལ་ལེ་ཧྲིག་གེ་བ་འདི་རྫོགས་སྐུ། རྩལ་རང་འབྱུང་རང་ཤར་རང་གྲོལ་དུ་ཁྲོལ་ལེ་བ་འདི་སྤྲུལ་སྐུ་ཡིན་ཏེ། གཞི་དེ་ལྟར་སྐུ་གསུམ་རང་ལ་རང་ཆས་སུ་གནས་པ་ལ། ཉམས་སུ་བླངས་པས་ལམ་གྱི་སྐབས་སུ་རྒྱུད་ལ་ཤར་བྱུང་ཐེབས་ཡོད་ཤེས་ངོ་ཤེས། ཉམས་སུ་སྐྱོང་འོག་ཏུ་ཚུད་པ་དེ་འཆར་(p.113)ཚུལ་ལམ་གྱི་སྐུ་གསུམ་དེ་ལ་རྩལ་རྫོགས་ཤུགས་ཐོན་ཐག་ཆོད་ངེང་ཐོབ་མངོན་དུ་གྱུར་པ་དེ་ནི་མཐར་ཐུག་འབྲས་བུ་སྐུ་གསུམ་སྟེ། བླ་ཆེན་གྱི་གསུངས་ལས། སྟོང་པ་སྣང་གསལ་ལ་སྐུ་གསུམ་དུ་ངོ་སྤྲད། མི་གཡོ་མཉམ་གསལ་ལ་སྐུ་གསུམ་དུ་གཟེར་གདབ། བརྗོད་བཅོས་རྩོལ་མེད་ལ་སྐུ་གསུམ་དུ་ལ་བཟླ་གསུངས། ཡང་ན་རིག་པ་རྟོག་མེད་བདེ་གསལ་གྱི་ངང་ལ་མ་གཡོས་རྒྱུན་ཆགས་སུ་གནས་པ་དེ་ལ་བྱུང་ཚོར་གྱི་འགྱུ་བས་མ་བསླད་པ་ནི་བོན་སྐུ། ཐེམ་རིག་འཕྲོལ་བ་ལྷ་སྐུ་རིགས་སྟོབས་ཡེ་ཤེས་ཤར་ཅིང་གྲོལ་བ་ནི་རྫོགས་སྐུ། ལུས་ངག་གི་བྱ་བྱེད་རྫོགས་སུ་སྤྱོད་ཅིང་རྩོལ་བཅས་ཀྱི་མཚན་མ་གྲོལ་བ་ནི་སྤྲུལ་སྐུ་སྟེ། རང་རིག་ཡེ་ཤེས་ཀ་དག་བོན་གྱི་སྐུ་ལུས་སེམས་འབྲེལ་བ་ལོངས་སྤྱོད་རྫོགས་པའི་སྐུ། བྱ་བྱེད་སྣ་ཚོགས་ཅེར་ཡང་སྤྲུལ་པའི་སྐུ། ཞེས་རྫོགས་ཆེན་སྙན་རྒྱུད་ལས་གསུངས་སོ། དེ་བཞིན་དུ་ཕྱི་གཟུགས་སོགས་ཚོགས་དྲུག་གི་འཆར་ཚུལ་ཐམས་ཅད་ཀྱང་གང་ཤར་བའི་ངོ་བོ་དེ་རང་བཞིན་གྱི་སྟོང་ཆ་ནི་བོན་སྐུ། འགག་མེད་དུ་གསལ་གྱིས་གསལ་ཆ་ནི་རྫོགས་སྐུ། ཆོ་འཕྲུལ་སྣ་ཚོགས་སུ་ཤར་གྱིས་གཡོས་ཆ་ནི་སྤྲུལ་སྐུ་སྟེ། སྐུ་གསུམ་གྱི་ངོ་བོར་འདུ་འབྲལ་མེད་པར་གནས་པ་ཡིན། ནང་དུའང་ཧོལ་སྐྱེས་ཀྱིས་བསམ་དྲན་ཅི་གཡོས་ཀྱང་། སྟོང་ཆ་ནི་བོན་སྐུ་སྣང་ཆ་ནི་རྫོགས་སྐུ་གསལ་ཆ་ནི་སྤྲུལ་སྐུ་སྟེ། ཐམས་ཅད་ཤེས་ན་སྐུ་གསུམ་གྱི་བདག་ཉིད་དེ། ཡར་མེ་བའི་ཞལ་ནས། ཞེ་སྡང་སྐྱེས་པ་སྟོང་པ་ཡིན། སྟོང་པའི་ངོ་བོ་གསལ་བ་ཡིན། གསལ་སྟོང་གཉིས་མེད་བོན་སྐུ་ཡིན་

གསུངས་པ་དང་མཐུན་ནོ། དེ་ལྟར་ཡིན་ན་འཁྲུལ་ཞིང་འཁོར་བ་སྣམས་ན། ངོ་ཤེས་མ་ཤེས་དང་རྟོགས་མ་རྟོགས་ཀྱི་ཁྱད་པར་ཏེ། འདི་མཐོང་རྣམས་ཀྱིས་འདི་མ་རྟོགས། དེ་རྟོགས་རྟོགས་ཁྱད་པར་ཆེ། ཞེས་ལུང་དྲུག་ལས་གསུངས་སོ། དེ་ལྟར་གྱི་(p.114)གདམས་པ་རྣམས་དང་པོར་ངོས་ཟིན་ཅིང་གོ་བ། བར་དུ་རྒྱུད་ལ་འབྱོར། ཐ་མར་ཉམས་སུ་སྐྱོང་། བཀའ་ལུང་ལས་གསུངས་སོ། ཐ་མས་བསྟན་པ། སྐྱོང་བ་ལ་ཤར་བ་གསུམ་པོ་དེ་གཅིག་ཐོག་ཏུ་གཅིག་བབ་ཅིང་ཕྱི་ཆུ་འདྲེས། མ་བུ་འཕྲོད་དེ་རུས་འབྱོར་ངོ་ཤེས་ཉམས་སྐྱོང་དང་ཆས་པ་ནང་ནས་ལྷངས་ཀྱིས་ཤར་ཡིད་ཆེས་ཧེང་ཐོབ་ཐག་ཆོད་གློང་དུ་གྱུར་པ་དེ་ལ་ངོ་འཕྲོད་པ་ཟེར་བ་ལགས་སོ། འགའ་ཞིག་སེམས་རྩུང་ཟད་ཟིན་པའམ་གནས་ཆ་རྩུང་ཟད་རྙེད་པའམ། གོ་བློ་ཕྱོགས་ཙམ་ཤར་བའམ། རིག་པ་སྣ་ཁ་འགྱུར་ཙམ་ལ། ངོ་ལོགས་པར་འཕྲོད་ཟེར་བ་མཐོང་སྐེ་འཛོལ་དོགས་ཡོད། དེ་ལྟར་ངོ་འཕྲོད་པའི་དོན་དེ་ལ་གཟའ་གཏད་མཐའ་བྲལ་དུ་ལྟ་བ་དེ་ལྟ་བ། དེ་མ་ཡེངས་རྒྱུན་ཆགས་སུ་བསྒོམ་པ་དེ་བསྒོམ་པ། དེ་འགག་མེད་རྒྱ་ཡན་དུ་སྤྱོད་པ་དེ་སྤྱོད་པ། དེ་དྲི་མེད་རང་སེམས་ལ་མི་འདའ་བ་དེ་དམ་ཚིག དེ་ཙམ་བྱས་གཞན་དོན་དུ་འགྱུར་བ་དེ་ཕྲིན་ལས། དེ་དག་ཀྱང་གདོད་ནས་རང་ཆས་འབྲལ་མེད་དུ་གནས་པ་དེ་གཞི། དེ་གསལ་བཏབ་རྒྱུད་ལ་སྦྱར་ཉམས་སུ་ལེན་པ་དེ་ལམ། དེ་ལ་རྩལ་རྫོགས་ཤུགས་ཐོན་གློང་དུ་གྱུར་པ་དེ་འབྲས་བུ། དེའི་ངང་ལས་མ་གཡོས་པ་དེ་མཉམ་བཞག དེ་རྒྱ་ཡན་དུ་ཁྱེར་བ་དེ་རྗེས་ཐོབ། དེ་རྒྱུན་ཆགས་སུ་གནས་པ་དེ་ཞི་གནས། དེ་གསལ་མདངས་སུ་ཤར་བ་དེ་ལྷག་མཐོང་། དེའི་ངོ་བོ་མངོན་དུ་གྱུར་པ་དེ་རྟོགས་པ། དེའི་རྣམ་པ་ཡོན་ཏན་དུ་ཤར་བ་དེ་ཉམས་ གཞི་གཅིག་ལ་བྱེད་པའི་ཁྱད་པར་གྱི་སོ་སོར་བརྡ་བཏགས་པ་ཡིན་ཏེ། ལྟ་བའི་སྟོབས་ཀྱིས་བསྒོམ་པ་དྲན། བསྒོམ་པའི་སྟོབས་ཀྱི་ལྟ་བ་དྲན། ལྟ་སྒོམ་གཉིས་སུ་ག་ལ་ཡོད་གསུངས་པ་དང་། གཞི་གང་ཡིན་པ་དེ་ལམ། ལམ་གང་ཡིན་པ་དེ་འབྲས་བུ་གསུངས་པ་དང་(p.115)མཐུན་ནོ། དེ་ནི་འབྲས་བུ་ངོ་སྤྲོད་ཀྱི་ཐུན་མཚམས་བཀའ་དྲིན་ཅན་གྱི་གསུངས་བཞིན་སྤྲིས་པ་སྟེ་བཅུ་བཞི་པའོ།། སྐབས་འདིར་ཡེ་ཤེས་ཟང་ཐལ་གྱིས་གདམས་པ་བསྟན་ལ་རྗེས་སུ་བསྔོ་བ་སྨོན་ལམ་དང་ཆས་པས་མཐའ་བརྟེན་པར་བྱས་ཏེ་ཐུན་མཚམས་བཅོ་ལྔ་པའོ། དེ་ལྟར་མན་ངག་ཁྲིད་ཀྱི་ལག་ལེན་གོ་རིམ་ཐུན་མཚམས་དང་བཅས་པ་འདི་ནི། རྗེ་རི་ཁྲོད་པ་ཡབ་སྲས་བརྒྱུད་པར་བཅས་པའི་མཛོད་སྤྱིལ་ལོ། འགྲོ་མགོན་གཡོར་མེ་དང་མཚན་ལྡན་བློ་གྲོས་རིན་པོ་

ཆེའི་ཐུགས་བཅུད་མཉམ་མེད་འདུལ་བ་རིན་པོ་ཆེའི་ཞལ་གདམས་ཕུག་ལེན་ཇི་ལྟ་བ་ལ། ལུང་དང་མན་ངག་གི་སྐབས་སྦྱར་ཉམས་མྱོང་གིས་གསལ་བཏབ་ནས་ཅུང་ཟད་གསལ་ཞིང་གོ་བདེ་བར་དཔེའ་ཐོབ་དོན་ཐོབ་ཀྱི་ཚུལ་དུ་ སློགས་མའི་བྲུ་བསྒོམ་རྒྱལ་བ་གཡུང་དྲུང་ལ་རྩེ་གཅིག་གི་ཉམས་ལེན་པ་འདུ་སྒོམ་སྒྲིན་པ་འོད་ཟེར་གྱིས་བསྐུལ་ནས་ རིན་ཆེན་སྤུངས་པ་མཁར་སྣའི་དགོན་དུ་བཀོད་པའོ། འགལ་འཁྲུལ་བཤགས་ཤིང་དགེ་བ་དབྱིངས་སུ་བསྔོ། དཔག་མེད་འགྲོ་བའི་དོན་དུ་འགྱུར་བར་ཤོག སྐལ་ལྡན་ཁྲིད་ཚར་བསྒོམ་ཕྱུག་མ་ཡིན་པར། རང་ཁར་སྤེལ་ཅིང་ཁྲིན་བུས་འདི་བསླད་ནས། དམ་ལས་འགལ་བཀའ་རྒྱ་མ་བཤིག་ཅིག ཅེས་བྲུས་ཏེ་མན་ངག་ཁྲིད་ཀྱི་རིམ་པ་རྫོགས་སོ།། སརྦ་མཾ་ག་ལམ།།

°གསས་མཁར་ཡེ་རྫོགས་མཆོག་གི་རྒྱུད་ལས། འདི་ལྟར་སྣང་བ་རྒྱུ་མའམ་རྨི་ལམ་ལྟ་བུ་ཁྱེར་ཤེས་ན། གསས་མཁར་གཡུང་དྲུང་དོན་རྟོགས་ནས། འབྲུས་རིག་འཛིན་ས་ལ་གནས། ཞེས་དང་ ཡོངས་རྫོགས་ལས། སྒྱུ་མའི་རང་བཞིན་རྨི་ལམ་ཡིན། ཞེས་དང་། ཡང་གསས་མཁར་ཐོ་ཐོག་རྒྱན་རྫོགས་དགུ་རིམ་ལས། སྐྱེས་བུ་གང་ཞིག་འཁྲུལ་བློ་བག་ཆགས་ཀྱིས། རྨི་ལམ་འཁྲུལ་པ་གང་ཡང་འབྱུང་། རྟོགས་ན་རྨི་ལམ་མཐོང་པ་ཡུལ་མེད་ཡིན། གཉིད་མ་སད་ན་རྟོགས་པ་ཡིན། (p.116)ཡང་ཁོད་སྤུངས་ཀྱི་སྒྲུབ་སྐོར་འཁྲུལ་པ་རྩད་གཅོད་ཞེས་པ་ལས། ད་ལྟ་ནི་མ་རིག་པའི་གཉིད་ལོག་པས་འདི་ལྟར་སྣང་བ་རྨི་ལམ་ཡིན་ཏེ། ཇི་སྲིད་མ་རིག་པའི་གཉིད་མ་སད་ཀྱི་བར་ལ་རྨི་ལམ་དུ་མི་གོ་སྟེ། དཔེར་ན་ད་ལྟ་ཡང་གཉིད་མ་སད་ཀྱི་བར་ལ་རྨི་ལམ་དུ་རྨི་ལམ་ཡིན་པར་མ་ཤེས་པ་ལྟར། མ་རིག་པ་རིག་པར་མ་ཤེས་པས་འཁོར་བར་འཁྲུལ། འཁྲུལ་པ་ལ་འཁྲུལ་པར་ཤེས་ན། མ་རིག་པའི་གཉིད་སད་དེ། རིག་པ་ཤར་བས་མཐོང་ལམ་སྐྱེས་ཏེ། དེའི་ཡོན་ཏན་ཤར་བས་སྔར་གྱི་དེ་རྣམས་འཁྲུལ་པར་འདུག་པས། སྐྱེ་འཆི་བདེ་སྡུག་གནས་མཐོ་དམན་གང་ལའང་འཛིགས་སྐྲགས་མེད་པར་འཁྲུལ་པའི་སྙིང་དུ། དོན་མེད་ལ་ཅི་ཙམ་འཁྲུམས་ཤིང་སྡུག་བསྔལ་ལ་སྤྱོད་འདུག་སྙམས་པ་འབྱུང་། དེ་ལྟར་ཤེས་ན་སྡུག་བསྔལ་ལས་གྲོལ་ལོ། ཞེས་དང་ མདོ་སྒྱུ་མ་གཏན་འབེབས་ལས། སྟོན་པ་གཤེན་རབ་མི་བོ་ནི། འོད་ཀྱི་ལྷ་རི་སྤོ་མཐོན་ན་བཞུགས་པའི་ཚེ། སྟག་གཟིགས་འོད་མའི་ཚལ་ནས་གཡུང་དྲུང་སེམས་དཔའ་དུ་མ་ཞིག་བྱོན་ནས། ཨུ་དུ་འབར་བ་ལས་སོགས་མཆོད་པ་དུ་མ་ཕུལ་ཏེ། བར་སྐལ་ཉི་ཤུ་ལ་མཆོད་པ་འབུལ།

ཉི་ཤུ་ལ་བོན་ཉན། ཉི་ཤུ་ལ་པཻ་དུ་རྱའི་སླེག་བམ་ལ་གུ་གེར་རྒྱུད། ཉི་ཤུ་ལ་དེ་དག་གི་དོན་བསྒོམ་སྐྱེ་རང་རང་གི་གནས་སུ་སོང་སོང་། དེ་ལ་ལྷའི་གནས་ཀྱི་ཉི་མ་གཅིག་ཏུ་མཐོང་། ཅེས་དང་། ཡང་དེ་ཉིད་ལས་ འོག་ཕྱོགས་དམྱལ་བའི་གནས་སུ་སྡིག་ཅན་གྱི་བུ་ཤན་པ་མེ་རུ་དམྱལ་ཟངས་སུ་བསྐལ་པ་གྲངས་མེད་པ་གཅིག་བཙོས། གྲངས་མེད་པ་གཅིག་འཁྲུག གྲངས་མེད་པ་གཅིག་གཏུབས་ཏེ་སྡུག་བསྔལ་སྨྱུངས། དེ་ལ་ལྷ་ཚེ་རིང་པོའི་ཕྱི་འཕྲེད་ཅིག་གོ ཞེས་དང་ དཔེ་ན་རང་རང སྣང་ངོར་ན་(p.117)གཉིས་ཀ་བདེན་ལ་དོན་དམ་དུ་གཉིས་ཀ་ལ་རང་བཞིན་མ་གྲུབ་པ་ཡིན་ནོ། ཞེས་དང་ ཡང་འབུམ་ལས་རྨི་ལམ་རུ་མ་འཕྲུལ་པོའི་བློ་ལ་མ་སྤྱོད་ཅིག སྤྱོད་ན་འཁོར་བར་ཕྱིར་ལྡོག་པའོ་ཞེས་ཀྱང་གསུངས་སོ། ད་ལམ་འདིར་ཐུན་མཚམས་བཅུ་གཅིག་པའི་སྐབས་ནས་ཟུར་དུ་བཀོད་པ་འདི་ཉིད་རྟོགས་ལྡན་ནམ་མཁའ་ལྷུན་གྲུབ་ཀྱི་ཕྱག་དཔེ་གསང་རྒྱུད་པོད་བཅུ་གཉིས་པའི་ནང་ཚན་ཨ་ཁྲིད་དང་ དོལ་པོ་ནས་གཡར་བའི་ཨ་ཁྲིད་གཉིས་ལ་འདི་ལྟར་མི་འདུག་པ་དང་། སྟོད་ཏྲེ་པ་དགོན་ནས་བྱུང་བའི་ཨ་ཁྲིད་གཞུང་ཞིག་ཡོད་པར་གསལ་བཞིན་ཟུར་དུ་བཀོད་པ་འདི་ཐུན་མཚམས་བཅུ་གཅིག་པ་གཞུང་དོན་ཡིན་མིན་གཞིག་རྒྱུ།